THEORIZING HISTORICAL CONSCIOUSNESS

Theorizing Historical Consciousness

Edited by Peter Seixas

UNIVERSITY OF TORONTO PRESS
Toronto Buffalo London

© University of Toronto Press Incorporated 2004
Toronto Buffalo London
Printed in Canada

ISBN 0-8020-8713-2

Printed on acid-free paper

National Library of Canada Cataloguing in Publication

Theorizing historical consciousness / edited by Peter Seixas.

Includes bibliographical references.
ISBN 0-8020-8713-2

1. History – Philosophy.   2. Historiography.   I. Seixas, Peter Carr, 1947–

D16.9.T48 2004   901   C2004-901811-6

University of Toronto Press acknowledges the financial assistance
to its publishing program of the Canada Council for the Arts and
the Ontario Arts Council.

University of Toronto Press acknowledges the financial support for
its publishing activities of the Government of Canada through
the Book Publishing Industry Development Program (BPIDP).

Contents

Acknowledgments

I want to acknowledge the generous support of the Canada Research Chairs program, the Peter Wall Institute for Advanced Studies, the Social Sciences and Humanities Research Council of Canada, and the Faculty of Education at the University of British Columbia. The contributors to this volume provided a stimulating community within which to work on difficult ideas. Many colleagues have been equally important in shaping the thinking behind this volume, including Jean Barman, Roland Case, Penney Clark, Marg Conrad, Gerry Friesen, David Lowenthal, Tom Morton, Walt Werner, and Sam Wineburg. This collection benefited immeasurably from the scrupulous attention of Ulrike Spitzer, who serves through her role not only as secretary but also as conference organizer, web-master, proofreader, typist, laboratory supervisor, equipment purchaser, bookkeeper, and friend. No piece of my academic accomplishment could have been achieved without the companionship, support, and love of Susan Inman.

Contributors

Kent den Heyer completed his doctoral studies at the University of British Columbia in Spring 2004, and is now Assistant Professor, Social Studies Education, at Kent State University, Ohio. He is a former high school history teacher with teaching, department leadership, and curriculum development experience in Canada, Colombia, and Japan. His research interests include the hermeneutics of historical consciousness, student and teacher conceptions of historical agency, and psychoanalytic approaches to anti-racist education.

Christian Laville is professeur associé of Didactique de l'histoire at Laval University. His research has focused primarily on the social function of history education. He has also written about the relationship between students' cognitive development and the study of history, and about the theory and the practice of history textbooks. Professor Laville is the author or co-author of many publications, including textbooks in national history, world history, and social science research methodology.

Peter Lee is a senior lecturer in education in the University of London Institute of Education, where he teaches research students and conducts research in the History Education Unit of the School of Arts and Humanities. His interests include research into students' understanding of history, curriculum development in history, and philosophy of history. Lee has co-directed research and curriculum development projects (including the Cambridge History Project and Project Chata). He has edited and contributed to books on history education, published papers on children's ideas about history, and is an editor of the *International Review of History Education.*

Jocelyn Létourneau is Canada Research Chair in the History and Political Economy of Contemporary Quebec at Laval University. His prize-winning *Passer à l'avenir: Histoire, mémoire, identité dans le Québec d'aujourd'hui* (2000) has been published in English as *A History for the Future: Rewriting Memory and Identity in Quebec Today* (2004). His latest book, *Le Québec, les Québécois: Un parcours historique,* is being released in the summer of 2004.

Chris Lorenz is Professor of Philosophy of History at the Free University Amsterdam. He has published widely on issues of theory and historiography (contributing articles to journals such as *History and Theory, Rethinking History, Journal of Contemporary History,* and *Geschichte und Gesellschaft*) and his publications have been translated into seven languages. His latest book, *Constructing the Past,* is forthcoming in 2005 with Princeton University Press.

Mark Salber Phillips is Professor of History at Carleton University. He is the author of *Society and Sentiment: Genres of Historical Writing in Britain, 1740-1820* (2000), as well as other studies of historical and political thought in the Italian Renaissance.

Jörn Rüsen is President of the Kulturwissenschaftliches Institut (Institute for Advanced Study in the Humanities) at Essen in the Wissenschaftszentrum of Northrhine-Westfalia. He is also Professor of General History and Historical Culture at the University of Witten/Herdecke. His books include *Studies in Meta-History* (1993), *Historische Orientierung* (1994), *Geschichte lernen* (1994), *Zerbrechende Zeit* (2001), *Geschichte im Kulturprozeß* (2002), *Kann Gestern besser werden?* (2003), and *History: Narration – Interpretation – Orientation* (forthcoming, 2004).

Peter Seixas is Professor and Canada Research Chair in Education at the University of British Columbia and Director of the Centre for the Study of Historical Consciousness. He taught high school social studies for fifteen years and earned a PhD in history from the University of California at Los Angeles. He is co-editor, with Peter Stearns and Sam Wineburg, of *Knowing, Teaching and Learning History: National and International Perspectives* (2000) and has published in journals such as the *Canadian*

Historical Review, Journal of Curriculum Studies, and the *American Journal of Education.*

Roger I. Simon is Professor at the Ontario Institute for Studies in Education, University of Toronto. Simon is the Faculty Director of the Centre for Media and Culture in Education and OISE/UT's Testimony and Historical Memory Project. He has written broadly on critical approaches to culture and education. Simon's work on cultural memory and the development of historical consciousness is part of his ongoing writing and teaching devoted to exploring the intersections of social and political theory, cultural practice, and pedagogy in regard to the problem of securing a public sphere which enables a just and compassionate society. His most recent book is *The Touch of the Past: Remembrance, Learning and Ethics* (forthcoming, 2005).

Tony Taylor is based in the Faculty of Education, Monash University, Australia. He taught history for ten years in comprehensive schools in the United Kingdom and was closely involved in the Schools Council History Project, the Cambridge Schools Classics Project, and the Humanities Curriculum Project. In 1999–2000 he was Director of the National Inquiry into School History and he was author of the Inquiry's report, *The Future of the Past* (2000). He is co-author with Carmel Young of *Making History: A Guide for the Teaching and Learning of History in Australian Schools.* Since 2001 he has been Director of the Australian Government's National Centre for History Education.

John Torpey is Associate Professor of Sociology and European Studies at the University of British Columbia. He is the editor of *Politics and the Past: On Repairing Historical Injustices* (2003) and author of *Making Whole What Has Been Smashed: On Reparations Politics* (forthcoming).

James V. Wertsch is the Marshall S. Snow Professor in Arts and Sciences at Washington University in St Louis. He received his PhD from the University of Chicago and has taught at Northwestern University, the University of California, San Diego, Clark University, and Washington University. Among his publications are *Voices of the Mind* (1991) and *Voices of Collective Remembering* (2002).

THEORIZING HISTORICAL CONSCIOUSNESS

Introduction

PETER SEIXAS

The trials and scandals of the 1990s that constructed the twenty-four-hour cable news networks, and which they helped to construct, have rendered the notion of 'breaking news' commonplace. After September 11, 2001, CNN regularly flashed the phrase on its multi-windowed broadcast screens. The 'break' connotes excitement and urgency, freedom and danger. In an era of 'breaking news,' when more people in more places can focus more uniformly on a smaller selection of media-worthy events, a new History News Network (http://hnn.us) has not coincidentally mobilized historians to write op-ed columns suitable for daily newspapers, to provide antecedents, roots, and historical background for the current, ever more foreshortened moment. History is invoked to provide context, meaning, and continuity, and, by the most optimistic, to nourish wisdom in making decisions in the present about the future.

Historians, of course, are not the only people who have stepped forward to provide connections to the past in a broken time. As historian David Lowenthal put it in *Possessed by the Past: the Heritage Industry and the Spoils of History*:

All at once heritage is everywhere – in the news, in the movies, in the marketplace – in everything from galaxies to genes. It is the chief focus of patriotism and a prime lure of tourism. One can barely move without bumping into a heritage site. Every legacy is cherished. From ethnic roots to history theme parks, Hollywood to the Holocaust, the whole world is busy lauding – or lamenting – some past, be it fact or fiction.[1]

This popular, market-oriented quest for the past has been mirrored in the academy, through the 'historiographic turn' and the explosive growth of memory studies, across the humanities and social sciences.

This was the *Zeitgeist* when, in January 2001, a research chair dedicated to the study of 'historical consciousness' was established at the University of British Columbia. While the term is relatively unfamiliar in English, it implicates historiography, collective memory, and history education (or, as the field is known in French and German, 'history didactics'). In August 2001 an inaugural symposium was held at UBC to move the theorizing forward. This volume builds on a number of the symposium papers, selected on the basis of their broad implications for the study of historical consciousness beyond the particular case of Canada.[2]

What do representations of the past do for people who experience the flow of events as 'breaking' and thus time as broken, in some sense, from the past? As new as breaking news seems to be, the disorientation that results from awareness of rapid change has been noted by social theorists throughout the modern era, as traditional continuities disintegrated in the face of capitalist social relations. 'All that is solid melts into air,' Marx and Engels observed.[3] The current malaise appears, however, to have a character sufficiently new to call it a 'postmodern condition.'[4]

In the modern era, the emerging discipline of history linked the past and future through national narratives. Disciplinary history, modernity, progress, and the nation were thus fundamentally joined. Once upon a time, one could tell the story of historiography (as J.H. Plumb did) as a progressive tale of increasing freedom from narrow prejudice and blind tradition.[5] The plot line was already familiar to those who knew the story of modernity, as told by J.B. Bury in *The Idea of Progress*.[6] In this story, professionalization brought history into the realm of disinterested, scientific practice through the historicized uses of evidence, the grounding of interpretation in archival sources, and the scrutiny and accountability of peer review. Looking backwards, the national narrations told by historians once thought to be emerging into the light of universal history may now look crudely partial. So the stories with the progressive plot lines have been overtaken by other interpretations: the failure of the discipline to live up to the ideal of objectivity that it professed, the poverty of the ideal in the first place, historians' implication in colonial projects, and the affinities – rather than the disjunctions – between what trained historians and their untrained contemporaries do.[7] A critical take on historiography opens the door to consideration of more complex causal explanations for changes in the forms and content of historical writing, and to analysis of the impact of changing social and cultural conditions on the production of professional history. Announcements of the 'death of the past' (in J.H. Plumb's sense) were clearly premature, given the cultural developments of the past couple of decades. But notwithstanding the postmodern assault on the authority of historians, so, too, are pronouncements about 'the death of history.' As virtually all of the symposium participants agreed, the historians' tools and dispositions continue to have an important role, even as they are subject to the historicists' discount.

Collective Memory

Historiography has been both challenged and enriched by a whole different approach to the study of our changing ways of making sense of the past. 'Memory studies,' starting not with a focus on the practices of historians but with the beliefs of everyone else, have seen explosive growth in the past decade and a half. 'Memory,' as Nancy Wood notes, 'is decidedly in fashion.'[8] With roots traced to French sociologist Maurice Halbwachs's 'collective memory,' its scholars have examined the structures that enable societies to hand down beliefs about the past from one generation to the next, the purposes for which those beliefs are mobilized, their nature and shape, and the ways that they change over time.[9]

Scholars from a range of disciplines have examined institutions such as museums, monuments, schools, archives, and commemorations. Throughout much of this work, the ties between institutions for the preservation of memory in the modern era and the project of nation building remain fundamental. But a broader view of the field of memory studies sets the predominant national memory in the context of other memory projects, in the family, religious communities, local and regional units, and social and political movements.[10] Beyond these purposeful uses of the past, others have noted the unconscious structural mechanisms that contribute to the preservation of the past in the present, in laws, language, habits, and customs.[11]

A common past, preserved through institutions, traditions, and symbols, is a crucial instrument – perhaps *the* crucial instrument – in the construction of collective identities in the present. As John R. Gillis notes, 'the notion of identity depends on the idea of memory, and vice versa.'[12] Belief in a shared past opens the possibility for commitments to collective missions in the future. In order to serve these purposes powerfully, memories organized as narratives include a temporal dimension, conveying an idea of origins and development, of challenges overcome, with collective protagonists and individual heroes confronting difficult conditions and threatening enemies. The narratives provide actors' roles with a moral valence, in accordance with belief in an enduring set of ideals or common character traits. The narrative thus defines a boundary between members who share the common past and those who do not. Its telling potentially invokes debts of the current generation to its collective forbears, while marking injustices perpetrated by or on others outside of the group. In this way the narrative provides a larger justificatory context for collective actions to be taken in response to current challenges. Recognition of the common features of these narratives opens the possibility for comparison across nations, cultures, and other collectivities.[13]

Examination of collective memory over time raises questions not only about how narratives themselves vary, but also about how and why their forms and uses change over time. The defeat of Germany and Japan after the Second World War, the destruction of the Berlin Wall, the fall of the Soviet Union, the accession to power of the African National Congress – all required a scrapping of the national narratives that had explained the collective mission of the old regimes. An American history survey textbook, scheduled for publication in September 2001, was delayed not only so the events of September 11 could be included, but so that the story up to that point could be revised.

Cross-cultural comparisons of collective memory also introduce the question of whether there are fundamentally different approaches to and uses of the past, and if so, how to define and organize them. Virtually all schemes suggest modernity itself as the critical dividing line. Friedrich Nietzsche's 'On the Uses and Disadvantages of History for Life,' the key nineteenth-century counter-progressive work, vilifies modern, scientific approaches to the past as undermining authentic engagement with life.[14] Indeed, Nietzsche attributes to scientific history the roots of all that is wrong with the culture of modernity: 'The war is not even over before it is transformed into a hundred thousand printed pages and set before the tired palates of the history-hungry as the latest delicacy.'[15] Knowledge is not produced in the service of life, but rather vice versa: 'The work never produces an effect but only another "critique"; and the critique itself produces no effect either, but again only a further critique.'[16] Legitimate uses of the past, in Nietzsche's scheme, include the 'monumental,' to exalt former heroes and to inspire their emulation, the 'memorial,' to preserve relics of the past in the service of cultural continuity, and the 'critical,' to tear down the past, in order to build anew. In contrast to 'scientific' history, which he locates as being in 'our own time,' he does not specify particular periods for these legitimate uses, but his argument is that different approaches suit the needs of different eras.

how so

If Nietzsche is the nineteenth-century precursor, then Pierre Nora is the contemporary author whose work, the massive *Realms of Memory: The Construction of the French Past*, provides the benchmark for collective memory studies in the current era. Modernity enters Nora's analysis through his fundamental contrast between pre-modern French agrarian culture, characterized by *milieux de mémoire*, and modern French culture, where the past is remembered through *lieux de mémoire*, 'sites of memory.' Throughout Nora there is a vaguely implied subtext mourning the loss of traditional culture, with *lieux de mémoire* serving as the always inadequate tools to commemorate what has been lost: 'Memory is constantly on our lips because it no longer exists.'[17] He leaves the chronological dividing line vague and suggestive: in Tony Judt's review, the decisive loss of *milieux de mémoire* in French culture is as late as the 1970s.[18]

Building upon Nora in a recent critique of collective-memory studies, Gabrielle Spiegel uses Jewish history and memory to divide approaches to the past into two: 'liturgical time' and 'historical time.'[19] The first, essentially pre-modern consciousness, understands events (and traumatic events, particularly) as instances in a series of cyclically repeating occurrences. The latter, in contrast, understands 'unique events unfolding within an irreversible linear time.'[20] She sees recent academic interest in collective memory as a problematic return to pre-modern practices in a post-Holocaust (and thereby postmodern) era:

> To the extent that memory 'reincarnates,' 'resurrects,' 're-cycles,' and makes the past 'reappear' and live again in the present, it cannot perform historically, since it refuses to keep the past in the past, to draw the line, as it were, that is constitutive of the modern enterprise of historiography.[21]

The ostensibly binary schemes articulated by Nora and Spiegel imply a third category. If memory (Nora) and liturgical time (Spiegel) characterize pre-modern societies, and history predominates in the modern era, then there is something new at hand when the urge to return to liturgical memory coincides with an avalanche of often-contentious commemorative and reparative campaigns. This postnational, postmodern era – a conjunction of technological globalization, demographic and economic instability, and political challenges to national regimes, tempered by a post-Holocaust sensibility – demands and has resulted in new orientations towards the past. Echoing Nora, John Gillis remarks:

> As the world implodes upon us, we feel an even greater pressure as individuals to record, preserve, and collect ... memory has simultaneously become more global and more local ... never before has remembering been so compulsive, even as rote memorization ceases to be central to the educational process. What we can no longer keep in our heads is now kept in storage.[22]

In a crude way, then, we might posit three approaches to the past – traditional, modern, and postmodern – the transitions between which signal deep cultural shifts.

Historical Consciousness

If the term 'collective memory' has served well to open up the study that David Lowenthal suggested was so neglected twenty years ago – the study of how ordinary people beyond the history profession understand the past – then what, if anything, is gained by the use of 'historical consciousness'?[23] In some instances, it appears to be virtually synonymous with collective memory. Thus, when the term 'historical consciousness' appears in Herbert Gutman's influential essay 'Historical Consciousness in Contemporary America' (written before the recent outpouring of collective memory work), he means simply how Americans think about the past.[24]

An important contrasting usage of 'historical consciousness' comes from German writers. In 'The Problem of Historical Consciousness,' Hans-Georg Gadamer calls the appearance of historical consciousness 'likely the most important revolution among those we have undergone since the beginning of the modern epoch,' more significant, indeed, than the revolution in technological innovation.[25] In his usage, historical consciousness is a specific cultural development located in the modern era. Its achievement is 'the full awareness of the historicity of everything present and the relativity of all opinions,' and thus the breaking of the hold of tradition.

> Modern consciousness – precisely as historical consciousness – takes a reflexive position concerning all that is handed down by tradition. Historical

consciousness no longer listens sanctimoniously to the voice that reaches
out from the past but, in reflection on it, replaces it within the context
where it took root in order to see the significance and relative value proper
to it.[26]

Similarly, in *The Holocaust in American Life*, Peter Novick associates
historical consciousness with the critical historicism of disciplinary history, and contrasts it with collective memory in much the same terms as
Spiegel's: 'Historical consciousness, by its nature, focuses on the *historicity* of events ... Memory, by contrast, has no sense of the passage of time;
it denies the "pastness" of its objects and insists on their continuing
presence.'[27]

This sort of contrast works well in the kind of application for which
Novick intended it. The ubiquitous distinction between memory and
history is here directly transferred to the field through the terms 'collective memory' and 'historical consciousness.'[28] The latter, informed by
the cultural tools developed in professional history, becomes the form of
memory characterized by modernity. With this specification of the term,
certain populations 'achieve' historical consciousness, as a result of
cultural development, intercultural contact, or education. There are at
least two problems with this approach. First, such a definition has the
flavour of a baldly Eurocentric model of progress, where the modern
West 'has' historical consciousness, and the rest do without, until they
achieve Western modes of understanding. And second, this approach
may foreshorten exactly those important discussions about the interplay
between history and memory that the term 'historical consciousness'
potentially opens up, and which are centrally important for our own
cultural moment, where the two are tangled and confounded.

It will serve our purposes, therefore, to adopt an inclusive notion of
historical consciousness by incorporating all those modes of understanding that are included in 'collective memory.' At the same time, this
notion should allow for the coexistence in any one culture and, indeed,
in any one individual, of fundamentally different *types* of historical consciousness.[29] These may (or may not) be related to the tools and practices of professional, disciplinary history, as broadly construed as written
communication, or as specialized as commitment to a historicized critique of sources and interpretations. Thus, we will use the term historical
consciousness to maintain collective memory's attention to broad popular understandings of the past, bringing to the forefront, nevertheless,
the problematic relationships between the distinctly modern, disciplin-

ary practices of historiography and the memory practices of broader populations across different cultures and across different eras, including – but not limited to – our own. The valorizing of particular types of historical consciousness is both unavoidable – most pressingly so for those concerned with any form of history education – and fraught with difficulty.

In taking this stance, we are aligned with the abbreviated definition of historical consciousness presented by the journal *History and Memory*, as 'the area in which collective memory, the writing of history, and other modes of shaping images of the past in the public mind merge.'[30] It is also consistent with the definition growing out of the extensive work on European historical consciousness: individual and collective understandings of the past, the cognitive and cultural factors that shape those understandings, as well as the relations of historical understandings to those of the present and the future.[31]

Five Principles

What, then, is needed in order to push the theorizing of historical consciousness further in this cultural moment? Five principles, each of which will be elaborated further below, can guide the way:

1. The relationship between academic and popular history. Theorizing historical consciousness has to recognize the complex relationship between the professional practice of history, which claims to advance historical knowledge, and the popular practice of history, where the past is mobilized for a wide variety of purposes including, to name a few, identity projects, policy justifications, reparations claims, public education, and profit-making entertainment.

2. The relationships among theory, empirical research, and practice. Theorizing historical consciousness cannot take place in an empirical or practical vacuum: it needs to be systematically tested and applied, reformulated, and reworked in the light of findings in the field.

3. The comparative imperative. Theories of historical consciousness need to be capacious enough to account for radically different ways of understanding and using the past, from different cultures and subcultures around the world, without using a Western lens to lock them into a developmental hierarchy.

4. The need for value commitments. In order to contribute to curriculum and other public-policy applications (notwithstanding the catholicity of principle no. 3), scholars of historical consciousness must accept

the burden of normative judgments: different forms of historical consciousness are supported by and, in turn, promote different social and political arrangements. Promoting an open, democratic, and just society implies certain value commitments in respect to historical consciousness.

5. Historicizing the study of historical consciousness. Scholars of historical consciousness must historicize their own practice. We need to locate the questions, methods, findings, and policy implications of our work in a particular historical, political, and cultural conjuncture in order to understand their genealogy as well as their contingent nature.

These principles can be pictured as a series of ropes for scholars to grab onto in order to advance the theorizing of historical consciousness. Some theorists have more leverage on one or two of the ropes. But the collaboration, the sum of the effort, is what will ultimately move the beast. Our hope is that in this giant, lurching, collaborative effort the lines are pulling – ever so roughly – in the same direction.

The Relationship between Academic and Popular History

Academic history writing itself provides a vast field for exploring possible variations in the construction of our understanding of the past. The field of historiography – traditionally the study of history writing by professional historians – provides ample scope not only for examining how the record and communication of history has changed over time, but also for making cultural comparisons, examining narrative and non-narrative structures for organizing historical knowledge, and defining the role of spatial and temporal scale in providing a sense of the past. One way of theorizing historical consciousness involves the recognition that many of the kinds of questions that grow out of the examination of academic historiography can be fruitfully extended to a broader arena.

Moving from a linear narrative of the development of historiographic change within the Western tradition to the challenge of drawing comparisons among various different national historiographies poses a central problem in the study of historiography. But this problem immediately entails the examination of the larger historical identity in which any nation's professional history writing is rooted, and thus the key academic/popular problematic is engaged from the outset. Chris Lorenz's chapter provides some preliminary guideposts for this kind of exploration. Even in his historiographically oriented chapter, the dynamic interaction between academic history and broader historical consciousness is understood as operating in both directions. Jocelyn Létourneau and Sabrina Moisan's chapter is structured across the same divide, but they start from the other end with young people telling the story of Quebec history as they themselves understand it. The authors interrogate the disjunction between these popular accounts and those presented by the recent academic historiography of Quebec. What accounts for the staying power of older ideas, in the face of historiographic change in the academy? Again, the relationship between the two is a major theme of the study.

Scholars have long recognized the problem of temporal and spatial scale in historical writing. Historiographic innovations frequently tackle the question of scale head-on, from the *longue durée* of the French *Annales* school to the Italian micro-historians. Robert Bain has taken historians' attention to scale and transported it to the teaching of history outside of academia, with the argument that flexibility and self-consciousness with respect to the scale of our pictures of the past are crucial competencies.[32] Alongside temporal and spatial scale, a third variable, relatively unrecognized in writing about historical representation, is that of the distance constructed between the past and the present. The fictional time machine imagines the impossible: re-experiencing the past itself. Short of that experience, every piece of historical writing provides a metaphorical bridge from present to past, but the sense of proximity or distance, and notions about what constitutes *appropriate* distance, vary by medium, genre, culture, author, and period. Variations in historical distance are also at work in popular representations of the past from movies and museums to Civil War re-enactments, legal battles over reparations, and Holocaust video testimony. Yet these are little remarked upon. Mark Phillips's chapter in this collection exemplifies the value of moving back and forth across the academic/popular divide to initiate a discussion of this previously tacit aspect of historical consciousness.

My own work on conceptualizing the growth of historical understanding has drawn from academic historiography to frame questions about young people's understanding of historical epistemology, evidence, significance, and interpretation.[33] Like the work of the British Schools Council History Project of the 1980s, this research is sometimes misconstrued and criticized as promoting 'mini-historians' in the school classroom by measuring students' historical thinking against standards from academia. In fact, in this model, the relationships among history in everyday life, history in academia, and history in the classroom are mutual and interpenetrating. The rationale for turning to academic historiography to analyse young people's historical cognition is precisely that the habits of mind underpinning historians' handling of the past may provide useful components for young people in their everyday orientation in time.

Theory, Empirical Research, and Practice

Theorizing the practice of history has most characteristically come from philosophers of history or from the pens of historians themselves, despite their lack of training in methods other than historical. While the philosophy of history can contribute to the theorizing of historical consciousness, the methods for investigating historical consciousness also draw from psychological, social-scientific, and educational-research traditions that value the gathering of empirical data. In the field of cultural studies, theorists have sometimes relied upon their 'readings' of museum displays, architecture, memorials, monuments, and other social texts in order to explore their meanings. Others in the field argue that these texts are the locus of multiple readings and that it is dangerous to infer how particular audiences interpret a monument without actually asking them about it. On the other hand, getting at what audiences do with historical texts is never as simple as 'asking them about it.' Qualitative empirical research traditions point to the reciprocal relationship between theory and research: the theories speak to the data and vice versa.

In this collection, James Wertsch, with a background in psychology, mobilizes empirical research in post-Soviet Russia to build a distinction between underlying 'schematic narrative templates' and the more transitory 'specific narratives' that structure understandings of the past. The methods of Létourneau and Moisan also exemplify the contribution of empirical research in the theorizing of historical consciousness. But perhaps the most systematic in this regard, among those represented in this collection, is the work of Peter Lee, whose multi-year investigations of young people's ideas about history (built on a rich tradition of British history education research) are mobilized here to engage the theoretical scheme put forward by Jörn Rüsen, which, in turn, has informed much of the German writing on the subject.[34]

The Comparative Imperative

As Lorenz's piece convincingly argues, our understanding of historical consciousness is most likely to be furthered by examinations that incorporate a comparative dimension. Comparison promotes the examination of unarticulated assumptions and throws aspects of historical consciousness that might otherwise have escaped notice into sharp relief. Comparison helps to challenge unfounded claims of uniqueness drawn from one national setting; conversely, it challenges unfounded claims of universality. Lorenz's own comparatively framed review of *The Killing of Canadian History* exposes the flaws in Jack Granatstein's assumptions of Canadian exceptionalism.[35] Similarly, Keith Barton's work with elementary-school children in a comparative study of Northern Ireland and the United States revealed deep, structural differences in their constructions of the past: the progressive narrative of change founded on individual achievement and invention, ubiquitous among American children, was largely absent from the Irish.[36]

While large, comparative studies can contribute to theorizing historical consciousness, they also depend on it. The massive, pioneering comparative effort *Youth and History* in Europe, involving 31,000 subjects in twenty-four countries, would likely have benefited from some of the theoretical work now being undertaken.[37] At the same time, it helped to alert researchers to some of the difficulties of comparative work. With the increasing empirical sophistication being developed by Peter Lee, Ros Ashby, and their international colleagues and students, and with the large-scale national projects being undertaken in the wake of Rosenzweig and Thelen's *Presence of the Past*, we can look forward to reaping some of the benefits of international, comparative work in the coming years.[38] The contributions of Lorenz, Wertsch, Phillips, and others in this volume will alert researchers to important comparative dimensions that must be accounted for as these projects are undertaken.

Comparative research in Europe and North America is challenging enough, but there is a further need to develop frameworks that can encompass a much broader group of nations and cultures, including those labelled 'peoples without history,' that is, lying outside the historiographic traditions of Western nations.[39] In doing so, the problem is to develop comparative frameworks that will be capacious enough to begin such work without implicitly elevating Western historical consciousness to an a priori ideal of development. Historians and anthropologists rooted in their own disciplinary concerns have begun to tackle this project in a piecemeal way, but there is, to date, no large coordinated research effort that places questions of contemporary historical consciousness at the centre of the project.[40]

The Need for Value Commitments

The search for broad frameworks that will encompass a wide variety of approaches to the past faces other threats from a diametrically opposed quarter. It should not dissolve into a laissez-faire refusal to assess these approaches in relation to the value commitments of an open, democratic, and just society. High levels of migration combined with rapidly developing technologies of communication necessitate both openness to change and acceptance of others. These requirements are particularly difficult to reconcile with practices of collective memory that seek to draw immutable boundaries around groups by establishing fixed identities based on biological difference or on moral codes rooted in the revelations of canonical texts. Some forms of historical consciousness that may have been acceptable for relatively homogeneous cultures pose òbstacles to the negotiation of inter-group relations and adaptation to rapid change that characterize postmodern global culture.

The problems of atavistic, fundamentalist historical consciousness are particularly insistent for those scholars – well represented among the contributors to this volume – whose research is intended to inform public policy in arenas such as school curriculum. Indeed, Christian Laville here voices concern that the term 'historical consciousness' itself carries baggage that is antithetical to the aims and achievements of liberal education. Those studying the problems of intercultural or international reconciliation or remembrance in the wake of historical crimes generally frame studies with implicit policy objectives, which have implications for the forms of historical consciousness likely to achieve them.[41]

Historicizing the Study of Historical Consciousness

It would be ironic if those studying historical consciousness did not also attempt to historicize their own work. Why the issues addressed in this field have achieved such currency in recent years, how current political struggles over history education and collective memory have shaped the research agenda, and perhaps even how the field's accomplishments are likely to appear in retrospect: these are questions that scholars need to address as they pursue studies about contemporary historical consciousness.

Much of the current writing on historical consciousness pays attention to such issues. In both the first and last volumes of *Realms of Memory*, Pierre Nora asks what prompts interest in the past in the current moment (and offers somewhat different answers in each volume). Indeed, the question is ubiquitous: this volume begins (at the outset of this introduction) and ends (in John Torpey's more extended analysis) with it. The difficult task of historicizing present scholarship can also extend to questions of why the answers we propose are satisfying – or not – in current circumstances. There has also been extensive writing on the closely related issue of the politics of historical consciousness, particularly in respect to history in the schools. Accounts of the history wars – few of them disinterested – have been offered from a variety of positions in several different national settings.[42] Museums and monuments have received similar treatment.[43] In most jurisdictions, however, placing these accounts in a broader historical trajectory remains to be done.

This volume makes a preliminary contribution to all of these principles. By setting debates about history education in the broader context of collective memory practices, it helps to move the debates about teaching and learning history beyond the relatively narrow terms within which they have been pursued to date. At the same time, it introduces the normative concerns and questions that have been at the forefront of history education scholarship to the discourse on collective memory. The chapters herein do not resolve the thorny question of defining an 'advanced' historical consciousness, but they bring some of the leading thinkers on these issues into dialogue with each other, and thus provide a solid basis for ongoing theoretical debate and empirical research both in national settings and in larger, comparative frames.

Notes

1 David Lowenthal, *Possessed by the Past: The Heritage Industry and the Spoils of History* (New York: Free Press, 1996), ix.
2 'Canadian Historical Consciousness in International Context: Theoretical Perspectives,' 27–29 August 2001, was generously funded by the Peter Wall Institute for Advanced Studies, the Canada Research Chairs program, and the Social Sciences and Humanities Research Council of Canada. The program may be viewed at www.cshc.ubc.ca. Other participants in the symposium, not represented in this volume, were Rosa Bruno-Jofre, Penney Clark, Margaret Conrad, Richard Menkis, Kevin O'Neill, Theresa Rogers, Kim Schonert-Reichl, Veronica Strong-Boag, Jonathan Vance, and Sam Wineburg.
3 Marshall Berman, *All That Is Solid Melts into Air: The Experience of Modernity* (New York: Simon and Schuster, 1982).

4 David Harvey, *The Condition of Postmodernity* (Cambridge, MA: Blackwell, 1989); Jean-François Lyotard, *The Postmodern Condition: A Report on Knowledge*, trans. Geoff Bennington and Brian Massumi (Minneapolis: University of Minnesota Press, 1984).

5 J.H. Plumb, *The Death of the Past* (Boston: Houghton Mifflin, 1969).

6 J.B. Bury, *The Idea of Progress* (New York: Dover, 1932).

7 Peter Novick, *That Noble Dream: The 'Objectivity Question' and the American Historical Profession* (Cambridge: Cambridge University Press, 1988); Lyle Dick, 'The Seven Oaks Incident and the Construction of a Historical Tradition, 1816–1970,' *Journal of the Canadian Historical Association* 2 (1991): 91–113; David Harlan, *The Degradation of American History* (Chicago and London: University of Chicago Press, 1997); John Willinsky, *Learning to Divide the World* (Minneapolis: University of Minnesota Press, 1998); Ashis Nandy, 'History's Forgotten Doubles,' in Philip Pomper, Richard H. Elphick, and Richard T. Vann, eds, *World History: Ideologies, Structures, and Identities* (Malden, MA: Blackwell, 1998), 159–78; David Lowenthal, *The Past Is a Foreign Country* (New York: Cambridge University Press, 1985); Mark Salber Phillips, *Society and Sentiment: Genres of Historical Writing in Britain* (Princeton, NJ: Princeton University Press, 2000).

8 Nancy Wood, *Vectors of Memory: Legacies of Trauma in Postwar Europe* (Oxford: Berg, 1999), 1.

9 Kerwin Klein has called the entire field 'the new structural memory studies.' See Kerwin Lee Klein, 'On the Emergence of Memory in Historical Discourse,' *Representations* 69 (2000): 127–50. For reviews of the field's growth, see also James Wertsch, *Voices of Collective Remembering* (New York: Cambridge University Press, 2002); Raphael Samuel, *Theatres of Memory* (London: Verso, 1994); Michael Kammen, 'Review of Iwona Irwin-Zarecka, Frames of Remembrance: The Dynamics of Collective Memory,' *History and Theory* 34, no. 3 (1995): 245–61; and Wulf Kansteiner, 'Finding Meaning in Memory: A Methodological Critique of Collective Memory Studies,' *History and Theory* 41, no. 2 (May 2002): 179–97.

10 See, e.g., James Green, *Taking History to Heart: The Power of the Past in Building Social Movements* (Amherst: University of Massachusetts Press, 2000); Yosef Hayim Yerushalmi, *Zakhor: Jewish History and Jewish Memory* (New York: Schocken Books, 1989).

11 Harald Welzer, ed., *Das soziale Gedächtnis: Geschichte, Erinnerung, Tradierung* (Hamburg: Hamburger Edition, 2001); Michael Schudson, *Watergate in American Memory: How We Remember, Forget, and Reconstruct the Past* (New York: Basic Books, 1993).

12 John R. Gillis, 'Memory and Identity: The History of a Relationship,' in J.R.

Gillis, ed., *Commemorations: The Politics of National Identity* (Princeton, NJ: Princeton University Press, 1994), 3.

13 Thus, for example, Gérard Bouchard recognizes the quest for ancient origins as an explanation for a variety of strategies in the construction of the collective memories of newer nations of the Americas: one adopts the origins of the European settler country as being the origins of one's own; a second sees origins in political ideals that antedate the demographic reality; another sees the origins of the nation threading back to the culture of aboriginal peoples who occupied the land before European settlement. Gérard Bouchard, *Génèse des nations et cultures du nouveau monde: Essai d'histoire comparée* (Quebec: Boréal, 2000).

14 In Daniel Breazeale, ed., *Untimely Meditations* (Cambridge: Cambridge University Press, 1997), 59–123.

15 Ibid., 83.

16 Ibid., 87.

17 Pierre Nora, *Realms of Memory: The Construction of the French Past*, trans. Arthur Goldhammer (New York: Columbia University Press, 1996), 1.

18 Tony Judt, 'A la recherche du temps perdu,' *New York Review of Books* 45, no. 19 (1998): 51–8.

19 Gabrielle M. Spiegel, 'Memory and History: Liturgical Time and Historical Time,' *History and Theory* 41, no. 2 (2002): 149–62.

20 Ibid., 152.

21 Ibid., 162.

22 John R. Gillis, 'Memory and identity,' 14.

23 Lowenthal, *The Past Is a Foreign Country*.

24 Herbert Gutman, 'Historical Consciousness in Contemporary America,' in H. Gutman, ed., *Power and Culture: Essays on the American Working Class* (New York: Pantheon, 1987).

25 Hans-Georg Gadamer, 'The Problem of Historical Consciousness,' in Paul Rabinow and William M. Sullivan, eds, *Interpretive Social Science: A Second Look* (Berkeley: University of California Press, 1987), 89.

26 Ibid., 90.

27 Peter Novick, *The Holocaust in American Life* (Boston: Houghton Mifflin, 1999), 4.

28 Lowenthal, *Possessed by the Past*.

29 For example, I have in mind the student who performed a sophisticated reading of Pierre Nora one week, using all of the critical tools available for textual critique at the turn of the 21st century, and then participated in the ritual incantations of traditional memory at his son's bar mitzvah the next.

30 http://www.tau.ac.il/humanities/publications/index.html/history.

31 Sharon Macdonald and Katja Fausser, 'Towards European Historical Consciousness,' in S. Macdonald, ed., *Approaches to European Historical Consciousness: Reflections and Provocations* (Hamburg: Koerber Stiftung, 2000), 10.

32 Robert B. Bain, 'Using Multiple Levels of Analysis in the World History Classroom,' paper presented at the American Historical Association, Washington (1999).

33 Peter Seixas, 'Conceptualizing the Growth of Historical Understanding,' in David Olson and Nancy Torrance, eds, *Handbook of Education and Human Development: New Models of Learning, Teaching, and Schooling* (Oxford, UK: Blackwell, 1996), 765–83.

34 See, e.g., Carlos Kolbl and Jurgen Straub, 'Historical Consciousness in Youth: Theoretical and Exemplary Empirical Analysis,' *Forum: Qualitative Social Research* 2, no. 3 (2001): http://www.qualitative-research.net/fqs.

35 C.F.G. Lorenz, 'Comparative Historiography: Problems and Perspectives,' *History and Theory* 38, no. 1 (1999): 25–39.

36 Keith Barton, 'A Sociocultural Perspective on Children's Understanding of Historical Change: Comparative Findings from Northern Ireland and the United States,' *American Educational Research Journal* 38, no. 4 (2001): 881–914.

37 Magne Angvik and Bodo von Borries, eds, *Youth and History: A Comparative European Survey on Historical Consciousness and Political Attitudes among Adolescents* (Hamburg: Körber-Stiftung, 1997). Also see Joke van der Leeuw-Roord, ed., *The State of History Education in Europe* (Hamburg: Koerber-Stiftung, 1998), 12.

38 Roy Rosenzweig and David Thelen, *Presence of the Past: Popular Uses of History in American Life* (New York: Columbia University Press, 1998).

39 Carlos Kolbl and Jurgen Straub, in 'Historical Consciousness in Youth,' have confronted this problem head-on, arguing, controversially, that historical consciousness 'is not a universal anthropological fact, but a result of the development of occidental cultures and societies.'

40 See, e.g., anthropologist Julie Cruikshank, *Reading Voices* (Vancouver, BC: Douglas & McIntyre, 1991) and historians Dipesh Chakrabarty, *Provincializing Europe: Postcolonial Thought and Historical Difference* (Princeton, NJ: Princeton University Press, 2000) and Ranajit Guha, *History at the Limit of World-History* (New York: Columbia University Press, 2002).

41 See, e.g., Roger Simon in this volume.

42 See, e.g., Keith Windschuttle, *The Killing of History: How Literary Theorists and Social Critics Are Murdering Our Past* (New York: Free Press, 1997); Gary B. Nash, Charlotte Crabtree, and Ross Dunn, *History on Trial: Culture Wars and the Teaching of the Past* (New York, 1997); Jack Granatstein, *Who Killed Cana-*

dian History? (Toronto: HarperCollins, 1998); Peter Gathercole and David Lowenthal, eds, *The Politics of the Past* (London: Unwin Hyman Ltd, 1990); Rob Phillips, *History Teaching, Nationhood and the State: A Study in Educational Politics* (London: Continuum, 1998).

43 Tony Bennett, *The Birth of the Museum* (New York: Routledge, 1995); Eilean Hooper-Greenhill, *Museums and the Shaping of Knowledge* (London: Routledge, 1993); Darryl McIntyre and Kirsten Wehner, eds, *National Museums: Negotiating Histories* (National Museum of Australia, 2001).

PART I

Historiographies and Historical Consciousness

In the first chapter of this collection, Chris Lorenz treats the professional historian as both producer and product of more generalized collective memory, and thus makes an important contribution to the understanding of historical consciousness, without making the term itself central. Thanks to his care in the handling of the role of professional historiography in the construction of historical identity among populations in general, his contribution makes a most appropriate first chapter in this volume. Lorenz uses the case of Quebec and Canada as a vehicle for the exposition of a capacious and wide-ranging analytical framework, with 'historical identity,' or identity developed over time, as the central concept. He maps relationships among key issues that need to be confronted in order to conduct cross-national and cross-cultural comparisons. After an introduction to the notion of 'normal' and 'abnormal' historiographies, the first part of his chapter explores the concept of historical identity. Because the concept is fundamentally relational, Lorenz argues, any particular expression of historical identity (national or otherwise) at least implicitly rests on a comparative foundation. He distinguishes between Enlightenment (universalist) and Romantic (particularist) bases of comparison. The second part of the chapter examines spatial and temporal aspects of historical identity, as well as religious, racial, class, and gender identities. The three succeeding chapters in this section provide conceptual tools with which to expand and elaborate the comparative work in historical consciousness advocated by Lorenz.

James Wertsch has found that, beneath the specific narratives that may change dramatically as one political regime is supplanted by the next, there are ongoing continuities, expressed in 'schematic narrative templates,' which are culturally specific and relatively enduring over time.[1] Specific narratives, in this account, change because new official versions of the past are invoked in support of new regimes. Wertsch has explored, elsewhere, the disjunctions between officially sanctioned and promoted collective memories and those narratives that are believed by the populations living under those official regimes. This consideration reminds us of the importance of studying not only the production of the narratives of collective memory and the structures within which they are preserved and promoted, but also their reception by various populations.[2] If 'schematic narrative templates' prove to be a fruitful analytical tool, then it will be because they lie deep enough beneath the surface that they shape not only the official versions of the past, but also the believed versions that may vary from group to group.

Jörn Rüsen's contribution to this volume is a revised version of an essay first published in English in 1989. The scheme he lays out in this chapter has been foundational in German and European studies, but it has had much less circulation in English.[3] He posits a hierarchy of four types, each representing a different stance towards the past as a means of moral orientation in the present. To summarize, in highly abbreviated form:

- Historical consciousness can support the continuity of fixed and unchanging moral obligations, without acknowledging any significant change over time (the 'traditional' type).
- It can draw on particular events and people from the past as a source of cultural universals, which apply across temporal change, as in the celebratory history of heroes to inspire strong character in the present (the 'exemplary' type).
- It can turn towards the past in order to break from it, as in women's history that helps to undo the past's oppressive gender relations (the 'critical' type).
- It can acknowledge the ongoing legacy of the past, at the same time. that it comprehends radically changed present circumstances and mores (the 'genetic' type).

Rüsen proposes this typology as a hierarchy in terms of cognitive and moral complexity, and thus a lens through which to examine both individual psychological (or 'ontogenetic') and socio-cultural development. There are clearly both tremendous risks and potential rewards from such a theoretical linkage of individual development and socio-cultural development. Rüsen is fully aware of the danger of an overly linear and one-dimensional model of progress, with the cultural tools and dispositions of modern Europe, on the socio-cultural side, taken as the goal for all cultures. There is also a risk in fashioning psychological models of development a priori from socio-cultural models, without the empirical work necessary to substantiate and justify the 'types' as they are defined. Rüsen himself points out the difficulty in locating any particular individual along this range: indeed, he writes, 'elements of all four types are operatively intermixed in the procedure that gives practical life a historical orientation in time.'

Though it has provided crucial elements for the study of historical consciousness, Rüsen's scheme leaves largely undefined the relationship between the disciplinary practices of historians and the types of historical consciousness. The 'traditional' type appears to be pre-historiographic in its failure to comprehend change over time. The exemplary and critical types bear some prima facie correspondence to progressive and the 'new' historiography of the 1970s, respectively, in North American terms. And the 'genetic' type, opening up 'the possibility of a multiplicity of standpoints,' as well as complexity in relation to historical identity and patterns of historical significance, looks compatible with historiographic trends of the past two decades. But the types are defined in terms of the experience of time, perceptions of historical significance, and moral judgments, values, and reasoning. Rüsen does little to relate these orientations explicitly to other fundamentally defining practices of historians such as the reading of textual evidence. Further work is necessary to define the relationships between disciplinary history and 'advancement' in historical consciousness, as framed by Rüsen. As uncomfortable as such phraseology may be – and here Rüsen's work is crucial – *some* notion of 'advancement' must undergird normative prescriptions for history education that answer the question, 'What should we cultivate in the way of historical consciousness in the next generation?' Rüsen's ambitious answer takes us far beyond the ubiquitous but empty answer 'Teach more history.'

Nobody who studies historiography, of course, works under the illusion that professional historians provide a single model for understanding the past. Mark Phillips draws attention to the dangers of unexamined assumptions about an 'ideal' stance for historiography by pointing to a dimension of historical representation that generally remains tacit: that of historical distance. While historians have been quite silent on this subject, there is nevertheless a broad, though unexamined agreement about what appropriate distance is and where its value lies: the modern, professional consensus closely identifies genuine historical knowledge with a position of relative detachment. This chapter challenges this consensus by (a) noting that historical distance is not so much given as constructed, (b) defining several kinds of distance in historical representation (formal, affective, ideological, and cognitive), and (c) providing examples of variations in 'appropriate' historical distance. By articulating and mapping this heretofore largely implicit dimension of historical representation, Phillips opens up the possibility of more deliberate use of distance as a variable in the study of historical consciousness.

Notes

1 In addition to his chapter in this volume, see also Wertsch, *Voices of Collective Remembering* (New York: Cambridge University Press, 2002), esp. chap. 3, 'Collective Memory: A Term in Search of a Meaning.'

2 Wulf Kansteiner, 'Finding Meaning in Memory: A Methodological Critique of Memory Studies,' *History and Theory* 41, no. 2 (2002): 179–97; Stuart Hall, 'Encoding/Decoding,' in David Graddol and Oliver Boyd-Barrett, eds, *Media Texts: Authors and Readers* (Clevedon, Avon, UK: Open University, 1994), 200–11.

3 In addition to his chapter in this volume, see also Rüsen, *Historische Orientierung: Über die Arbeit des Geschichtsbewußtseins, sich in der Zeit zurechtzufinden* (Köln: Böhlau, 1994); Rüsen, *Historisches Lernen. Grundlagen und Paradigmen* (Köln: Böhlau, 1994); Rüsen, *Zerbrechende Zeit: Über den Sinn der Geschichte* (Köln: Böhlau, 2001); Bodo von Borries and Jörn Rüsen, eds, *Geschichtsbewußtsein im interkulturellen Vergleich* (Pfaffenweiler: Centaurus, 1994); and Rüsen, ed., *Geschichtsbewußtsein: Psychologische Grundlagen, Entwicklungskonzepte, empirische Befunde* (Köln: Böhlau, 2001).

Towards a Theoretical Framework for Comparing Historiographies: Some Preliminary Considerations

CHRIS LORENZ

In his recent book *Making History in Twentieth-Century Quebec*, Montreal historian Ronald Rudin starts his introduction with the following somewhat paradoxical observation:

> The point has often been made that history occupies a privileged place in Quebec culture. The motto of the province – *Je me souviens* (I remember) is but one indicator of this reverence for the past. Another is the special status still reserved in Quebeckers' collective memory for Abbé Groulx, the first full-time university professor of Quebec history, more than twenty-five years after his death. In spite of this interest in the past, however, no single volume has yet been dedicated to a comprehensive analysis of Quebec historical writing over the course of the twentieth century. During this period historical writing was increasingly carried out, throughout much of the Western world, by people who viewed themselves as professionals engaged in a 'scientific endeavour.'[1]

And then, of course, the author informs his readers that the book they are about to read is the first book containing this comprehensive analysis of Quebec historiography.

Now, assuming for the moment that Rudin's observations about Quebec are correct, he points to the remarkable fact that at the end of the twentieth century the privileged place of *history* in Quebec does not imply a similar privileged place for Quebec *historiography* (the history of history writing).[2] Rudin develops an explanation for this apparent contradition, which goes something like this: the 'Quiet Revolution' that has revolutionized Quebec society since the 1950s has also revolutionized Quebec historiography by producing 'revisionist' historians. These 'revisionist' historians have been promoting themselves as 'scientific experts,' meanwhile profiting from the unprecedented expansion of the universities. At the same time, however, they turned their back on Quebec's specific traditions. Instead of emphasizing the continuing particularity of 'the French fact' in Anglo-Saxon North America, as most of their predecessors had done, the revisionists started stressing Quebec's essential 'normality.' They replaced Quebec's traditional discourse of difference, which emphasized *la survivance*, with a brand-new discourse of normality, emphasizing Quebec as a normal modern, Western society.

This change from a fixation on Quebec's difference to a fixation on Quebec's essential normality was a real 'paradigm shift,' and Rudin interprets this shift both as a product and as a producer of a new collective identity of Quebec. Traditional Quebec history, centred on the French period and the subsequent defeats by the British, was pushed aside by the history of 'modern' Quebec, starting around the 1850s and centred on the unfolding process of industrialization, urbanization, and economic rationalization.

At the end of his book Rudin signals a recent but growing unease among younger Quebec historians with this type of revisionist approach, because the revisionists' apparent obsession with Quebec's 'normality' obscures its particular historical and cultural characteristics. In addition, Rudin criticizes the revisionists for their lack of a sound reflection on their own trade, Quebec historiography itself. Their lack of reflexivity manifests itself in a contradiction: *if* it is true, as the revisionists say, that Quebec has been surprisingly 'normal' and modern for at least one century and a half, then how can it be that Quebec has produced a 'normal' scientific historiography *only* since the rise of revisionism, that is, after the 'Quiet Revolution'? This last conviction has also been part and parcel of revisionist writings: that the predecessors of revisionism had been amateurs and partisan historians, while the revisionists were the first real 'scientific' historians of Quebec. Rudin thus ends his book by criticizing the revisionist historians for their lack of self-reflection.

Here I have chosen Rudin's analysis of revisionist Quebec historiography in order to introduce some general problems of comparative historiography, which are relevant for theorizing historical consciousness. However, I must inform the reader from the outset that my remarks do *not* constitute a theoretical framework in any stringent sense. The most I can offer are some clarifications of questions and concepts that may be useful when comparing historiographies.[3] Most of the real work is still ahead, but that is what research projects are about.

Now, which general problems of comparative historiography am I referring to? The first general theme brought up by Rudin is the relationship between historical consciousness in a broader societal and cultural sense – sometimes identified by the nebulous term collective memory (criticized in John Torpey's contribution to this volume) – on the one side and professional history on the other.[4] This relationship needs to be addressed because professional historians are far from being the only producers of historical consciousness. From its beginning professional history has been in competition with several other representational forms of history, such as myth, literary fiction, and 'amateur' history (including the histories handed over from generation to generation in families and 'Stammtisch'-histories).[5] Moreover, since the sudden rise of cultural studies, the study of the past has also been practised by professionals other than historians, such as literary critics and anthropologists, a trend that has evoked some alarmist reactions.[6] Since television and film have replaced the book as the most important media of information, the non-professional forms of historical representation have been gaining an ever-increasing influence on the formation of historical consciousness. In this arena no professional book can compete with films such as *JFK* or *Schindler's List*. Thus, the *media* of representation have had a profound influence on the *content* of representation of the past.

This theme, which is explicitly addressed by Christian Laville in this volume, is an important one for at least two reasons. The first is that it concerns the relationship between the production and consumption of historical representations (including the schoolbook versions of professional history). The issue here is that we can only determine the influence of professional historiography on historical consciousness in relation to other influences.[7] The second reason is that the relationship between the production and consumption of the various sorts of historical representations may also tell us something important about the contents of professional historiography. It is my hypothesis that one important problem of professional history nowadays is its neglect of several domains of human experience that are regarded as crucial for our modern age. I am hinting at experiences of facing the extreme, also labelled as liminal, catastrophic, and traumatic experiences or the experience of the sublime. These domains of experience seem to escape the grips of 'normal' professional history, probably because such types of experience usually leave few controllable documentary traces – except for the individual stories about them. This circumstance may explain why the experience of trench warfare has primarily been documented in (memoir) literature written by former participants and not in 'normal' history books.[8] It may also explain why the experiences of modern concentration and extermination camps has been dominated by literary and not by historical representations.[9]

However this may be, I shall argue that the relationship between professional historians and their societies can be analysed in a fruitful way by the concept of collective identity. Although the concept of identity, including collective identity, is also hotly debated, I think it is fundamental for the analysis of the practical functions of history.[10] Through the concept of identity, the three time dimensions of past, present, and future can plausibly be connected, as also indicated by Jörn Rüsen, Jocelyn Létourneau, and John Torpey in their contributions to this volume. The basic idea is that professional historians are both products *and* producers of the collective identities of the cultures of which they are part (the very same idea that Rudin formulated in relation to Quebec).

The second general theme brought up by Rudin is the practical function of historiographical discourse. In identifying both the traditional discourse of difference and the revisionist discourse of normality in Quebec historiography, he touches on the relationship between history and collective identity. Difference simply presupposes sameness or identity and the same holds for normality. Now, whenever the normality of a nation or of a state turns into an issue, this is the surest indication of a widespread suspicion of its *ab*normality. Only people whose normality is being questioned seriously – by themselves or by others – are inclined to debate the issue. The post-war obsession of Germany with its *Normalität* is a paradigmatic example.

The same story holds for the discourse of difference: whenever individuals and collectives transform their difference into an issue, this is the surest indication that their experience of being different is under threat. This circumstance may explain why the discussions about identity issues are unevenly distributed in space and time. Thus, both the discourses of normality and the discourse of difference are symptoms of perceived threats to identity. From a comparative point of view it may be worthwhile to note that we find these discourses not only in Quebec historiography, but also in English-Canadian historiography – in the discussion about 'limited identities' – and extensively in German historiography.[11] So Rudin's second theme leads to questions about the relation between history and identity.

I shall deal with the relation between history and identity in two steps. First, I shall dwell on some of the conceptual characteristics of the slippery notion of identity in order to elucidate its fundamentally multiple character. This multiplicity is essential for our understanding of multiplicity in historiography. In the second step I shall fill the concept of historical identity with some material content, addressing the relationship between different forms of collective identity, especially national identity, religious identity, and class identity. Further I shall identify some categories and problems that appear useful when comparing historiographies.

The Concept of Historical Identity

When we are referring to the identity of individuals and collectives, we refer to the properties that make them different from each other in a particular frame of reference. It is on the basis of their particular set of properties that we can identify them as individuals and tell them apart. Identity or sameness and difference or otherness, therefore, presuppose each other: without identity there is no difference and without difference there is no identity. For example, the notion of personal identity or of a 'self' presupposes the notion of the 'non-self' or the 'other.' Therefore, there can be no Other in any absolute sense, because the concepts of the Self and of the Other are conceptually related.[12] Identity and difference are thus fundamentally relational concepts and are, as such, fundamentally opposed to essentialist concepts (which imply that, for instance, nationhood and ethnicity are invariant essences). Sam Wineburg's enlightening location of historical understanding between the poles of familiarity and strangeness can directly be connected to the dichotomy of Self (familiarity) and Otherness (strangeness).[13] And the fundamental multiplicity of descriptions of identity can also be connected to its relational quality, because one can relate any Self to various Others (as is observed in James Wertsch's contribution to this volume on the function of 'aliens' in Russian self-definitions, and also in Peter Lee's contribution).

This relational quality, of course, also holds for the notion of collective identity. We can identify an 'in-group' – a 'we' – only in relation to an 'out-group' – a 'they.' There can only be inclusion in a collective if there is at the same time exclusion. The notion of a 'limited identity,' which has popped up in the English-Canadian discussion, is therefore a category mistake because identity is limited by definition. The abdication of this notion by Ramsay Cook was certainly justified.

In history we can observe the relational character of collective identity concretely because we can trace the demarcations of in-groups from out-groups *in statu nascendi*. The discourses on national identity are a case in point. For instance, the discourse on German national identity in the early nineteenth century was conducted by opposing characteristics of the Germans to characteristics of the French. In the discourses on Dutch identity, to take another example, we observe a change from opposing the Dutch to the French in the early nineteenth century to opposing the Dutch to Germans from the late nineteenth century onwards. Similar observations pertain to the discourse on the Canadian identity, where the United States often functions as the identity *ex negativo*. So we can observe that representation of collective identity is closely related to other particular collective identities in a negative way. Identity is constructed by negation, as Spinoza, Hegel, and Foucault argued some time ago. This also holds for the special cases in which a new identity is constructed by negating one's own former identity. This phenomenon is not unusual in the aftermath of traumatic experience: both individuals and collectives may try to start a 'new life' by adopting a new identity. This transformation is usually accompanied by publicly acknowledging past 'mistakes' and by trying to make up for them. The Federal Republic of Germany offers a clear historical example because it defined itself politically as the democratic negation of totalitarian Nazi Germany. Because undoing the past is impossible by definition, material reparations for past misdeeds and mourning – *Trauer* – is all that is left in the end.

In history, this negative bond between collective identities is often connected to some sense of being under threat and is therefore embedded in power relations. The Germans and the Dutch in the early nineteenth century, for instance, had recently had bad experiences with France, but later in the century many Dutch started worrying more seriously about the expanding German empire. Since mighty neighbours are usually perceived as (at least potentially) threatening, the negative aspects of collective identities are probably most outspoken among the less powerful collectives. And because power relations may change over time, we can also expect parallel changes in the discourses of national identities.

This negative bond between different collective identities – this need of a 'negation' in articulating one's own identity – also helps to explain another important historical phenomenon, that of the collective exclusion of minorities by majorities – ranging from discrimination to expulsion and annihilation – especially in periods of crisis. Such minorities are usually represented as some kind of aliens or strangers who pose a threat to the very identity of the majority.[14] From this angle, the simultaneous rise of nationalism and of popular anti-Semitism in the nineteenth and twentieth centuries is not accidental, nor is the fact that anti-Semitism was especially virulent in regions with suppressed forms of nationalism, like in east-central Europe. As we shall see in the second part of my contribution, weak nations may also adapt to mighty neighbours in another way by defining themselves as 'blends' of neighbouring cultures or as international mediators. Their collective identity is then defined not primarily by negating other identities but instead by absorbing them.[15] Nevertheless, the need to specify the core identity in the mix of others still remains.

Before we turn to the concept of historical identity, it is important to keep in mind that historical identity is just one type of identity among others. Individuals, for instance, can also be identified through their biological identity, that is, their DNA profile. Moreover, in a not so distant past, serious attempts have been made in order to identify collectives in terms of racial identity. Thus, the identification of individuals and collectives in terms of historical identity is not self-evident and therefore requires an explanation. Many historians are inclined to forget this fact, because it means that doing history needs an explanation and a justification. In this volume the chapters by Torpey and Rüsen address this issue, so I shall not deal with it here.[16]

Be that as it may, when we are talking about the historical identity of individuals and collectives, we refer to a type of identity that is defined by its development in time. The paradigm case of historical identity can therefore be conceived on the model of personal identity (although we must always be very careful not to attribute the properties of individuals to collectives). The identity of a subject consists of the set of characteristics that the subject develops over time in interaction with its environment and that set it apart from similar subjects. This set of characteristics is not random, if we are talking about historical and personal identity, but must relate to important characteristics. It is also possible in principle to identify individuals through their fingerprints or iris, but we would not associate personal identity with properties of that kind.

The same holds for the concept of historical identity. In both cases, identity does not just mean telling individuals apart from each other (i.e., describing numerical identity); rather, it means a characterization of individuality (i.e., describing a qualitative identity). It is no accident, therefore, that the biography, in which an individual develops a personal identity in time, has often been regarded as the paradigm of doing history (by Dilthey, for instance).

Historical identity thus has a paradoxical quality, because it is identity through change in time. When we are referring to the historical identity of Canada, we are thus referring to a collective that retained a particular identity over time in its interactions with its environment – although this same Canada changed at the same time. Historical identity is therefore essentially persistence through change or the identity of identity and non-identity, to quote the apt Hegelian formulation of Odo Marquard.[17]

Historical Identity between Particularism and Universalism

The fact that individuals and collectives can be described in terms of particular characteristics, constituting unique identities, does not of course mean that collective identities can be described in just one way. The mode of description is always dependent on the frame of reference that is used by the historian. Through the frame of reference the historian constructs implicit or explicit relations between his case and others. Within the framework of Canada, for instance, Quebec can be described as the province with a French-speaking majority or as the only province with a formal status as a 'distinct society' – thus constructing a contrasting relation between Quebec and the other provinces of Canada. Within the framework of the new nations, however, Quebec can simultaneously be described as the only new nation in the New World that did *not* attain political sovereignty (as Gérard Bouchard recently argued).[18] Bouchard thus constructs a contrasting relation between Quebec and new nations like New Zealand and Australia. History itself does not force a historian to use the former or the latter frame of reference. It is, rather, the other way around: what history looks like is more or less defined by its representations (although, of course, history in turn defines the range of plausible representations). The frame of reference in representations is entirely dependent on the choice of the historian (although the choice may be an unconscious one, when the historian lacks the imagination to see the past differently from the way he or she does).[19]

The fact that individuals and collectives can be described in terms of unique identities does not imply that they cannot be described as similar. Actually, this emphasis on similarity instead of on particularity was dominant in Enlightenment historiography, when the diversity of so-called 'national characters' was basically seen as variety within a common human species. The variety of 'national characters' was basically interpreted as the variety of their location on the developmental path of 'civilization.' Only after the Enlightenment, under the influence of Romanticism, was the particularity of each 'national character' anchored in a particular language; next this particular language was transformed into a nation's essence. What the various 'national characters' had in common – their common humanity – then faded into the background (only making its comeback in our 'post-national' rediscovery of universal human rights). The politically emancipatory contents of the idea of the nation also evaporated after 1815; after all, the idea of the nation had been the justification of modern representative democracy and was criticized by conservatives precisely for that reason. Only in the second half of the nineteenth century was nationalism discovered by conservatism as an effective ideology in its struggle against universalism and democracy.

To all appearances, the opposition between the universalist outlook of the Enlightenment and the particularistic outlook of Romanticism is still with us in historiography today. This opposition may be located in the various weights a historian attributes to the factor of ethnicity within the nation. Civic representations of nationhood are a direct offspring of Enlightenment universalism, while ethnic representations owe more to the particularism of Romanticism.[20] The same tension can be located in the debate about so-called post-national identities (like the 'European identity' and perhaps even a 'NAFTA identity'), an issue brought up in Laville's contribution to this volume.

When we stick to the representation of national identity, the case of Canada offers an example. One can write a history of Canada as the history of *the* Canadian nation – the only legitimate way to write Canadian history according to historians like Granatstein. By contrast, many Quebec historians seem to prefer to write the history of Canada as the history of a federation originating in *two* nations – the British and the French. According to others – and Margaret Conrad is among those – this representation of Canada is inadequate, because the First Nations were here long before the French and the British arrived. Therefore, the history of Canada is the history of a multitude of ethnic groups and can better be written as the *History of the Canadian Peoples* – in the plural.[21]

Canada's past can thus be represented from a national, a bi-national, and a multi-ethnic perspective or frame of reference, each with its own blend of universalism and particularism. Therefore, in historiography we are faced with the problem of how to integrate the different perspectives, if we are not satisfied with the observation that historical narratives just look different. As a ground rule, representations that integrate more relevant perspectives than competing representations in a coherent and balanced manner are to be preferred. The more distinct voices of relevant 'Others' are included in a collective identity, the better is the quality of its representation. To be brief, I can introduce my view on multiple perspectives in historiography with three observations.

First, the fundamental fact that historians are faced with a choice among different perspectives does not mean that this choice is free from empirical considerations, that is, free from the evidence. It only means that although historical evidence does not determine the choice of perspective in history, the evidence restricts the choices. Second, the role of empirical considerations does not mean that the choice of perspective is free from normative considerations. This would be very implausible a priori, because representations of identity offer an orientation in time (as Rüsen rightly emphasizes) and time implies past, present, and future. The choice among perspectives can therefore usually be connected to the identity politics of the historian (and neither the 'end of ideology' nor 'the end of history' has changed this fundamental fact of historiography, as Torpey and Létourneau have rightly observed in their contributions). As Rüsen states in his chapter, historical identity is a matter both of factual and of normative arguments *at the same time.*

The choice between multiple perspectives, therefore, is not arbitrary; nor does the possibility of choice mean that one perspective is as good as another. The 'underdetermination' of the perspectives by the evidence and the role of normative considerations only implies that historians are forced to justify their perspectives explicitly by arguments. This, again, can only be done by arguing for one perspective in relation to others. Since history has lost what we could call its 'epistemological innocence' – that is, the idea that historians are capable of 'just telling it like it really was' – historians are forced to become self-reflective, whether they like it or not. 'Doing history' has become more 'philosophical' in this sense, because representing history implies presenting a debate, that is, presenting the various ways in which the past has been represented in time. The borderlines between 'plain' history and historiography have therefore become more porous than before.

Third, and last, respect for the evidence (and for the methodological rules) remains paramount as long as historical representations claim to be scientific, that is, are presented as claims to knowledge with a universal validity.[22] This claim to universal validity is the basis of all scientific historical debates. Although history is about identity, therefore, 'identity history is not enough,' to quote Eric Hobsbawm.[23] So much for the problem of multiple perspectives in historiography for the moment.

Bouchard's description of Quebec as the only new nation that did *not* attain statehood, by the way, offers a concrete illustration of what I have said earlier on about the role of negation in the construction of collective identity. Bouchard's description of Quebec is a clear example of a collective that is characterized in terms of a negative property, that is, in terms of what a collective is lacking in comparison to others; in Bouchard's case, statehood. Here there is a remarkable parallel between Quebec and German historiography, because Germany has long been characterized by historians like Hans-Ulrich Wehler as the only modern society in the West that did not develop some kind of parliamentary democracy on its own. In this sense Germany is contrasted with other 'modern' countries, like France, England, and the United States. Instead of a democracy, Germany developed aggressive authoritarian regimes, like the German empire of 1871 and, last but not least, the Third Reich.[24]

This comparison between the historiography of Quebec and of Germany suggests that when a collective identity is explicitly characterized in terms of a 'missing' property, this is a property that is highly valued by the historian – statehood in Bouchard's history of Quebec and parliamentary democracy in Wehler's history of modern Germany. In both cases the 'missing' property is represented as a consequence of a 'false' development in comparison with 'good' developments elsewhere. So both cases show nicely how the construction of a collective identity is negatively related to other collective identities and is thus based on comparisons – implicit or explicit. Both cases illustrate that history writing may be comparative, even when it is concerned with one particular case.

Historical Identity: Ingredients for the Comparison of Historiographies

I come now to the second part of my contribution, which concerns the empirical forms of historical identity as we confront them in historiography. Here I want to address the question of how we can bring some order to the multiplicity of historical representations. In order to do so we have to develop some framework in which historiographies can be 'marked' and compared to each other. For this task we need some ways to classify historiographies and thus some kind of conceptual matrix. My aim is to suggest some dimensions for such a matrix and to identify some of the problems we are likely to face.[25] Alas, we shall soon discover that there are quite a few of those.

For reasons of efficiency, I shall take national historiographies – history writing in the frame of the nation-state – as a general point of reference, because that is the most usual point of departure in professional historiography. I shall propose to use the axes of space and time as the first and most general dimensions for ordering the different sorts of historiography. Because history implies a location in space and time, all objects of historical representation have spatial and temporal characteristics, which can in principle be used as a basis for comparison. Next to space and time I shall propose some other non-spatial dimensions, like religion, class, race, and gender. At the end of my contribution, I will deal with some aspects of the dimension of time.

The Spatial Classification of Historiographies: Problems with the Nation

When we take the historiography of the nation-state as our point of spatial reference, we can differentiate between historiographies on a *sub-national* level – such as villages, cities, and regions – and units on a *supra-national* level – such as multinational empires, particular subsets of nations (like the new nations), continents, cultures, civilizations, and, last but not least, the world. So we can construct an orderly scheme containing a sub-national, a national, and a supra-national level. When this scheme is applied to concrete forms of historiography, however, we confront at least three kinds of problems that complicate it in practice. The first problem is that of the ideological load of various spatial concepts; the second is the problem of the double meaning of some spatial concepts; and the third and last problem is that of the essentially contested nature of some spatial concepts, the nation in particular.

The first problem, that of the ideological load of some spatial concepts, has been put on the agenda by Edward Said in his analysis of the notion of the 'Orient.' He showed that although most spatial concepts look quite neutral and innocent at first sight, they often have carried important ideological and political implications. As politics has traditionally contained a very important spatial dimension, this political dimension of spatial orderings was perhaps to be expected. Like 'the Orient,' the notion of 'the primitive,' 'the savage,' and the 'barbarian' have fulfilled similar ideological functions in the colonial encounter, because – like 'the Orient' – they were used as the justification of the domination of 'the primitive' by its supposed opposite: the 'civilized' part of the world ('the Occident'). In European history of the twentieth century spatial concepts like 'Mitteleuropa' and 'Asia' have fulfilled similar ideological functions, implying claims of political hegemony. Perhaps the spatial notion of 'the wilderness,' versus 'civilization,' has played a similar role in North American history.

The second problem with the spatial scheme is that the spatial scope of a historical work is not always what it seems. This realization is important when, for instance, we would like to assess the relationship between regional and national historiographies in, say, Canada. What makes such an assessment complicated is the fact that historians may cloak the history of a region as the history of a nation. In that case, the micro-cosmos of the region functions as a stand-in for the macro-cosmos of the nation. For instance, a history of Holland – the western province of the Netherlands – has been presented as the history of the whole Netherlands. In a similar manner, the history of Prussia has been presented as the history of Germany. And maybe there are histories of Ontario parading as histories of Canada. The spatial unit, therefore, may function as a *pars pro toto*. This problem may seriously complicate the classification of historiographies on the basis of spatial markers.

The third and perhaps most troubling problem in our spatial scheme is the essentially contested character of its central concept: the nation. The nation belongs to the same category as notions like 'freedom' and 'democracy,' which also refuse unambiguous definition. Therefore, I can only signal the problem here, which is, fundamentally, that in the discourse on the nation, the nation does not necessarily coincide with the state or even with the nation-state. Sometimes spatial units at a sub-state level, like provinces (Quebec, for instance) or tribal areas (the First Nations, for instance) are represented as nations. And sometimes nations (like the British or the German nations in the nineteenth and the first half of the twentieth centuries, or the Albanian and the Kurdish nations in the present) are represented as supra-national units, that is, as units exceeding the borders of a nation-state. The nation therefore has a very fuzzy extension.

To make the definitional problems of the nation worse still, there are a few collectives identified as nations without a 'place of their own,' that is, without an identifiable spatial anchor. The Jews, the Sinti, and Roma are well-known examples in European history. So, although the rule is that nations are usually associated with some spatial location, there are also exceptions to this rule.

These definitional issues could perhaps be regarded as only annoying if there were no serious practical problems attached to them. This happens to be the case, however, because the issue of collective identity – and especially of national identity – is firmly connected to the issue of collective rights. Since collective identity is regarded as the basis and as the justification of collective rights – including political autonomy – issues of collective identity may have serious political implications. The history of nationalism presents a clear case (and Laville in his chapter rightly points at the intimate relationship between the rise of the historical profession and that of the nation-state). Because representations of collective identity are usually anchored in the past, the representation of historical identity may have serious political implications too. This is, of course, evident in Canada, where the claim to political autonomy of the Québécois has always been based on the representation of the French-speaking majority as a nation.[26] By implication, according to this view, Canada *is* not a nation, but only contains nations – in the plural (as Létourneau emphasizes in his chapter).[27]

The First Nations offer another clear example of the political implications linked to the representation of collective identity: the Nisga'a Treaty of 1998, which restored the collective rights of this First Nation to its former heartland, offers a clear example, underscoring the practical dimension of historical representation.[28]

Of course it is not the task of professional historians to solve these practical issues – this is a matter of politics – but I do think that it is a task of professional historians to clarify the historical roots of political problems. (I do not say this is their only task, only that it is a very important one.) In practice, this amounts to the identification and the integration of the different and often conflicting perspectives pertaining to present-day issues. This identification and combination of perspectives is the most practical meaning of striving for objectivity in history that I know of. Striving after objectivity in this sense is a necessary condition for scientific history, because striving after truth is not enough.[29] This, by the way, would at the same time be my interpretation of furthering the cause of 'historical consciousness,' because 'objective' history in this sense furthers the understanding of the historical origins of present-day problems.

The attempt to classify historiographies on the basis of the spatial dimension has thus led us to and through the swamps of the nation into the battlefields of historiography. We can conclude that, to a certain degree, the battles for space in the past are still continued in their present-day historiographical representations. This circumstance suggests that it is neither realistic nor reasonable to expect consensus in historiography. As in politics, the most we can strive for is a sound knowledge of the different points of view, leading to a maximum of empathy and to mutual understanding of past and present positions. This can only be achieved, as I argued earlier on, by presenting history in the form of a debate among different and often conflicting representations. This mode of presentation is fit not only for university classes, but also for history education in school. I must admit that to me this is a new insight, because I have often heard the argument that young children must first get one picture of the past before raising the problem of alternative pictures.

Overlapping and Competing Identities

The battle for space, however, is far from being the only serious battlefield in historiography. The multiple representations of what constitutes a nation are just one instance of the general phenomenon of overlapping and competing identities in historiography. This phenomenon was to be expected because, as I have argued earlier, historical identity can be represented in various (though not arbitrary) ways. Now national identities usually overlap and sometimes compete with other spatial identities – such as regional identities or they may compete with other national identities (especially in borderlands).[30] However, they may also compete with non-spatial types of collective identity, such as religious, racial, class, and gender identities. And to complicate this complex situation still further, different representations of the same collective identity may compete and conflict with one another – as in the case of conflicting ethnic and civic definitions of the nation.[31]

Since the Reformation and the separation of Protestantism from Catholicism, there has often been a close relationship between religious and national collective identities. Especially since the nineteenth century among nations with a problematic existence as a political entity, like the Poles, the Irish, the Italians, and the Hungars, this relationship between nationality and religion has been especially close. Quebec is far from unique seen in this frame of reference.

In the context of an analysis of 'historical consciousness' in the broad sense, the interrelations between national and religious identity may require further attention, because they have more in common than is usually assumed. Recently it has been argued that nationalism and religion are basically comparable phenomena, fulfilling similar cultural functions and using similar cultural mechanisms. The cult of the nation bears a clear resemblance to religious cults: both are centred on a sacred dogma and a sacred object – God and the Nation. Both have sacred symbols and both have a fixed calendar and fixed places for their rituals – the churches and the national monuments. Both worship special persons, who are regarded as mediators between the worlds of the sacred and the profane. In religious cults these special persons are the saints and martyrs; in national cults they are national heroes, especially the ones who founded the Nation and those who sacrificed their lives for the Nation. In both violent death in defence of the Sacred Cause is represented as worthy and meaningful – as a sacrifice – because it helps the community to continue its cult and its existence.[32] Thus, in both cases we usually encounter a reverence for the dead. Both essentially define moral communities that define the borders of human solidarity. The concept of character can thus be regarded as the secularized version of the concept of the soul and this also applies to the idea of 'national character.' The relation and competition between national and religious identity therefore is an important one from a comparative perspective.

The competition of national and ethnic identities with class, racial, and gender identities is of more recent date than their competition with religious identity. Racial identity has competed with national identity in all colonial encounters (outside and inside Europe) and whenever national identity was conceived of in biological terms, as in the Nazi period. Class identity has only been a competitor of national identity in the nineteenth century and under twentieth-century communism. Gender identity is quite another case: gender has not been so much a collective identity in competition with the nation as it has been an analytical category used to determine the gendered nature of representations of the nation (think of the notion of the Fatherland!).

Thus, collective identity can be defined in terms of spatial marks, in terms of non-spatial marks, and also in terms of combinations of spatial and non-spatial marks. And although pure geographic determinism nowadays finds few defenders, we should not forget that 'national characters' have for a long time been explained in terms of geography (and its correlate, the climate), implying a reduction of the non-spatial marks to the spatial ones. We still confront echoes of geographic determinism in the discourses on national identity; Montesquieu was certainly not the last thinker along these lines. For instance, the Dutch national identity has sometimes been located in the struggle of the Dutch against the surrounding waters, while Swiss national identity has sometimes been located in the Alps.[33] The spatial location of Canada's national identity in the construction of the Canadian Pacific Railway is thus not unique, and its mythical role may even be compared to that of the construction of the famous Dutch dikes (although the last achievement was never claimed by one company).

Openness and Closure of National Identity

Next to the characterization of collective identities in terms of spatial and non-spatial marks, it seems meaningful to analyse representations of national identity on the continuum between openness and closure in relation to other nations. In the first part of this chapter I mentioned the fact that some nations have defined their identity as being mediators of other cultures, emphasizing their openness to *other* national identities. The representation of Canada's national identity as a 'mosaic' is probably the clearest example of this fascinating phenomenon, but seen in a comparative perspective Canada is – again – far from unique.

It is probably significant that the national identities of Belgium, Switzerland, and the Netherlands (not a federal state!) have also at times been represented as mediating between various other cultures. In all these cases the nations that represent themselves as 'mediators' are those with powerful neighbour states. Therefore, the emphasis on the mediating functions and on the relative 'openness' of a nation is probably connected to its relative political weakness. The emphasis on a nation's absorbing qualities and its international mediating functions may therefore be interpreted as a sublimation of its relative political impotence. This, at least, can plausibly be argued for the history of several small European nations, an interpretation also backed up by international-relations theory. This sublimation even may lead to a redefinition of a nation's armed forces into a corps of UN peacekeepers (as is exemplified by the Netherlands, the Scandinavian countries, and Canada). However this may be, it seems worthwhile to test this hypothesis in an international comparison.

Historical Identity and Temporal Markers

Now that I have indicated some spatial and non-spatial marks of collective identity and also the relevance of openness and closure for comparative historiography, I want – at last! – to say a few words about the role of the axis of time. Since historical identity was defined here as identity through change in time, at least some clarification of the role of time in comparative historiography is needed. I shall touch on only two issues of historiography connected to time. The first is the issue of origins; the second issue concerns the relationship between time and space. For efficiency reasons I again shall take the historiography of the nation as my point of departure.

First the issue of origins. Because all representations of historical identity deal with changes in time, all historical representations are faced with the temporal problem of origins. Before the changes of national identity can be investigated, its existence and thus its genesis must be clarified – unless we presuppose that collective identities are naturally given and that their existence does not require explanation. In that case, however, we are by definition no longer dealing with history, so I can leave this possibility aside. Therefore, we expect that a history of a collective identity – say of the Canadian nation – will inform us about its origins in time. However, the question 'Where did the Canadian nation come from?' already presupposes what must be clarified, that is: the existence of a Canadian nation. But as we have observed (see also Létourneau's and Laville's chapters), the existence of the Canadian nation is essentially contested, and therefore we can expect the same contest concerning its origins. The two sorts of contests always go together and for good reasons. Canada shares this problem of contested origins with most of the other new nations (including those in the Old World that belonged to former multinational empires, like the nations of the former Habsburg empire). Other nations probably have less-contested origins, but this too is still a matter of empirical investigation.

The second and last temporal problem I want to signal is the relation of time and space in historiography. Although most histories are written within a national frame of reference – without explicit comparison to other nations – they usually contain many implicit temporal references to other nations. This temporal reference to other histories is contained in notions like being 'late' or 'modern,' or in notions of 'retardation' or of being 'ahead' and so on. In this way the time axes of different histories are often connected to each other and transformed into one time axis – that of world time. Sometimes this can be done in an explicit way, as it is by all sorts of developmental schemes and theories. Modernization theory is probably the best-known example. The Enlightenment conception of ongoing 'civilization' and the Marxist theories of history provide other examples of the construction of one time axis for the whole world.

Now the construction of one world time leads to a direct connection between space and time by transforming spatial relations into temporal relations, as the German historian Sebastian Conrad has pointed out in his ingenious comparison of German and Japanese historiography.[34] Through the introduction of world time, historians have interpreted the spatial variety of nations, economies, and so on in terms of different positions on the axis of time; that is, in terms of different phases of the same development. Differences in geography are thus transformed into differences in time: being culturally or economically different – for example, China in relation to the United States – is thus transformed into being 'late' or being 'early.' The result, in Conrad's terms, is a temporalization of space. So much for the temporal markers of historical identity.

Summary

In this contribution I have proposed some concepts that may be useful when we are comparing historiographies. (The question of why to compare historiographies I have dealt with elsewhere.)[35]

I have introduced some important general problems of comparative historiography using the example of Quebec historiography as analysed by Ronald Rudin. The first general theme concerns the relationship between historiography and historical consciousness in a broader, societal sense. The second and related general theme concerns the practical functions of historiographical discourse. I have argued that the debates among Quebec historians that were centred on the difference and/or the normality of Quebec society exemplified the identity-construing dimensions of historiography. Next, I suggested that both general themes can best be elucidated through the notion of historical identity. Thus, I have proposed to take the concept of historical identity as the bridge between historiography and society; it is introduced, therefore, as the central notion for the matrix of comparative historiography.

Next, I defined the concept of historical identity in order to highlight some of its fundamental features. I proposed to define historical identity basically as identity through change in time. Further I elucidated the fundamental relational nature of identity. The fundamental multiplicity of historical identity is a consequence of this relational nature.

Further to its multiplicity, I elaborated on the 'exclusive' nature of identity, leading to its 'negative bond' to other identities. Last but not least, I pointed at the circumstance that although identity implies particularity, the weighting and evaluation of particular and general characteristics is a completely different matter. The Enlightenment tradition tends to emphasize the general features, while the tradition rooted in Romanticism tends to put value on the particular features of identity.

In the second part of my contribution, I identified some fundamental dimensions of a matrix that can be used for classifying types of historiography. I suggested that the dimensions of space and time can be taken as the most general markers of historiography, although both types of markers show problems when applied. In theory the spatial dimension can be neatly differentiated into a sub-national, a national, and a supra-national level, but this order is threatened in practice by the essentially contested nature of its central level, that of the nation. I argued that representations of the nation are so contested because they are used as justifications of collective rights. Moreover, the spatial scope of historiography appears not always to be what it seems.

Next to the spatial markers of historiography, I identified non-spatial markers, like religion, race, class, and gender identities. By this route we confronted the phenomenon of overlapping and competing identities. Religious identity appeared especially to have more in common with national identity than is usually assumed.

The dimension of openness and closure of identities also turned out to be important in history. Nations with powerful neighbours especially may cultivate openness instead of closure, and I suggested that this may be interpreted as a sublimation of their relative political weakness.

The last two markers I addressed relate to the temporal dimension. First, I explored the fact that all representations of historical identity must face the problem of their origins. As a consequence, debates about historical identity always shade off into debates over origins. Second, I showed that spatial relations are sometimes transformed into temporal relations through the construction of world time. In that case, spatial differences are explained as different locations on one time axis. A matrix for comparing historiographies should therefore encompass this eventual 'temporalization of space.'

Notes

1 Ronald Rudin, *Making History in Twentieth-Century Quebec* (Toronto: University of Toronto Press, 1997).
2 I shall not go into the reception of and debate on Rudin's book here. See, for references to reviews, Rudin's answer to his critics in 'On Difference and National Identity in Quebec Historical Writing: A Response to Jean-Marie Fecteau,' *Canadian Historical Review* 80 (2000): 666–76. See also the quite different evaluations of Rudin by Ramsay Cook in *Histoire sociale / Social History* 33 (1999): 120–3 and by Jan Noel in *University of Toronto Quarterly* 68, no. 1 (1998–9): 523–5.
3 See, for comparative historiography, Chris Lorenz, 'Comparative Historiography: Problems and Perspectives,' *History and Theory* 38, no. 1 (1999): 25–39.
4 I regard the term 'collective memory' as highly problematic, because it presupposes a collective subject with the ability to reach back to unmediated collective past experience. The presupposition of both a unitary collective subject and an unmediated contact with some collective experience are not valid. Although similar objections could be raised against the concept of 'historical consciousness,' Peter Seixas's definition of historical consciousness avoids these problems by defining it in terms of the multiple ways in which the past is handled in collectives. See Kerwin L. Klein's fundamental critique in his 'On the Emergence of Memory in Historical Discourse,' *Representations* 69 (2000): 127–50.
5 In a research project of the University of Hanover concerning the representations of the Nazi period, it has been established that the family versions of the Nazi past often show very little similarity with the findings of professional history. See Harald Welzer et al., *Nationasozialismus und Holocaust im Familiengednächtnis* (Frankfurt; Fischer, 2002).
6 Granatstein's *The Killing of Canadian History* is matched in Australia by Keith Windschuttle's *The Killing of History: How Literary Critics and Social Theorists Are Murdering Our Past* (New York: The Free Press, 1997). In England, Richard Evans, *In Defence of History* (London: Granta Books, 1997), is a better-balanced critique of the textualistic approaches of cultural studies. Evans's book also lacks the nostalgia for good old national history that characterizes both Granatstein and Windschuttle. See, further, Tony Taylor's contribution to this volume.
7 Jonathan Vance, 'The Formulation of Historical Consciousness: A Case Study in Literature,' paper presented at UBC symposium, August 2001 (http://www.cshc.ubc.ca/viewabstract.php?id=19).

8 As Vance shows in 'The Formulation of Historical Consciousness,' on First World War literature.

9 As observed in Theresa Rogers, 'Understanding in the Absence of Meaning: Coming of Age Narratives of the Holocaust,' paper presented at UBC symposium, August 2001 (http://www.cshc.ubc.ca/viewabstract.php?id=11).

10 See, e.g., H. Berding, ed., *Nationales Bewußtsein und kollektive Identität: Studien zur Entwicklung des kollektiven Bewußtsein in der Neuzeit* (Frankfurt a.M.: Suhrkamp 1996); A. Assmann and H. Friese, eds, *Identitäten: Erinnerung, Geschichte, Identität* (Frankfurt a.M.: Suhrkamp, 1998); and Lutz Niethammer, *Kollektive Identität: Heimliche Quellen einer unheimlichen Konjunktur* (Hamburg: Rowohlt, 2000). I have dealt with this issue in my book *Konstruktion der Vergangenheit* (Cologne: Böhlau, 1997), 400–37.

11 I have developed this argument in 'Comparative Historiography.' For the discussion see Philip A. Buckner, '"Limited Identities" Revisited: Regionalism and Nationalism in Canadian History,' *Acadiensis* 30, no. 1 (2000): 4–16.

12 See Steve Galt Crowell, 'There Is No Other: Notes on the Logical Place of a Concept,' *Paideuma* 44 (1998): 13–29.

13 See Sam Wineburg, 'Historical Thinking and Other Unnatural Acts,' paper presented at UBC symposium, August 2001, (http://www.cshc.ubc.ca/viewabstract.php?id=21).

14 Simmel's sociology of the stranger is relevant in this context.

15 The Belgian historian Jo Tollebeek (Leuven) has identified this phenomenon in an unpublished paper, 'National Identity, International Eclecticism and Comparative Historiography,' presented in June 2000 in Oslo, Norway.

16 I have dealt with the functions and justification of history in my article 'History, Forms of Representation and Functions,' in Neil Smelser and Paul Baltus, eds, *International Encyclopedia of the Social & Behavioral Sciences* (Oxford: Elsevier, 2001), 10: 6835–42.

17 Odo Marquard, *Apologie des Zufälligen* (Stuttgart: Reclam, 1986), 361.

18 Gérard Bouchard, *Genèse des nations et cultures du Nouveau Monde: Essai d'histoire comparée* (Montreal: Editions de Boréal, 2000).

19 I have developed this argument at greater length in 'Historical Knowledge and Historical Reality: A Plea for "internal realism,"' in Brian Fay, Philip Pomper, and Richard T. Vann, eds, *History and Theory: Contemporary Readings* (Cambridge: Blackwell, 1998), 342–77.

20 Roger Brubaker's sharp dichotomy between (French) civic nationalism and (German) ethnic nationalism has, however, recently been under attack as too schematic. See Brubaker, *Citizenship and Nationhood in France and Germany* (Cambridge, MA: Harvard University Press, 1992) and Dieter

Gosewinkel, 'Staatsangehörigkeit in Deutschland und Frankreich im 19. und 20. Jahrhundert,' in J. Kocka and C. Conrad, eds, *Staatsbürgerschaft in Europa: Historische Erfahrungen und aktuelle Debatten* (Hamburg: Körber Stiftung, 2001), 48–62.

21 Margaret Conrad, Alvin Finkel, and Cornelius Jaenen, *History of the Canadian Peoples*, 2 vols (Toronto: Copp Clark Pitman, 1993).

22 See Jörn Rüsen, *Grundzüge einer Historik*, 3 vols (Göttingen: Vandenhoeck & Ruprecht, 1983–9) and my *Konstruktion der Vergangenheit*.

23 Eric Hobsbawm, 'Identity History Is Not Enough,' in Hobsbawm, *On History* (London: Abacus, 1997), 351–67.

24 For an overview of this German debate see my article 'Beyond Good and Evil? The German Empire of 1871 and Modern German Historiography,' *Journal of Contemporary History* 30 (1995): 729–67.

25 For a recent inventory see Stefan Berger's unpublished paper 'Construction and Deconstruction of National Historiographies' (Strasbourg, 2001) and Lex Heerma van Voss and Marcel van der Linden, eds, *Class and Other Identities: Entries to West European Labour Historiography* (New York: Berghahn Books, 2002).

26 See, e.g., Lawrence McFalls, 'Getrennt sind wir stark: Der kanadische Föderalismus als Modell?' *Komparativ* 8, no. 4 (1998): 15–31.

27 See Hamish Telford, *The Federal Spending Power in Canada: Nation-Building or Nation-Destroying?* (Kingston, 1998; Institute of Intergovernmental Relations, Working Paper Series 1999, 4), 12: 'Canadians outside Québec seem blissfully unaware that the federal bargain with Québec may have been broken. The majority of Canadians outside Québec have an identity that corresponds to the Canadian state. Indeed, they rather presumptuously regard Canada as the nation, much to the consternation of the Québécois. As nationalists, many Canadians outside Québec believe that sovereignty should be vested with the federal government. Many Canadians outside Québec have been highly suspicious of the federal principle and the concomitant notion of shared sovereignty, and they are strong supporters of federal social programs, especially Medicare. Indeed, health insurance seems to have become a part of the Canadian identity outside Québec.'

28 See the special issue on the Nisga'a Treaty of *BC Studies*, 120 (Winter 1998/9).

29 The basic argument is that truth is only a necessary but not a sufficient condition for objectivity. See my article '"You got your history, I got mine": Some Reflections on Truth and Objectivity in History,' *Österreichische Zeitschrift für Geschichtswissenschaften* 10, no. 4 (1999): 563–85.

30 See Margaret Conrad, 'Historical Consciousness, Regional Identity and

Public Policy,' paper presented at UBC symposium, August 2001 (http://www.cshc.ubc.ca/viewabstract.php?id=3); Buckner, '"Limited Identities" Revisited.'

31 In this context, the fact that Germany only recently changed its ethnic definition of nationhood into a civic one illustrates the actuality of this issue.

32 Vance's paper on the anti-war novel (see note 7) illustrates in an exemplary form what happens to those who cast doubt on this kind of Sacred Cause.

33 For the debate on Dutch identity see Rob van Ginkel, *Op zoek naar eigenheid: Denkbeelden en discussies over cultuur en identiteit in Nederland* (The Hague: SDU Publishers, 1999). For Swiss identity see Oliver Zimmer, 'In Search of Natural Identity: Alpine Landscape and the Reconstruction of the Swiss Nation,' *Comparative Studies in Society and History* 40 (1998), 637–65.

34 Sebastian Conrad, *Auf der Suche nach der verlorenen Nation: Geschichtsschreibung in Westdeutschland und Japan 1945–1960* (Göttingen: Vandenhoeck & Ruprecht, 1999).

35 Lorenz, 'Comparative Historiography.'

Specific Narratives and Schematic Narrative Templates

JAMES V. WERTSCH

As Peter Seixas notes in his introduction to this volume, contemporary analyses of historical consciousness draw on many disciplines and intellectual traditions. These include education, history, memory studies, psychology, and museum studies. This makes for an interesting and lively discussion, but it also presents a challenge when we are trying to find a shared focus. The range of voices is sometimes so wide that it is difficult to know whether they are all involved in the same discussion at all. Motivated by such concerns, Seixas argues for the need to find common and overlapping themes that will facilitate cross-fertilization.

In my view, a topic that presents itself as an excellent candidate in this regard is narrative. Bruner[1] has argued for the need to place narrative at the centre of cultural psychology and the analysis of human consciousness more generally, and scholars in literary studies,[2] psychoanalysis,[3] and the philosophy of history[4] have made similar claims. Such arguments about the importance of narrative for the human sciences apply nowhere more obviously than in the study of collective memory and historical consciousness.

A bold version of the sort of approach I have in mind can be found in Alasdair MacIntyre's assertion that 'man is in his actions and practice, as well as in his fictions, essentially a story-telling animal.'[5] MacIntyre expands upon this claim by arguing that individuals do not create these stories out of nothing, as if in some kind of totally original, creative act. Instead:

> We enter human society ... with one or more imputed characters – roles into which we have been drafted - and we have to learn what they are in order to

be able to understand how others respond to us and how our responses to them are apt to be construed. It is through hearing stories about wicked stepmothers, lost children, good but misguided kings, wolves that suckle twin boys, youngest sons who receive no inheritance but must make their own way in the world and eldest sons who waste their inheritance on riotous living and go into exile to live with the swine, that children learn or mislearn both what a child and what a parent is, what the cast of characters may be in the drama into which they have been born and what the ways of the world are ... [T]here is no way to give us an understanding of any society, including our own, except through the stock of stories which constitute its initial dramatic resources.[6]

MacIntyre's line of reasoning has several implications when we are thinking about the narrative organization of historical consciousness. The first of these concerns the importance of narrative in general. Like Bruner, MacIntyre stresses that a great deal of thinking, speaking, and other forms of action are fundamentally shaped by narratives. We are especially 'story-telling animals' when it comes to recounting and interpreting our own, and others', actions – the motives that lie behind them, the settings in which they occur, and the outcomes they produce.

Second, MacIntyre stresses that the narrative tools we employ in this connection are provided by the particular cultural, historical, and institutional settings in which we live. Just as Bruner claims that 'symbolic systems ... [are] already in place, already "there," deeply entrenched in culture and language,'[7] MacIntyre sees the narratives we use to make sense of human action as coming from a 'stock of stories' from which any particular individual may draw.

In what follows, I shall examine a particular socio-cultural setting that has been a major source of the stock of stories and cultural tool kits in our world, namely, the modern state. As I have argued elsewhere,[8] modern states have sponsored the most ambitious effort at creating collective memory ever witnessed, and for this reason they deserve special attention. They have particular tendencies and forms of power when it comes to this task. States not only attempt to provide their citizens with official accounts of the past, but they also seek to control the particular ways such accounts are used, as well as access to alternative versions.

In order to address any of these claims concretely, one must begin by trying to clarify what we mean when speaking of 'narrative.' This is a term that is notoriously difficult to pin down, and as a result it has taken on almost as many meanings as there are people using it. Providing a comprehensive review of this issue is a difficult, if not impossible, task and goes well beyond the scope of what I wish to undertake in this chapter. Instead, I shall limit myself to a single major distinction that I believe to be useful when one is trying to understand the role of states in promulgating collective memory: the distinction between 'specific narratives' and 'schematic narrative templates.'

In the terminology I shall employ, specific narratives are the focus of history instruction in schools and deal with 'mid-level' events that populate textbooks, examinations, and other textual forms found in that context. In contrast, schematic narrative templates involve a much more abstract level of representation and provide a narrative framework that is compatible with many instantiations in specific narratives. But let me take up these two levels of narrative analysis in turn.

Specific Narratives

Under the heading of specific narratives I have in mind items such as those MacIntyre lists when he alludes to stories about 'wicked stepmothers, lost children, good but misguided kings,' and the others.[9] These are narratives in the Western tradition that have specific settings, characters, and sequences of events.

Specific narratives can be analysed in terms of the 'episodic' and the 'configurational' dimensions outlined by Ricoeur. The first of these is grounded in chronology and the temporal order and 'characterizes the story insofar as it is made up of events.'[10] In contrast, the second dimension involves emplotment and is what 'transforms the events into a story.'[11] It entails the act that '"grasps together" the detailed actions or ... the story's incidents. It draws from this manifold of events the unity of one temporal whole ... [and] extracts a configuration from a succession.'[12]

The notion of a specific narrative that I shall outline rests squarely on these two dimensions, but it also goes beyond Ricoeur's description in certain respects. Consistent with his account of the episodic dimension, specific narratives involve a temporally ordered set of explicitly mentioned and differentiated events. An additional characteristic of specific narratives is that they are organized around 'mid-level' events.[13] Such events are presented as having specific temporal and spatial boundaries, and the actors are typically groups or particular individuals who act on behalf of, or as leaders of, political collectives. The specific narratives produced by states usually constitute political history. Prototypes can be found in school textbooks that focus on major events such as wars, revolutions, and other political happenings.

As is often the case with narrative analyses, it is difficult, if not impossible, to pursue this line of reasoning very far by relying solely on abstract categories. For that reason I shall develop my claims about specific narratives and how they differ from schematic narrative templates by using illustrations. These come from a natural laboratory for the study of collective memory and historical consciousness, namely, Russia as it made the transition from Soviet to post-Soviet times. As I have outlined elsewhere,[14] this is a setting that witnessed a transition from strict, centralized control over collective memory to open, if not chaotic, public debate and disagreement. In the years following the break-up of the Soviet Union teachers were confronted with all sorts of proposals for what should be taught as history, and students encountered a host of interpretations of the past, both in and out of school. One of the hallmarks of this period has been that the past is now presented in textbooks and history instruction in ways that differ radically from Soviet practices. Indeed, much of what is presented would have been considered heretical during the Soviet period and discussing such matters publicly would have resulted in severe punishment.

Such radical reinterpretation is evident when one considers episodes such as the 1917 Revolution and the Russian Civil War. Accounts of these events were rewritten such that heroes were turned into villains and vice versa. More important, the events themselves were re-emplotted such that they no longer were triumphs over powerful and evil adversaries. In the post-Soviet rewriting, these events became grand tragedies that could have been averted had actors had more courage and foresight. One important event that has *not* been fundamentally re-emplotted, however, is the Second World War. The most plausible reason for this is that it serves as the 'dominant myth'[15] that continues to be positively viewed in post-Soviet Russia.

The basic plot of this dominant myth involves the treacherous invasion of the homeland by Germany, followed by great suffering and near disaster, followed by triumph against overwhelming odds through Soviet or Russian heroism, and concluding with the expulsion of the German enemy from the homeland and the march to Berlin. This skeletal plot has changed little in the transition to the post-Soviet era. What *has* changed is the identity and characterization of the heroes. Instead of Stalin or the Soviet Communist Party, the story today is formulated such that the masses, especially the Russian masses, are the heroes.

As I have outlined elsewhere,[16] this pattern of retaining the basic plot while changing the heroes of the dominant myth of the Second World War can be found in the official Russian state history as presented in post-Soviet textbooks. It also is reflected in what Russians seem to rely on when asked to speak or write about this war. A fairly standard account of this dominant myth can be found in the following essay written in 1999 by a thirty-five-year-old man from the Siberian city of Novosibirsk. It was written in response to the request to 'write a short essay on the theme: "What was the course of the Second World War from its beginning to end?"'

On September 1, 1939 German forces invaded the territory of Poland.

By the second month they had seized all of Poland. The result of the occupation of Poland was that all of 6 million Poles (30% of the whole population) perished.

In 1940 the seizure of France and the Benelux countries took place.

In 1941 the USSR was attacked. By the end of October 1941 the Germans approached Moscow along a 100-kilometer front. At the price of incredible suffering the Soviet forces were able to throw the Germans back from Moscow at the end of 1941. 1942 was the year of massive resistance. It was the year in which our forces were surrounded at Kharkov and the year of the battle of Stalingrad. The turning point came in 1943. This was the year of the struggle at the Kursk salient, the huge tank battle. In 1944 the second front was opened, and there was a rapid advance toward the west. 1945 saw the atomic bombing of Hiroshima and Nagasaki and the end of the Second World War.

This text clearly meets the criteria for Ricoeur's episodic dimension in that it lists several differentiated and temporally organized events. As is the case for subjects from various studies that colleagues and I have conducted over the past several years, this essay writer separates the beginning of the Second World War (September 1939) from the beginning of the Great Patriotic War (22 June 1941). It is clear from his account that the major story to be told, in his view, has to do with the latter. There is a basic set of events that appear repeatedly in Soviet and post-Soviet textbooks and other official accounts, as well as in subjects' essays and interviews about the Second World War. As is the case for this subject, other events also appear, but the following core events of the Great Patriotic War must appear in any official account:

• German invasion of USSR on 22 September 1941
• Battle of Moscow, winter of 1941–2

- Battle of Stalingrad, winter of 1942–3
- Soviet victory over German army and the march to Berlin and victory, May 1945

The fact that this thirty-five-year-old subject structured his narrative around these basic events is not surprising, given that he had received his education and lived much of his life in the Soviet system. It is worth noting, however, that he also included a few 'post-Sovietisms.' For example, he made note of specific groups, namely Poles, as opposed to the Soviet people, who were at the heart of official history in the Soviet era.

For my present purposes, however, the most important point is that this individual included the four basic events that had to be included in an official account of either the Soviet or post-Soviet period. These are mid-level events in that they have specific temporal and spatial boundaries and involve concrete collective actors. Furthermore, taken together, they form an identifiable plot and hence reflect the configurational, as well as episodic, dimensions of narrative.

Schematic Narrative Templates

One of the most striking findings to emerge from the study of collective memory for the Second World War in Russia is the difference between generations who grew up and attended school during the Soviet era ('Soviet generations'), on the one hand, and those who did so in the post-Soviet era ('post-Soviet generation'), on the other. This difference is usually characterized in terms of how little the post-Soviet generation knows about the past. Strikingly, older Russians routinely complain, 'The younger generation knows nothing about history these days.'

At first glance, empirical findings suggest that this assessment has much to recommend it. Individuals in the post-Soviet generation were generally unable to provide the sort of specific narratives about the Second World War that were readily available to older people. The difference was so great that members of Soviet-educated generations are often appalled at the paucity and inaccuracy of details in the post-Soviet generation's account of the war. They view many of the younger people's accounts as pathetic, laughable, and even blasphemous.

As an example of the sort of account provided by members of the post-Soviet generation, consider the following essay written by a fifteen-year-old boy from Moscow in 2000:

The beginning [of the war] was very unexpected for the whole world except for Hitler. Also unexpected was the massive amount of bloodshed, the human losses, the Fascist concentration camps. The emergence of a second Napoleon, Adolf Hitler, was also unexpected and strange. The course of the war was hard for the countries of the defenders. Terrible, hard, bloody.

The difference between this account and the one outlined earlier is striking. And if anything, this difference understates the case when we consider the difference between the Soviet and post-Soviet generations. Many members of Soviet generations provided much longer and more elaborate accounts of the Second World War than the one I reported above, while many members of the post-Soviet generation provided much shorter accounts (some saying they didn't know and therefore could not respond at all). Furthermore, the younger subjects often made mistakes that virtually never appeared in older subjects' responses.

Such striking, systematic differences between the generational groups' accounts of the war indeed seem to support the older group's dismissal of younger Russians as not knowing anything about the past. More generally, I have argued that such differences support the view that the post-Soviet Russian state largely lost control of collective memory, at least temporarily.[17]

This interpretation, however, is unsatisfactory because it provides only a negative characterization of the post-Soviet generation. In this view, the younger subjects are understood solely in terms of the standards they are not living up to, the implication being that they were trying to do the same thing as older Russians, but were simply less good at it. In fact, members of the post-Soviet generation often included items in their accounts that never appeared in those of older subjects, which suggests they were doing something distinct from their older counterparts.

It is in this connection that the notion of schematic narrative templates becomes useful. It provides a means for understanding differences as well as commonalities between the two generations. As understood here, the notion of a schematic narrative template can be traced to several sources. One of the most important is the Russian folklorist Vladimir Propp.[18] In developing his line of reasoning about Russian folk tales, Propp argued for the need to focus on the generalized 'functions' that characterize a broad range of narratives, as opposed to the particular events and actors that occur in specific ones. From this perspective, 'recurrent constants' or functions 'of dramatis personae are basic components of the tale.'[19] This focus on abstract function means that several specific events and individuals may fit under the heading of a particular function in a narrative. In this view, *'Functions of characters serve as stable, constant elements of a tale, independent of how and by whom they are fulfilled.'*[20]

Propp identified an extensive network of generalized functions, including items such as 'THE VILLAIN RECEIVES INFORMATION ABOUT HIS VICTIM' and 'THE VILLAIN IS DEFEATED.'[21] From my perspective, the primary value of Propp's ideas about narrative functions concerns his general line of reasoning rather than his detailed claims (developed in connection with Russian folk tales) about particular functions. Specifically, I am concerned with the notion that a generalized narrative form underlies a range of specific narratives in a cultural tradition. This viewpoint changes the focus from analysing a list of specific narratives to analysing an underlying pattern that may be instantiated in any one of several ways.

If we switch from folklore to psychology, an analogous line of reasoning may be found in the writings of Frederic Bartlett.[22] His classic book *Remembering* spawned a host of research efforts that continue to this day in the psychology of memory. Although there is no reason to assume that he was familiar with Propp's writings, Bartlett did develop some similar claims. In his view, human cognitive functioning is usually more of a 'constructive' process[23] than a product of stimuli, and this belief led him to examine the generalized patterns or 'schemata' brought to this process by the agent doing the constructing.

Bartlett took as a starting point for his inquiry the assumption that one can 'speak of every human cognitive reaction – perceiving, imagining, remembering, thinking and reasoning – as an *effort after meaning.'*[24] This effort is grounded in 'tendencies which the subject brings with him . into the situation with which he is called upon to deal.' Bartlett discussed these tendencies in terms of 'schemes' that are 'utilised so as to make [the subject's] reaction the "easiest," or the least disagreeable, or the quickest and least obstructed that is at the time possible.'[25] He also noted that these schemes are often used in a 'completely unreflective, unanalytical and unwitting manner.'[26]

Bartlett's general line of reasoning continues to have a powerful impact on memory research in psychology to this day. An example of this influence can be seen in the writings of Michael Ross[27] on 'implicit theories.' Ross is concerned with the formation of autobiographical memory, which is 'depicted as an active, constructive, schema-guided process.'[28] Like many psychologists of memory, Ross assumes that remembering is typically not very accurate with regard to details. Instead, he sees the construction of personal histories as being shaped by a host of biasing factors, including implicit theories. In this account, '[i]mplicit theories are schemalike knowledge structures that include specific beliefs.'[29] Furthermore, '[t]hese theories are implicit in that they encompass rarely discussed, but strongly held beliefs.'[30]

The writings of Propp, Bartlett, and Ross contribute different elements of an understanding of schematic narrative templates. The main point is that narrative templates are schematic in the sense that they concern abstract, generalized functions of the sort that Propp discussed in his structural analysis of folk tales and that Bartlett and Ross discuss under the heading of 'schemalike knowledge structures.' These involve narrative, a point that is explicit in Propp's writings and consistent with what Bartlett and Ross propose. And the notion of template implies that these abstract structures can underlie several different specific narratives, each of which has a particular setting, cast of characters, dates, and so forth. This viewpoint suggests that collective memory comprises not a long list of specific narratives about the past as separate items, but a cultural tool kit that includes a few basic building blocks.

The writings of Propp, Bartlett, and Ross suggest a few additional properties worth keeping in mind when we deal with schematic narrative templates. First, they are not some sort of universal archetypes. Instead, they belong to particular narrative traditions that can be expected to differ from one cultural setting to another. Second, narrative templates are not readily available to conscious reflection. As Bartlett noted, they are used in an 'unreflective, unanalytical and unwitting manner,'[31] and according to Ross, they are 'rarely discussed.'[32]

In the case of the Russian texts about the Second World War that are of concern here, the particular schematic narrative template involved can be termed the 'triumph-over-alien-forces' narrative. This is a narrative template that may be instantiated using a range of concrete characters, events, dates, and circumstances, but its basic plot remains relatively constant and contains the following items:

- an 'initial situation'[33] in which the Russian people are living in a peaceful setting where they are no threat to others is disrupted by
- the initiation of trouble or aggression by an alien force, or agent, which leads to
- a time of crisis, great suffering, and almost total defeat, which is

- overcome by the triumph over the alien force by the Russian people, acting heroically and alone

To many it will appear that there is nothing peculiarly Russian about this narrative template. It may be found just about anywhere. For example, if we replace 'Russian' with 'American,' the template would seem to provide a foundation for American collective memory of the Japanese attack on Pearl Harbor in 1941. My claim is not that this particular narrative template is available *only* to members of the Russian narrative tradition or that this is the only schematic narrative template in this tradition. Obviously, this is a cultural tool employed by many people around the world. However, there are some points that suggest that this template plays a particularly important role and takes on a particular form in the Russian narrative tradition and hence in collective remembering.

The first of these concerns its ubiquity. Whereas the United States and many other societies have accounts of past events that fit this narrative template, it seems to be employed more widely in the Russian tradition than elsewhere. It forms the basic plot line for several of the most important events in Russian history, including the Mongol invasion in the thirteenth century, the Swedish invasion in the eighteenth century, Napoleon's invasion in the nineteenth, and Hitler's invasion in the twentieth century. Indeed, many would say that this narrative template is *the* underlying story of Russian collective remembering, and hence contrasts with the narratives that people from other nations might employ. For example, it contrasts with the American 'mystique of Manifest Destiny'[34] or 'quest for freedom' narrative.[35]

Of course, one obvious reason for the ubiquity of this narrative template in Russian collective remembering is that it reflects actual experience. Over its history Russia clearly has been the victim of several invasions and other acts of aggression, and my intent is not to argue that this narrative is without foundation. Instead, it is to examine how this narrative template is organized and how it plays a role in shaping new accounts of the past.

Returning to the two texts provided above, there is evidence that the triumph-over-alien-forces schematic narrative template is at work in both cases. The thirty-five-year-old's account positions the USSR as being the victim of an unexpected and uncalled-for attack and then goes on to talk about throwing back the Germans 'at the price of incredible suffering' by the Soviet forces. It then lists other major battles that eventuated in a 'rapid advance toward the west' and the end of the war in Europe. In short, this is a specific narrative built around concrete, mid-level events, all of which are organized or motivated by the triumph-over-alien-forces schematic narrative template.

On the face of it, the fifteen-year-old's account of the war looks completely different. It is not a specific narrative built out of mid-level events. Instead, the items mentioned involve either unique personalities (Hitler) or general observations that hardly qualify as events at all ('the massive amount of bloodshed, the human losses, the Fascist concentration camps'). So few specific events are included here that there is little to the episodic dimension of the narrative. And without that dimension it is difficult to know what the configurational dimension would be. It is precisely such texts by the post-Soviet generation that lead their older Russian counterparts to shake their heads and say this generation knows nothing about history.

On the other hand, this fifteen-year-old includes some items in his text that were never found in those of the older subjects. Of particular interest is his mention of 'a second Napoleon, Adolf Hitler,' something not mentioned in older subjects' essays. For someone from the United States, Canada, or many other countries, the reason for including this comment is difficult to fathom. The juxtaposition of Napoleon and Hitler in this young man's text is probably something that Westerners seldom, if ever, have encountered. It is something, however, with which both the Soviet and the post-Soviet generations of Russians are familiar. Indeed, it was included in a few other essays by post-Soviet subjects.

What did this young man have in mind, then, when he included this reference in his essay? The answer is to be found in the schematic narrative template that he and others of his generation use when trying to provide an account of the Second World War. Even though he cannot provide a detailed specific narrative about the events of the war, like many others in the post-Soviet generation, he continues to use the triumph-over-alien-forces schema. While he may not be able to provide the standard fare of dates and mid-level events found in older subjects' accounts, he can emphasize the general plot involved in his account. It is as if he can provide the configurational, but not the episodic, dimension of a narrative about the Second World War. He does this by suggesting the plot is the familiar one that has applied to many previous episodes in Russian history. The names, faces, events, and dates may change, but the basic outline of the story is available in template form, as he suggests by calling Hitler the 'second Napoleon.'

This idea that the Second World War is another version of the same basic story that Russia has encountered time and again in its history reflects this post-Soviet subject's reliance on the triumph-over-alien-forces schematic narrative template. Other young subjects used other devices to come up with accounts that reflect the same basic pattern. As with their older counterparts, the triumph-over-alien-forces narrative template guided their efforts, but unlike them, the younger subjects often could rely on little other than this narrative template.

What this comparison suggests is that the generational transition at issue is one that involves striking change as well as underlying continuity. If we take essays such as the ones I have provided above as reflecting collective memory of the Second World War, then there are grounds for saying that this memory has undergone a radical change over the past decade or two. Such is the assessment of people who complain that the younger generation in Russia no longer knows anything about history. Yet if we consider that the post-Soviet generation is relying on the same basic schematic narrative template as the older subjects did, then there is reason to assert that little has changed in collective memory in this setting.

Conclusion

My general purpose in this chapter is not to provide details about the specific narratives and schematic narrative templates unique to Soviet or post-Soviet Russia. This is a task that I have taken up elsewhere, and it is a topic that deserves much more attention in the future. Instead, my purpose is to introduce the distinction between two different levels of narrative organization and demonstrate the need to recognize this distinction in discussions of historical consciousness and collective memory. It will not do to speak simply of the narrative organization of collective memory. If we leave it at that, we would have no means for understanding the striking differences, *and* underlying continuities, that characterize generational transitions in collective memories, such as those of the Second World War in Russia.

I suspect that similar issues underlie many of our discussions about other areas of collective memory and historical consciousness. While it may be the case that narrative can provide an important theme that can rein in centrifugal tendencies in the discussions about these phenomena, confusion will continue to surface if we do not have a way of distinguishing between specific narratives involving mid-level events, on the one hand, and schematic narrative templates, on the other.

Notes

The writing of this chapter was assisted by a grant from the Spencer Foundation. The statements made and the views expressed are solely the responsibility of the author.

1 Jerome S. Bruner, *Actual Minds, Possible Worlds* (Cambridge, MA: Harvard University Press, 1986).
2 R. Scholes and R. Kellogg, *The Nature of Narrative* (London: Oxford University Press, 1966).
3 Roy Schafer, 'Narration in the Psychoanalytic Dialogue,' in W.J.T. Mitchell, ed., *On Narrative* (Chicago: University of Chicago Press), 25–49.
4 Louis O. Mink, 'Narrative Form as a Cognitive Instrument,' in R.H. Canary and H. Kozicki, eds, *The Writing of History: Literary Form and Historical Understanding* (Madison: University of Wisconsin Press, 1978), 129–49; Hayden White, *The Content of the Form: Narrative Discourse and Historical Representation* (Baltimore: Johns Hopkins University Press, 1987).
5 Alasdair MacIntyre, *After Virtue: A Study in Moral Theory* (Notre Dame, IN: University of Notre Dame Press, 1984), 216.
6 Ibid., 216.
7 Jerome S. Bruner, *Acts of Meaning* (Cambridge, MA: Harvard University Press), 11.
8 James V. Wertsch, *Voices of Collective Remembering* (New York: Cambridge University Press, 2002).
9 MacIntyre, *After Virtue*, 216.
10 Paul Ricoeur, *Time and Narrative*, 3 vols, trans. Kathleen McLaughlin and David Pellauer (Chicago: University of Chicago Press, 1984), 1: 66.
11 Ibid.
12 Ibid.
13 Wertsch, *Voices of Collective Remembering*.
14 Ibid.
15 A. Weiner, 'The Making of a Dominant Myth. The Second World War and the Construction of Political Identities with the Soviet Polity,' *The Russian Review* 55 (1996): 638–60.
16 The following is based on research explored in Wertsch, *Voices of Collective Remembering*.
17 Ibid.
18 Vladimir Propp, *Morphology of the Folktale*, trans. Laurence Scott (Austin: University of Texas Press, 1968).
19 Ibid., 21.
20 Ibid., 21; italics in the original.

21   Ibid., 28, 53; capitals in the original.
22   Frederic C. Bartlett, *Remembering: A Study in Experimental and Social Psychology* (Cambridge: Cambridge University Press, 1995; first published 1932).
23   Ibid., 312.
24   Ibid., 44
25   Ibid., 44.
26   Ibid., 45.
27   Michael Ross, 'Relation of Implicit Theories to the Construction of Personal Histories,' *Psychological Review* 96, no. 2 (1989): 341–57.
28   Ibid., 341–2.
29   Ibid., 342.
30   Ibid.
31   Bartlett, *Remembering*, 45.
32   Ross, 'Relation of Implicit Theories,' 342.
33   Propp, *Morphology of the Folktale*, 26.
34   David Lowenthal, 'Identity, Heritage, and History,' in John R. Gillis, ed., *Commemorations: The Politics of National Identity* (Princeton, NJ: Princeton University Press, 1992), 41–57.
35   James V. Wertsch, 'Struggling with the Past: Some Dynamics of Historical Representation,' in Mario Carretero and James F. Voss, eds, *Cognitive and Instructional Processes in History and the Social Sciences* (Hillsdale, NJ: Lawrence Erlbaum, 1994), 323–38; James V. Wertsch and Kevin O'Connor, 'Multi-voicedness in Historical Representation: American College Students' Accounts of the Origins of the US,' *Journal of Narrative and Life History* 4, no. 4 (1994): 295–310.

Historical Consciousness: Narrative Structure, Moral Function, and Ontogenetic Development[1]

JÖRN RÜSEN

> Question: What comes immediately into your mind, when you think history?
> Answer: Today will tomorrow be yesterday.[2]

A Narrative in Four Variations

The ancient castle of Col is located in the highlands of Scotland. It is the ancestral residence of the chiefs of the Maclean clan and is still in the possession of a member of the Maclean family, who lives in the castle. On the wall is a stone engraved with the following inscription: *If any man of the clan of Maclonich shall appear before this castle, though he come at midnight, with a man's head in his hand, he shall find here safety and protection against all.*

This text is from an old Highlands treaty concluded upon a highly memorable occasion. In the distant past, one of the Maclean forefathers obtained a grant of the lands of another clan from the Scottish king; that clan had forfeited its land by giving offence to the king. Maclean proceeded with an armed force of men to take possession of his new lands, accompanied by his wife. In the ensuing confrontation and battle with the other clan, Maclean was defeated and lost his life. His wife fell into the hands of the victors, and was found pregnant with child. The chief of the victorious clan transferred the pregnant Lady Maclean to the custody of the Maclonich family with a specific stipulation: if the child born should be a boy, it was to be killed immediately; if a girl, the baby should be allowed to live. Maclonich's wife, who also was pregnant, gave birth to a girl at about the same time Lady Maclean gave birth to a boy. They then switched the children.

The young boy Maclean, having by this ruse of transposition survived the death sentence passed on him before birth, in time regained his original patrimony. In gratitude to the Maclonich clan, he designated his castle a place of refuge for any member of the Maclonich family who felt himself in danger.

This narrative is contained in Samuel Johnson's *Journey to the Western Islands of Scotland*, first published in 1775.[3] It is my intention in this chapter to utilize this story in order to demonstrate the nature of narrative competence and its various forms, and the importance of such competence for moral consciousness. To approach this demonstration in a concrete manner, let us envisage this narrative within the context of an actual situation in which moral values are challenged, and where their use and legitimation require historically based argumentation.

Imagine you are a member of the Maclean clan living now in the ancestral castle: one dark night a member of the Maclonich clan – let us call him Ian – knocks at your door asking for help. He tells you he is being sought by the police because of a crime he is alleged to have committed. How would you react? Would you help hide him from the police, or decide on some other course of action? Imagine that later on you find it necessary to explain what is going on to a friend of yours who chances by and is unfamiliar with the ancient clan narrative. Whatever your action in respect to Ian Maclonich, you are obliged to narrate to your friend the tale about the switched infants in order to make plausible to him (and thus interpretable) the situation in which you find yourself and the decision you have made. Your narration of this clan legend will probably differ depending on the nature of that decision. Moreover, your original decision itself depends on our interpretation of the ancient clan legend about the transposed infants.

I submit that there are four principal possibilities for such an interpretation:

1. You can hide Ian Maclonich because you feel there is a *binding obligation* on your part to honour the ancient Highland agreement. In this case, you will tell your friend that you – as a Maclean – feel obliged to assist Ian because you regard as binding the ancient and still existent ties between the two clans. You then proceed to narrate the legend of the transposed infants, with the conclusion that you will hide Ian Maclonich from the police in keeping with the ancient clan treaty, thus renewing

and continuing its long validity in the relationship between the two clans.

2. You can hide Ian Maclonich, yet do so for a variety of other reasons. Thus, you can say that you have helped Ian because in the past a Maclonich once aided a member of the Maclean clan, and you now feel obliged to reciprocate on the basis of a *general principle* of reciprocity of favours. Or you can say that you are coming to his aid in order to fulfil the obligation of a treaty between clans: because treaties have to be kept as such, that is, they are binding qua treaty. Then you go on to narrate the legend, concluding with a remark that mutual aid or the keeping of a treaty between clans is a guiding and important moral principle for you, as proven already when the male baby was rescued.

3. You can refuse to hide Ian Maclonich. Then you first have to explain his request for help by narrating the tale of the infants and the stone with its inscription. But you will comment on this story by stating that you do not believe it, that it is merely a 'myth' or 'legend' devoid of any evidence or binding validity, and that it does not obligate you morally in any way. Or you can argue that since the introduction of modern English law, those old clan treaties have lost the validity they once had, and are outdated. In this case, you present a series or combination of *critical historical arguments* to relieve yourself of the obligation to keep the ancient treaty. You argue historically in order to sever any bonds between you and the Maclonich clan, which may have been valid and binding in the past.

4. You can decide to convince Ian Maclonich that it is fruitless to hide from the police and that it would be better for him to surrender himself to the authorities. You, in turn, promise to do whatever you can to assist him, for example, by hiring the best lawyer available. In this case, you narrate the tale of the infants, but circumscribe it by adding the following argument: the legal system has gone through an enormous transformation from the clan law of the pre-modern age to our modern period. You still feel obliged to help someone from the Maclonich clan, but wish to do so in a way based on *modern considerations*, and not as the ancient treaty prescribes.

This ancient clan narrative dealing with the Macleans, the Maclonichs, and the exchanged infants in its four variations provides the point of departure for my arguments here. The tale indicates the need for historical consciousness in order to deal with moral values and moral reasoning. Its four variants, I hope to demonstrate, reflect four stages of development by learning.

The Relationship between Historical Consciousness
and Moral Values and Reasoning

In the situation depicted in our narrative, we must decide upon a course of action. Such a decision is dependent on values. These values are general principles, guidelines for behaviour, key ideas, or perspectives that suggest what should be done in a given situation where various options exist. Such values function as a source of arbitration in conflicts and as objectives guiding us when we act.

What does it mean to term such values 'moral'? Our perspectives shape action systematically, acknowledging the social relationship within which we live and have to decide upon a course of action to be taken. They express this social relationship as an obligation for us, addressing us at the core of our subjectivity and calling upon our sense of responsibility and conscience.

How does history enter into this moral relationship between our action, our self, and our value orientations? The narrative sketched at the outset of the chapter can serve to furnish an answer: when moral values are supposed to guide the actions we take in a given situation, we must relate them to this situation, interpret the values and their moral content with respect to the actuality in which we ·apply them, and evaluate the situation in terms of our code of applicable moral values. For such a mediation between values and action-oriented actuality, historical consciousness is a necessary prerequisite. Without that consciousness, we would not be able to understand why Ian Maclonich has asked us to hide him from the police. Without such consciousness as a prerequisite to action, we would be unable to deal with the situation and arrive at a decision that appears plausible to all parties involved – Ian, my visiting friend, and myself as a Maclean.

But why should historical consciousness be a necessary prerequisite for orientation in a present situation requiring action? After all, such consciousness by definition is pointed toward events in the past. The simple answer is that historical consciousness functions as a specific orientational mode in actual life situations in the present: it functions to aid us in comprehending past actuality in order to grasp present actuality. Without narrating the ancient story of the exchanged infants, it would be impossible to explain to my visiting friend the 'actual situation' and justify – which is to say legitimate – my decision. Moreover, the narrative's explanatory power serves to ground the situation not only for the uninformed outsider, but for myself as well as an involved party, a Maclean clansman.

What then is specifically 'historical' in this explanation, this interpretation of the situation and its legitimation? In its temporal orientation, historical consciousness ties the past to the present in a manner that bestows on present actuality a future perspective. This implied reference to future time is contained in the historical interpretation of the present, because such interpretation must enable us to act – that is, it must facilitate the direction of our intentions within a temporal matrix. When we say we feel bound or obligated by the ancient treaty, we define a future perspective on our relationship to the Maclonich clan. The same is true of all other historical explanations and legitimations associated with our decision.

I wish to derive a general characteristic of historical consciousness and its function in practical life from the narrative example given.[4] Historical consciousness serves as a key orientational element, giving practical life a temporal frame and matrix, a conception of the 'course of time' flowing through the mundane affairs of daily life. That conception functions as an element in the intentions guiding human activity, our 'course of action.' Historical consciousness evokes the past as a mirror of experience within which life in the present is reflected and its temporal features revealed.

Stated succinctly, history is the mirror of past actuality into which the present peers in order to learn something about its future. Historical consciousness should be conceptualized as an operation of human intellection rendering present actuality intelligible while fashioning its future perspectives. Historical consciousness deals with the past qua experience; it reveals to us the web of temporal change in which our lives are caught up and (at least indirectly) the future perspectives toward which that change is flowing.

History is a meaningful nexus between past, present, and future – not merely a perspective on what has been, *wie es eigentlich gewesen*. It is a translation of past into present, an interpretation of past actuality via a conception of temporal change that encompasses past, present, and the expectation of future events. This conception moulds moral values into a 'body of time' (e.g., the body of the continuing validity of an ancient treaty). History clothes values in temporal experience. Historical consciousness transforms moral values into temporal wholes: traditions, timeless rules of conduct, concepts of development, or other forms of comprehension of time. Values and experiences are mediated by and synthesized in such conceptions of temporal change.

Thus, the historical consciousness of a contemporary member of the Maclean clan translates the moral idea that treaties are binding and must be fulfilled into the concrete form of an actual treaty valid over time. Historical consciousness amalgamates 'is' and 'ought' into a meaningful narrative that informs about past events to help render the present intelligible, and to bestow upon present activity a future perspective. In so doing, historical consciousness makes an essential contribution to moral-ethical consciousness. The sense-creating procedures of historical consciousness are necessary for moral values, and for moral reasoning as well if the plausibility of moral values is at stake. The reference here is not to a *logical plausibility* of values (in respect to their coherence, for example); rather, it is to plausibility in the sense that values must have an acceptable relationship to reality.

Historical consciousness has a practical function:[5] it bestows upon actuality a temporal direction, an orientation that can guide action intentionally by the agency of historical memory. This function can be termed a 'temporal orientation.' Such an orientation occurs in two spheres of life, involving (a) external practical life and (b) the internal subjectivity of the actors. The temporal orientation of life has two aspects, one external, the other internal. The external aspect of orientation via history discloses the *temporal dimension of practical life*, uncovering the temporality of circumstances as shaped by human activity. The internal aspect of orientation via history discloses the *temporal dimension of human subjectivity*, giving self-understanding and awareness a temporal feature within which they take on the form of historical identity, that is, a constitutive consistency of the temporal dimensions of the human self.

By means of historical identity, the human self expands its temporal extension beyond the limits of birth and death, beyond mere mortality. Via this historical identity, a person becomes part of a temporal whole larger than that of his or her personal life. Thus, the role of a member of the Maclean clan of today presupposes a historical family identity, which extends back to the ancient time when clans battled over a king's gift of territory. By giving Ian Maclonich assistance today, we affirm this identity of what it means to be a Maclean in respect to the future. A more familiar example of such 'temporal immortality' (as historical identity can be characterized) is national identity. Nations often locate their wellsprings in a hoary and ancient past, and project an unlimited future perspective embodying national self-assertion and development.

The Narrative Competence of Historical Consciousness

The linguistic form within which historical consciousness realizes its function of orientation is that of the narrative. In this view, the operations by which the human mind realizes the historical synthesis of the dimensions of time simultaneous with those of value and experience lie in narration: the telling of a story.[6] Once the narrative form of the procedures of historical consciousness and its function as a means of temporal orientation are clear, it is possible to characterize the specific and essential competence of historical consciousness as 'narrative competence.'[7] Such competence can be defined as the ability of human consciousness to carry out procedures that make sense of the past, effecting a temporal orientation in present practical life by means of the recollection of past actuality.

This general competence concerned with 'making sense of the past' can be divided into three sub-competencies. These can be best defined in terms of the three elements that together constitute a historical narrative: form, content, and function. In respect to *content*, one can speak of the 'competence of historical experience'; in respect to *form*, the 'competence of historical interpretation'; and in respect to *function*, the 'competence of historical orientation.'[8]

1. Historical consciousness is characterized by the 'competence of experience.' This competence entails an ability to have temporal experience. It involves the capacity of learning how to look at the past and grasp its specific temporal quality, differentiating it from the present. A more elaborate form of such competence is 'historical sensitivity.' In terms of our narrative, it is the competence to understand the stone in the wall of the Maclean castle and the need to take note of its inscription: that is, that it bears information important for the members of the Maclean family.

2. Historical consciousness is further characterized by the 'competence of interpretation.' This competence is the ability to bridge time differences between past, present, and future through a conception of a meaningful temporal whole comprising all time dimensions. The temporality of human life functions as the principal instrument of this interpretation, this translation of experience of past actuality into an understanding of the present and expectations regarding the future. Such a conception lies at the core of the meaning-creating activity of historical consciousness. It is the fundamental 'philosophy of history' active within the meaning-creating activities of historical consciousness,

shaping every historical thought. In terms of our narrative, it entails the competence to integrate the event of the exchange of infants into a concept of time which links that ancient period with the present, giving this complex a historically weighty significance for the Macleans in their relationship with the Maclonichs. Such a concept could be embodied either in the notion of the unbroken validity of the treaty or in the evolution of law from a pre-modern form to its modern manifestation.

3. Historical consciousness, finally, is characterized by the 'competence of orientation.' Such a competence entails being able to utilize the temporal whole, with its experiential content, for the purposes of life orientation. It involves guiding action by means of notions of temporal change, articulating human identity with historical knowledge, and interweaving one's own identity into the concrete warp and woof of historical knowledge. In terms of the Highlands narrative, it entails the ability to utilize the interpretation of the treaty in order to deal with the current situation and determine a course of action: that is, to decide whether or not to hide Ian, or assist him in some other way, and to legitimate this decision – in each instance using a 'good historical reason' related to one's identity as a member of the Maclean clan.

Four Types of Historical Consciousness

In the preceding sections, an attempt was made to explicate the basic operations of historical consciousness, its relationship to moral consciousness, and its main competencies. Now we turn to the question of *development.*

The various incisive theories on the development of moral consciousness worked out and empirically confirmed by such thinkers as Piaget, Kohlberg, and others are familiar from the literature on cognitive development.[9] My intention here is to propose an analogous theory of development concerning the narrative competence of historical consciousness, so crucial for relating values to actuality or morality to activity by a narrative act: the telling of a story about past events.

In order to find stages of structural development in historical consciousness, it is necessary, first of all, to distinguish basic structures within the procedures involved in making historical sense of the past. I propose to explicate such basic structures in the form of a general typology of historical thinking. This typology conceptually encompasses the entire field of its empirical manifestations, and can therefore be utilized for comparative work in historiography, including intercultural comparisons.[10]

The typology is already implicit in the four different modes of historical argumentation briefly alluded to above in connection with the request by Ian Maclonich to seek refuge from the police. What then is the typological meaning of these four modes?

My starting point is the function of historical narration. As already mentioned, such narration has the general function of serving to orient practical life within time. It mobilizes the memory of temporal experience, developing the notion of an embracing temporal whole, and bestows on practical life an external and internal temporal perspective.

Historical consciousness realizes this general function in four different ways, based on four different principles for the temporal orientation of life: (a) affirmation of given orientations, (b) regularity of cultural patterns and life patterns (*Lebensformen*), (c) negation, and (d) transformation of topical orientating patterns. These are all brought about via the agency of historical memory.

There are six elements and factors of historical consciousness in terms of which these four types can be described. These are displayed in table 1.

The Traditional Type

Traditions are indispensable elements of orientation within practical life, and their total denial leads to a sense of massive disorientation. Historical consciousness functions in part to keep such traditions alive.

When historical consciousness furnishes us with traditions, it reminds us of origins and the repetition of obligations, doing so in the form of concrete factual past occurrences that demonstrate the validity and binding quality of values and value systems. Such is the case when, for example, in our role as a member of the Maclean clan, we feel an obligating link to an ancient treaty. In such an approach, both our interpretation of what occurred in the past and our justification for hiding Ian Maclonich are 'traditional.' Some other examples of such 'traditionality' are commemorative public speeches, public monuments, or even private stories narrated by individuals to each other with the purpose of confirming their personal relationship. Thus, both you and your partner will indeed be 'enamoured' of the narrative describing how you first fell in love – if indeed you still love each other.

Traditional orientations present the temporal whole, which makes the past significant and relevant to present actuality and its future extension as a continuity of obligatory cultural and life patterns over time.

TABLE 1   The four types of historical consciousness

	Traditional	Exemplary	Critical	Genetic
Experience of time	Repetition of an obligatory form of life	Representing general rules of conduct or value systems	Problematizing actual forms of life and value systems	Change of alien forms of life into proper ones
Patterns of historical significance	Permanence of an obligatory life form in temporal change	Timeless rules of social life, timeless validity of values	Break of patterns of historical significance by denying their validity	Developments in which forms of life change in order to maintain their permanence
Orientation of external life	Affirmation of pregiven orders by consent about a valid common life	Relating peculiar situations to regularities of what had happened and should happen	Delimitation of one's own standpoint against pregiven obligations	Acceptance of different standpoints within a comprising perspective of common development
Orientation of internal life	Internalization of pregiven life forms by limitation – role taking	Relating self-concepts to general rules and principles – role legitimation by generalization	Self-reliance by refutation of obligations from outside – role making	Change and transformation of selfconcepts as necessary conditions of permanence and self-reliance – balance of roles
Relation to moral values	Morality is dictated by obligatory orders; moral validity as unquestionable stability by tradition	Morality is the generality of obligation in values and value systems	Breaking the moral power of values by denying their validity	Temporalization of morality; chances of further development become a condition of morality
Relation to moral reasoning	The reason of values is their effective pregivenness, enabling consent in moral questions	Arguing by generalization, referring to regularities and principles	Establishing value criticism and ideology critique as important strategies of moral discourses	Temporal change becomes a decisive argument for the validity of moral values

Traditional orientations guide human life externally by means of an affirmation of obligations requiring consent. Such traditional orientations define the 'togetherness' of social groups or whole societies in the terms of maintenance of a sense of common origin. In regard to internal orientation, such traditions define historical identity, the affirmation of predetermined cultural patterns of self-reliance and self-understanding. They shape identity formation as a process in which roles are assumed and played out.

The importance of tradition for moral values is clear. Traditional historical orientation defines morality as tradition. Traditions embody morality as an unquestioned stability of *Lebensformen*, cultural and life patterns over time and its vicissitudes.

With respect to moral reasoning, traditions are reasons upholding and underpinning the moral obligation of values. If practical life is orientated predominantly in terms of traditions, the reason informing values lies in the permanence of their actuality in social life, a permanence that history serves to bring to our recollection.

The Exemplary Type

It is not traditions we utilize here as argument – but rather rules. The story of the struggles between the clans and the transposition of the two infants stands here for a general timeless rule: it teaches us what course of action to take, and what to refrain from doing.

Here historical consciousness deals with the experience of the past in the form of cases representing and embodying rules of temporal change and human conduct. The horizon of time experience is significantly expanded in this mode of historical thought. Tradition moves within a rather narrow frame of empirical reference, but historical memory structured in terms of exempla is open to process an infinite number of past events, since they do not possess any specific significance in themselves, but rather only in relation to an *abstract idea of temporal change and human conduct*, valid for all times, or whose validity is at least not limited to the specific event.

The pattern of significance involved here has the form of timeless rules. History in this conception is viewed as a past recollected with a message or lesson for the present, as didactic: *historia vitae magistra* is a time-honoured apothegm in the Western historiographical tradition.[11] It teaches rules, their derivation from specific cases, and their application.

The mode of orientation realized by historical consciousness in this exemplary type is rule-focused: it entails the application of historically derived and proven rules to actual situations.

Many classical examples of historiography in a variety of differing cultures reflect this type of historical significance. In the ancient Chinese tradition, the best example is the classic by Suma-Kuang, *Tzu-chih t'ung-chien (A Mirror for Government)*. Its very title indicates how it conceives of the past as exemplum: political morality is taught in the form of cases of governments that have succeeded or failed.

In respect to the internal orientation of life, exemplary historical thinking relates life roles and principles, and functions to legitimate such roles by abstract reasoning. Historical identity is here constituted by one's assuming the regularity of cultural and life patterns. Historical identity is given the shape of prudence (*prudentia*). Exemplary historical thinking provides competence in deriving general rules from specific cases and applying them to other cases.

Such a mode of historical consciousness makes a significant contribution to moral reasoning. Exemplary historical thought discloses the morality of a value or value system culturally embodied in social and personal life by proving its generality: that is, that it has a validity extending beyond its immediate concrete eventfulness, a validity extending to a gamut of situations. Morality is conceptualized as having timeless validity.

The contribution of this mode of historical interpretation to moral reasoning is clear: history teaches moral argument by means of the application of principles to specific and concrete situations – such as a knock on the door by a member of the Maclonich clan in the dead of night.

The Critical Type

The decisive argument in the critical version of our narrative is that as a member of the Maclean clan, we feel no obligation whatsoever to its presumed 'binding' quality. For us, it is an ancient tale that has lost any relevance for present action and actuality. Yet this is not automatically so: as a Maclean, we are still somehow a part of this story, for the ancient stone indeed bears its inscription upon our wall. Thus, we must discredit the story if we do not wish to help Ian in his distress. We must present a new interpretation that – by means of historical reasoning – denies the validity of the treaty.

The easiest way to do this is to state that the story is untrue. In order to be convincing, however, we must muster evidence, and that requires us to engage in critical historical argumentation, establishing the plausibility of the contention that there are no historical reasons that could motivate us to offer help to Ian Maclonich.

We can develop an ideological critique, stating that there was a ruse involved, a trick by the Maclonichs to trap the Macleans into a kind of moral dependence on them. We can argue that even in that ancient period, it was prohibited to murder infants, which is the pivotal motif on which the narrative turns. Such argumentation is based on offering elements of a 'counter-narrative' to the one behind the stone engraving. By means of such a 'counter-narrative' we can unmask a given story as a betrayal, debunk it as misinformation. We can also argue critically in another way, contending that the treaty engraved on the stone has lost its current validity, because new forms of law have since emerged. Then we can narrate a brief 'counter-story,' that is, the story of how laws have changed over time.

What are the general characteristics of such a mode of historical interpretation? Here, historical consciousness searches for and mobilizes a specific kind of experience of the past: evidence provided by 'counter-narratives,' deviations that render problematic present value systems and *Lebensformen.*

The concept of an embracing temporal totality including past, present, and future is transformed in this mode into something negative: the notion of a rupture in continuity still operative in consciousness. History functions as the tool by which such continuity is ruptured, 'deconstructed,' decoded – so that it loses its power as a source for present-day orientation.

Narratives of this type formulate historical standpoints by demarcation, distinguishing them from the historical orientation entertained by others. By means of such critical stories we say *no* to pregiven temporal orientations of our life.

In regard to ourselves and our own historical identity, such critical stories express a negativity; what we do not want to be. They afford us an opportunity to define ourselves unentangled by role determinations and prescribed, predefined patterns of self-understanding. Critical historical thinking clears a path toward constituting identity by the force of negation.

Its contribution to moral values lies in its critique of values. It challenges morality by presenting its contrary. Critical narratives confront moral values with historical evidence of their immoral origins or consequences. For example, modern feminists criticize the principle of moral universality. They claim that it channels us into overlooking the nature of 'otherness' in social relations in favour of an abstract universalization of values as a sufficient condition of their morality. They contend that such 'universalization' is highly biased and ideological, serving to establish the male norm as the general human norm and disregarding the uniqueness qua gender of men and women as a necessary condition of humanity.[12]

Critical historical thinking injects elements of critical argumentation into moral reasoning. It calls morality into question by pointing to cultural relativity in values contrasted with a presumed and specious universality, by uncovering temporal conditioning factors as contrasted with a bogus 'timeless' validity. It confronts claims for validity with evidence based on temporal change, highlighting the relativizing power of historical conditions and consequences. In its most elaborate variant, such critical thinking presents moral reasoning as an ideology-critique of morality. Two classic examples of such an enterprise are Marx's critique of bourgeois values[13] and Nietzsche's *Genealogie der Moral*.[14]

The Genetic Type

At the core of these procedures for making sense of the past lies change itself. In this framework, our argument is that 'times have changed': we thus deny both the option of hiding Ian owing to traditional or exemplary reasons and of critically negating the obligation to this old story as a reason for refusing to hide him. In contrast, we accept the story, but place it in a framework of interpretation within which the type of obligation to past events has itself changed from a pre-modern to a modern form of morality. Here *change* is of the essence, and is what gives history its sense. Thus, the old treaty has lost its former validity and taken on a new one; consequently, our behaviour necessarily differs now from what it would have been in the distant past. We understand it within a process of dynamic evolvement.

We therefore choose to help Ian Maclonich, but in a way different from that prefigured in the treaty preserved in stone on the wall of our castle. We allow the story to become part of the past; at the same time, however, we bestow upon it another future. It is change itself that gives history its meaning. Temporal change sheds its threatening aspect, instead becoming the path upon which options are opened up for human activity to create a new world. The future surpasses, indeed 'outbids,' the past in its claims on the present – a present conceptualized as an intersection, an intensely temporalized mode, a dynamic transition. This is the quintessential form of a kind of modern historical thought shaped by the category of progress, though it has been thrown into radical doubt by speculations on postmodernity by a certain segment of the contemporary intellectual elite.

Historical memory in this mode prefers to represent the experience of past actuality as transformational, such that alien cultural and life patterns evolve into more positive 'modern' configurations.

The dominant pattern of historical signification here is that of development, where patterns change in order, paradoxically, to maintain their very permanence. Thus, permanence takes on an internal temporality, becoming dynamic. In contrast, permanence by tradition, by timeless exemplary rules, by critical negation – that is, the rupture of continuity – is in essence static in nature.

This mode of historical thinking views social life in all the profuse complexity of its sheer temporality. Differing standpoints are acceptable because they can be integrated into an embracing perspective of temporal change. Returning to our narrative, we as the modern Maclean are eager to persuade the modern Maclonich that it would be wisest for him to turn himself over to the police, and then accept our aid. His expectations and our reaction must intersect, and we believe that this intersection is part of the historical interpretation within which we deal with the actual situation. This mutual acknowledgment is part of the future perspective we derive from the past through our decision in the present not to offer him refuge, but rather to help him in a way we believe is more in keeping with the tenor of our times: 'I know a good lawyer.'

In respect to our self-understanding and self-reliance, this type of historical consciousness imbues historical identity with an essential temporalization. We define ourselves as being a cross-point, an interface of time and events, permanently in transition. To remain what we are, not to change and evolve, appears to us as a mode of self-loss, a threat to identity.[15] Our identity lies in our ceaseless changing.

Within the horizon of this kind of historical consciousness moral values become temporalized, morality shedding its static nature. Development and change belong to the morality of values conceptualized in terms of a pluralism of viewpoints and the acceptance of the concrete 'otherness' of the other and mutual acknowledgment of that 'otherness' as the dominant notion of moral valuation.

According to this temporalization as a principle, moral reasoning relies here essentially on the argument of temporal change as necessary or decisive for establishing the validity of moral values. Thus, one can move on from the final stage in the Kohlbergian scheme of the development of moral consciousness to a higher stage: moral principles include their transformation within a process of communication. It is here that they are realized concretely and individually, engendering difference; those differences, in turn, activate procedures of mutual acknowledgment, changing the original moral form. One fascinating illustration of this stage of moral argumentation, which cannot be elaborated on in the context of this essay, is the example of the relations between the sexes. The idea of universal human rights is another key example demonstrating the plausibility of this genetic mode of argumentation in reference to moral values.[16]

This typology is meant as a methodological and heuristic tool for comparative research. Insofar as morality is connected with historical consciousness, we can utilize the typological matrix to help categorize and characterize the cultural peculiarities and unique features of moral values and modes of moral reasoning in different times and places. Since elements of all four types are operatively intermixed in the procedure that gives practical life a historical orientation in time, we can reconstruct complex relations among these elements in order to pinpoint and define the structural specificity of empirical manifestations of historical consciousness and their relationship to moral values.[17]

The Development of Narrative Competencies

It is not my intention here to focus on the comparative method in historiography. Instead, I wish to make use of the typology in order to construct a theory of the ontogenetic development of historical consciousness. Such a theory is familiar from psychological studies on cognitive development,[18] but to my knowledge there has been no serious attempt to date to widen this psychological perspective by investigating historical consciousness and its cognitive competencies. Since historical consciousness can be conceptualized as a synthesis of moral and temporal consciousness, it might appear to be a relatively simple matter to develop a genetic theory of historical consciousness. Unfortunately, however, we find that Piaget and his followers have pursued the category of time only within the framework of the natural sciences,[19] so that their work remains basically silent on questions of historical consciousness.

To embark upon an investigation of historical consciousness and its essential relationship with moral consciousness it is first necessary to clear the ground, as it were: that is, a theoretical framework must be constructed that defines the field and explicates in conceptual terms what the basic questions are. It is my view that the typology sketched above can effectively serve such a purpose. It defines fundamentally and discloses the procedures of historical consciousness, even affording some basic notions as to what the development of historical consciousness might entail.

What conceptions of development can indeed be derived from the typology? We can come closer to answering this by logically ordering the types in a sequence defined by the *principle of precondition*.

The traditional type is primary, and does not presuppose other forms of historical consciousness, yet it constitutes the condition for all other types. It is the font, the beginning of historical consciousness. The logical sequence of types, each the precondition for the next is as follows: *traditional, exemplary, critical, genetic.* Though this sequence is based on logical criteria, it may have empirical applications, and there is reason to assume it is also a structural sequence in the development of historical consciousness.

The sequence entails increasing *complexity* in several aspects. Stages in human evolution can also be described in terms of an increasing capacity to digest complexity.

1. Growth in complexity can be specified and differentiated following the logical ordering of preconditions. Thus, the extent of experience and knowledge of past actuality expands enormously as one moves from the traditional to the exemplary. The critical type requires a new qualification of temporal experience based on the distinction between 'my own time' and the 'time of the others.' Finally, the genetic type goes even beyond this quality by the temporalization of time itself: that is, 'my own time' is dynamic, altering, undergoing change, as is that 'of the others' as well.

2. There is also a growth in complexity with regard to the patterns of historical significance. There is no relevant difference between fact and meaning in the form of traditional historical consciousness. They diverge in exemplary historical consciousness. In the critical form, meaning itself undergoes differentiation, intensified into even more complex differentiation in the genetic form.

3. There is a similar growth in the degree of abstraction and complexity of logical operations.

4. In addition, there is an increasing complexity of external and internal orientation. In external orientation, this can be demonstrated

by the manner in which historical consciousness characterizes social life: traditions are exclusivistic, and present one's own cultural and life patterns as the only acceptable *Lebensformen*. Exemplary thinking enlarges upon this by generalization, while critical thought elaborates definite, critique-based standpoints and delimitations. Genetic thought clears the temporal ground for a pluralism of standpoints.

5. Moving through the typological series, there is growing complexity in relation to historical identity. It begins with the unquestioned form of historical self-understanding imprinted by tradition and extends on to the fragile balance engendered by multidimensional, multiperspectival genetic forms.

My arguments here have been principally theoretical, but there appears to me to be a certain amount of empirical evidence as well to substantiate the hypothesis that historical consciousness follows the typological order sketched here in its evolution.

6. Everyday observations demonstrate that the traditional and exemplary modes of historical consciousness are widespread and frequently encountered; critical and genetic modes, in contrast, are far more rare. This fact correlates with the degree of education and knowledge, and with the progress of the human intellect toward more complex capacities.

7. Experience in the teaching of history in schools indicates that traditional forms of thought are easiest to learn, that the exemplary form dominates most history curricula, and that critical abilities, and genetic abilities even more so, require enormous amounts of effort by both teacher and pupil.

Observations on Historical Learning and Empirical Research

In conclusion, I would like to turn to the question of historical learning. Learning can be conceptualized as a process of digesting experience, of absorbing it into competencies. Historical learning is a process of digesting the experience of time into narrative competencies.[20] 'Narrative competence' is here understood as the ability to narrate a story by means of which practical life is given an orientational locus in time. This competence consists of three principal abilities:

1 the ability to experience, which is related to past actuality;
2 the ability to interpret, related to the temporal whole, which combines (a) experience of the past with (b) understanding of the present and (c) expectations regarding the future; and

3 the ability to orient, related to the practical need to find a path
   through the straits and eddies of temporal change.

In theoretical terms, it is not difficult to explicate the development of
historical consciousness as a process of learning. Learning is conceptualized in this framework as a specific quality of the mental procedures of
historical consciousness. Such procedures are termed 'learning' when
competencies are acquired to (1) experience past time, (2) interpret it
in the form of history, and (3) utilize that interpretation for the practical
purpose of orientation in life.

Using the typology, historical learning can be explained as a process of
structural change in historical consciousness. Historical learning entails
far more than simply acquiring knowledge of the past and expanding
the stock of that knowledge. Seen as a process by which competencies
are progressively acquired, it emerges as a process of changing the
structural forms by which we deal with and utilize the experience and
knowledge of past actuality, progressing from traditional forms of thought
up to the genetic modes.

Thus, the typology offers a basis for a usefully differentiated theory of
historical learning. Such a theory combines three central elements of
narrative competence (experience, interpretation, orientation) and four
stages of their development. A theory of historical learning of this kind
can be of some significance for the theory of the development of moral
consciousness and moral learning.

Unfortunately, theory alone does not suffice for dealing with the
knotty questions of historical and moral consciousness. The proof of
theory lies in amassing empirical evidence substantiating its theses, and
here research still needs to be done. There have been empirical studies
on historical consciousness and historical learning,[21] but there is still no
comprehensive psychology of historical learning. No further study on
the relationship between historical and moral consciousness and learning seems to exist.

An investigation of this nature faces formidable obstacles; principal
among these is the intricate complexity of historical consciousness and
its competencies. The four types presented here are not strict alternatives, permitting a simple count of their distribution in manifestations of
historical consciousness. Normally, the types appear in complex admix-
tures, and it is necessary to discover their hierarchical ordering and
relationship in any empirically given manifestation of historical consciousness. Nonetheless, the typology can focus our sights, and function
heuristically in defining questions and preparing strategies for use in

empirical studies. Such a typology impresses on investigators that what is important to discover in regard to historical consciousness is not the extent of knowledge involved, but rather the framework and effective principles operative in making sense of the past.

How can these principles be found in empirical evidence? There is one basic, elicitation-oriented approach: let persons relate narratives that are relevant for the temporal orientation of their own personal lives, and then analyse the narrative structures of such stories. Such an investigative tack seeks to establish answers to questions such as these: what type (in the typology) do these elicited narratives seem to follow? Is there any relation between the dominant type and the age of the narrator? Or with his/her level of education?

Empirical experiments have been undertaken by our students using this approach in connection with the Highlands story.[22] They were told the clan tale of Maclean and Maclonich in a highly 'neutral' version. They were confronted with the current situation of Maclean and asked to decide what he should do in regard to Ian Maclonich's request for assistance, and to write a short justification of their decision containing a specific reference to the motif of the transposed infants. These texts were then analysed with regard to the patterns of historical interpretation they utilized. Empirically, the four types were indeed distinguishable, and it even proved possible to differentiate more sensitively between these basic types of the typology. It was established that there are significant correlations between the narrative patterns used, age of the respondent, and stage of education and learning.

This constitutes only one limited example of empirical research, and questions were not explored regarding the moral component of historical consciousness. Nonetheless, I would contend that any discussion of moral values and moral reasoning should also attempt to relate to the associated dimensions of historical consciousness and learning.

Notes

1   First published in *History and Memory* 1, no. 2 (1989): 35–60.
2   Answer of a student on a questionnaire concerning historical consciousness, February 1987 (cf. Jörn Rüsen et al. 'Untersuchungen zum Geschichtsbewußtsein vom Abiturienten im Ruhrgebiet,' in Bodo von Borries, Hans-Jürgen Pandel, and Jörn Rüsen, eds, *Geschichtsbewußtsein empirisch* (Pfaffenweiler: Centaurus, 1991): 221–344.

3 Samuel Johnson, *A Journey to the Western Islands of Scotland* (New Haven and London: Yale University Press, 1971), 133ff. The version of the tale presented here is simplified.

4 A summarizing description is given by Karl-Ernst Jeisman, 'Geschichtsbewusstsein,' in Klaus Bergman, Annette Kuhn, Jörn Rüsen, and Gerhard Schneider, eds, *Handbuch der Geschichtsdidaktik* (Düsseldorf: Schwann, 1985), 40–4; cf. Jeisman, *Geschichte als Horizont der Gegenwart: Über den Zusammenhang von Vergangenheitsdeutung, Gegenwartsverständnis und Zukunftsperspektive* (Paderborn: Schonigh, 1985), 43ff.

5 This question is discussed principally from the narrow perspective of the function of historical studies in social life, for example, by Jürgen Kocka, *Sozialgeschichte: Begriff – Entwicklung – Probleme*, 2nd ed. (Göttingen: Vandenhoeck & Ruprecht, 1986), 112–31. Also see Jörn Rüsen, *Lebendige Geschichte, Grundzüge einer Historik III: Formen und Funktionen des historischen Wissen* (Göttingen: Vandenhoeck & Ruprecht, 1989).

6 See Hayden White, *Metahistory: The Historical Imagination in Nineteenth Century Europe* (Baltimore: Johns Hopkins University Press, 1973); Jörn Rüsen, *Historische Vernunft: Grundzüge einer Historik I: Die Grundlagen der Geschichtswissenschaft* (Göttingen: Vandenhoeck & Ruprecht, 1983); Paul Ricoeur, *Time and Narrative*, 3 vols. (Chicago: University of Chicago Press, 1984–1988); and David Carr, *Time, Narrative and History* (Bloomington: Indiana University Press, 1986).

7 I have sketched an outline of a theory of narrative competence in respect to the question of the main objectives of historical learning in 'Historisches Lernen: Grundriß einer Theorie,' in *Historisches Lernen: Grundlagen und Paradigmen* (Köln: Böhlau, 1994), 74–121.

8 For a more detailed explication see Jörn Rüsen,'Historical Narration: Foundation, Types, Reason,' *History and Theory*, Beiheft 26: *The Representation of Historical Events* (1987), 87–97.

9 Jean Piaget, *Das moralische Unteil beim Kinde* (Frankfurt am Main: 1973); Lawrence Kohlberg, *Zur kognitiven Entwicklung des Kindes* (Frankfurt am Main: Suhrkamp, 1974); cf. R.N. Hallam, 'Piaget and Thinking in History,' in Marin Ballard, ed., *New Movements in the Study and Teaching of History* (Bloomington: Indiana University Press, 1970), 162–78.

10 For a more detailed explanation of this typology, see Jörn Rüsen, 'Die vier Typen des historischen Erzählens,' in *Zeit und Sinn: Strategien historischen Denkens* (Frankfurt am Main: Fishcer-Taschenbuch-Verlag, 1990), 153–230; and Rüsen, *Lebendige Geschichte, Grundzüge einer Historik III*, part I.

11 Cf. Reinhart Koselleck, 'Historia Magistra Vitae: Über die Auflösung des Topos im Horizont neuzeitlich bewegter Geschichte,' in R. Koselleck

Vergangene Zukunft: Zur Semantik geschichtlicher Zeiten (Frankfurt am Main: Suhrkamp, 1979), 38–66.

12 Cf. Seyla Benhabib, 'The Generalized and the Concrete Other: Visions of the Autonomous Self,' *Praxis International* 5, no. 4 (1986): 402–24.

13 E.g., human and civil rights, in his essay 'Zur Judenfrage.' In Karl Marx and Friedrich Engels, *Werke 1* (Berlin: Dietz Verlag, 1964).

14 Friedrich Nietzsche, 'Zur Genealogie der Moral' (1887), in Giogio Colli and Mazzino Montinari, eds, *Sämtliche Werke: Kritische Studienausgabe in fünfzehn Einzelbänden* (München: Deutscher Taschenbuch Verlag, 1988), 5: 245–412.

15 One of Bertolt Brecht's 'Stories of Mr. Keuner' illustrates this point beautifully: 'A man who hadn't seen Mr. Keuner for a long time greeted him with the remark: "You don't look any different at all." "Oh," said Mr. Keuner, and turned pale.' Bertholt Brecht, *Gesammelte Werke 12* (Frankfurt am Main: Suhrkamp, 1967), 383 (my translation).

16 Cf. Ludger Kühnhardt, *Die Universalität der Menschenrechte: Studie zur Ideengeschichtlichen Schlüsselbestimmung eines politischen Schlüsselbegriffs* (Munich, 1987). Jörn Rüsen, 'Menschen- und Bürgerechte als historische Orientierung,' in *Historisches Lernen: Grundlagen und Paradigmen* (Köln: Böhlau, 1994), 204–35.

17 An interesting contribution to such comparison with special respect to Chinese historiography is Changtze Hu, *Deutsche Ideologie und politische Kultur Chinas: Eine Studie zum Sonderwegsgedanken der chinesischen Bildungselite 1920– 1940* (Bochum: Studienverlag Brockmeyer, 1983).

18 Cf. note 7. In addition, see Hans G. Furth, *Piaget and Knowledge: Theoretical Foundations* (Englewood Cliffs, NJ: Prentice Hall, 1969).

19 Cf. Jean Piaget, *Die Bildung des Zeitbewußtseins beim Kinde* (Frankfurt am Main: Suhrkamp, 1974).

20 Cf. Jörn Rüsen, *Historisches Lernen: Grundlagen und Paradigmen* (Köln: Böhlau, 1994), passim.

21 Recent publications in this field in Germany include Bodo von Borries, Hans-Jürgen Pandel, and Jörn Rüsen, eds, *Geschichtsbewußtsein empirisch* (Pfaffenweiler: Centaurus, 1991); Bodo von Borries, Jörn Rüsen, et al., eds, *Geschichtsbewußtsein im interkulturellen Vergleich: Zwei empirische Pilotstudien* (Pfaffenweiler: Centaurus, 1994); Magne Angvik and Bodo von Borries, eds, *Youth and History: A Comparative European Survey on Historical Consciousness and Political Attitudes among Adolescents*, 2 vols. (Hamburg: Körber-Stiftung, 1997); Bodo von Borries, *Jugend und Geschichte: Ein europäischer Kulturvergleich aus deutscher Sicht* (Opladen: Leske & Budrich, 1999); Bodo von Borries, *Das Geschichtsbewußtsein Jugendlicher: Eine repräsentative Untersuchung über Vergangenheitsdeutungen, Gegenwartswahrnehmungen und*

Zukunftserwartungen von Schülerinnen und Schülern in Ost- und Westdeutschland
(Weinheim: Juventa Verlag, 1995); Bodo von Borries, 'Forschungsprobleme
einer Theorie des Geschichtsbewußtseins: Am Beispiel einer Studie zum
empirischen Kulturvergleich,' in Horst-Walter Blanke, Friedrich Jaeger, and
Thomas Sandkühler, eds, *Dimensionen der Historik: Geschichtstheorie, Wissen-
schaftsgeschichte und Geschichtskultur heute: Jörn Rüsen zum 60: Geburtstag* (Köln:
Böhlau, 1998), 139–52; and Bodo von Borries and Hans-Jürgen Pandel, eds,
*Zur Genese historischer Denkformen: Qualitative und quantitative Zugänge (Jahr-
buch für Geschichtsdidaktik* 4) (Pfaffenweiler: Centaurus, 1994).

22 Hans-Günter Schmidt, '"Eine Geschichte zum Nachdenken," Erzähltypolo-
gie, narrative Kompetenz und Geschichtsbewußtsein: Bericht über einen
Versuch der empirischen Erforschung des Geschichtsbewußtseins von
Schülern der Sekundarstufe I (Unter- und Mittelstufe),' *Geschichtsdidaktik* 12
(1987): 28–35.

History, Memory, and Historical Distance

MARK SALBER PHILLIPS

Questions of 'distance' have been debated in a number of disciplines, including aesthetics, theatre, narratology, and sociology. In history, however, the issue has generally been left to the quieter realms of practice, where craft rather than theory prevails. Even so, the question seems too important for historians to overlook. In the complex matter of constructing a past that we can engage with – one that is both true to our discipline and responsive to our interests – problems of proximity and distance arise at a multitude of levels. Nor need we limit the issue to traditional forms of historical narration, since similar problems of involvement and detachment, insight and overview are equally present in other forms of historical representation. In this essay, the specific reference will largely be to historical writing as such, but it would not be difficult to extend the analysis – allowing for appropriate adjustments to other media and genres – to museums, monuments, or film.[1]

The combination of centrality and silence is intriguing and I have allowed it to shape much of what follows. My goal is to give a preliminary view of this overlooked dimension of historical thought, stressing the variability of historical practice as well as the variety of distances at play in every representation of the past. Close attention to the complexities of distance, I want to suggest, allows us to explore a number of balances and tensions in historical representation – especially the convergence of formal, affective, ideological, and cognitive elements. The goal, in the first instance, will be a clearer understanding of individual texts and authors, but on another level the analysis of distance may also give us new ways of thinking about styles of historical reasoning and their changes over time.[2]

The absence of explicit discussion of historical distance does not mean that historians have been indifferent to the issue. On the contrary, I would argue that this silence indicates the presence of assumptions that are all the more effective for being tacit. Indeed, as will become clear when we turn to the issue of 'memory,' these assumptions are now so firmly embedded in our general understanding of the historian's craft that a prescriptive concept of distance seems hardly distinguishable from the idea of history itself. My purpose is to put this consensus under question, though not necessarily to overthrow conclusions that have come to be accepted as common wisdom. Indeed, to the extent that current assumptions represent the consolidation of a much lengthier and more comprehensive tradition of Western thought, it would be foolish to think we can simply opt for other ways of understanding and representing the past that would be equally compelling. It is ironic, nonetheless, that the history of historical thought has long resisted attempts to historicize its own foundations, preferring instead to follow implicit, but strongly held prescriptions about what constitutes proper forms of historical investigation or understanding. The consequence is that historians have excluded from sympathetic consideration many of the most salient forms of historical knowledge, both within and outside of the dominant Western tradition. The effect has been not only to make it more difficult to clarify many features of history and memory in the contemporary world, but also to obscure much of the richness of the Western inheritance of historical thought.

Defamiliarizing 'Distance'

To retrieve a descriptive idea of distance from so much prescription will require some defamiliarization of its own. Perhaps I can best start this process by recollecting my own first encounter with the question of distance in the expanded sense I want to give it. The occasion was a classroom discussion of the strengths and weaknesses of microhistory. One student made it plain that other courses had already introduced him to more than enough massacred cats, deluded millers, and long-lost 'husbands,' and my defence of microhistory as a way of representing ordinary lives and everyday experience was met with undisguised scepticism. 'Aren't you really saying that your generation came too late to write the really important stuff – the lives of people like Cosimo de Medici or Lorenzo the Magnificent – so there was not much left over except a bunch of odd balls and small potatoes like these?'

The question was reasonable enough and in its way not unexpected;

what did surprise me was the direction taken in my own reply. 'Let me put the question in a different way. Let's say I have two books here on the battle of Stalingrad. One is an overall tactical account of this crucial battle. It looks at events from the point of view of the general staff and it details the success of the Soviet command in outmanoeuvring the German army, so that they were encircled and starved into surrendering. The other book takes a very different point of view. It depicts the ordinary German soldier's experience by using letters captured by the Soviets – anguished letters written by men facing starvation and defeat in the depths of a Russian winter. Which of these two books (I asked) do you want to read?' The general response, predictably enough, strongly favoured the second, though one student astutely argued that there was no need to make a final choice. My point, of course, was not to suggest that there could be a right or wrong answer, but rather that there was something here worth thinking about as an index of contemporary interest in the past. In our histories as much as in our journalism or our museums, we seem to be strongly attracted to objects and stories that display the intimate texture of ordinary experience. Rather than deny this preference or moralize about it, perhaps we should understand it as a widely shared cultural choice and think further about its implications.

The student's objections to microhistory and my defence of it could have turned on any one of a number of small-scale histories that captured the interest of historians in the nineteen eighties or nineties. The truth is, however, that the discussion was about a book of my own,[3] a circumstance that undoubtedly has a great deal to do with its subsequent impact for me. Why, I began to ask, are so many historians (myself included) currently fascinated by the microhistorical approach? Was this simply a 'revival of narrative' (as Lawrence Stone famously called it at the time) or was my own work part of a larger shift in sensibility marked by a preoccupation with a sort of intimate or everyday experience that best lent itself to the close focus of microhistory? And if contemporary historical writing had been shaped in significant ways by something that – broadly speaking – could be called a new sentimentalism, what precedents or analogies could I find in the past? Did historians of different sorts (or perhaps of different eras) construct for their readers different forms of proximity to or distance from the past? What affective, ideological, or cognitive implications follow from such constructions?

Historians ordinarily think of 'distance' as a simple function of temporality and they generally assign it a strongly positive value. Distance, in this sense (often called 'objectivity') means a kind of clarity that comes with the passage of time. This view of historical distance, however, can only be a starting point, since a little consideration will make it clear that every history has to take on the task of positioning its audience in relation to a past. Thus distance is not simply given, but is also constructed, and the range of distance-constructions is really quite broad. In this expanded sense, distance is something the reader experiences as well as the historian; it also takes in all points along a gradient of distances, including proximity or immediacy as well as remoteness or detachment. (We have no trouble recognizing that both the bungalow and the skyscraper have height; equally, we can say that every representation of the past manipulates distance, however foreshortened or extended.) By the same token, distance as I want to develop the term refers not only to matters of form or rhetoric, but also to other significant dimensions of engagement or disengagement. As a result, questions about distance can be directed to a history's *ideological* implication as well as its *affective* coloration, its *cognitive* assumptions as well as its *formal* traits.

A second occasion pushed me to recognize ethical issues implicated in the question of distance. At a conference I listened to a paper concerning narratives of female incarceration. The historian argued that journalistic circulation of such stories offered genteel readers a voyeuristic thrill in an eminently respectable form. As the recitation continued, I found myself disturbed by the historian's failure to pose the same question of *our* interest in such stories – an interest that seemed to be part of a widespread fascination in current scholarship with the intimate description of painful experience. Afterwards, I asked whether it might be necessary to guard against the possibility that his own retellings of these stories could also have a titillating effect, and I came away wondering whether the pendulum of historical studies had swung so far that, in the present moment, the most evident moral trap has less to do with the much discussed issue of falsely objectifying the 'other' than with its sentimental opposite: the temptation to assume a position of unwarranted intimacy in the face of past suffering.

The dangers that accompany this posture are ones that we find easy to spot in journalism – the intrusive interview at the scene of private tragedy, the violent or pornographic thrill made respectable by the duty to report the news – but historical scholarship seems to have exempted itself from such self-questioning. What, I wondered, might be the historian's equivalent of the ethical permission forms for research on human subjects that have become a standard feature of work in medical, sociological, or anthropological contexts?

History and Memory

For anyone who doubts the significance of implicit assumptions of distance in our understanding of history and historical representation, a good place to begin may be the idea of 'memory.' In this widespread contemporary discussion, 'memory' is generally constructed by means of a contrast with the assumed norms of 'history' proper. Thus, for Pierre Nora, impresario of a massive archaeology of French national iconography, memory is 'always a phenomenon of the present, a bond tying us to the eternal present.' History, by contrast, is reconstructive, critical, and perpetually suspicious of memory.[4] Nora's discussion employs an elegaic tone that suggests some nostalgia for an earlier day before 'true memory' was replaced by the more artificial constructions he calls *lieux de memoire*. David Lowenthal, studying the same phenomenon, calls it 'heritage' and he too sets its foreshortening of the historical past in opposition to the critical perspectives of genuine history. Most people, he writes, cannot deal with a past that is too alien; instead, they enlist it for present causes, domesticating it with legends that 'project the present back, the past forward.' The result is a kind of 'communion' with the past that we think of as history, but is actually heritage. The distinction, writes Lowenthal, is vital. 'History explores and explains pasts grown ever more opaque over time; heritage clarifies pasts so as to infuse them with present purposes.'[5] Lowenthal accepts that there must be a place for the domesticated past that he calls 'heritage' as long as we do not confuse it with the more critical stance he identifies with an authentic historical outlook.

Peter Novick makes the same sharp separation, but (unsurprisingly in a study of the manipulation of Holocaust memory) he leaves no real room for choice:

[C]ollective memory is in crucial senses ahistorical. To understand something historically is to be aware of its complexity, to have sufficient detachment to see it from multiple perspectives, to accept the ambiguities, including moral ambiguities, of protagonists' motives and behaviour. Collective memory simplifies; sees events from a single, committed perspective; is impatient with ambiguities of any kind; reduces events to mythic archetypes. Historical consciousness, by its nature, focuses on the *historicity* of events – that they took place then and not now, that they grew out of circumstances different from those that now obtain. Memory, by contrast, has no sense of the passage of time; it denies the 'pastness' of its objects and insists on their continuing presence.[6]

For Novick, as for Nora and Lowenthal, memory is evidently a way of seeing the past that truncates or denies distance. What is more, this flattening is not simply temporal ('the pastness of its objects') but – to anticipate terms I will introduce later – is also ideological, affective, and cognitive. Thus memory is morally simplistic, mythic, analytically blunted – by implication an unreconstructed or perhaps primitive form of historical consciousness for which Novick, at least, has no nostalgia. History, by contrast, 'focuses on the *historicity* of events,' meaning (one has to presume) not only their pastness but also their complexity. Thus, the affective and ideological simplicities of a point of view that looks to the past only to find a 'continuing presence' is opposed by a critical historical spirit that might be defined as distance-consciousness.

In the end, what is most notable about all these discussions is not simply that they rely upon unexamined assumptions about what constitutes legitimate distance, but also that they set out their terms with an absoluteness that leaves no space to recognize the range and variability of historical writing. The simplified picture of the 'use and abuse of history' that results is all the more remarkable in that it comes from historians who have made important contributions to the study of historiography. Indeed, anyone interested in pursuing the variability and complexity of distance in recent times could do no better than to begin with Novick's iconoclastic history of the pretension to objectivity in the American historical profession or Nora's study of Ernst Lavisse as the principal organizer of the republican myth in French historiography.

Constructing Historical Distance

Conventionally, historians identify the idea of historical distance with the possibility of the new (and generally, it is thought, improved) perspectives that are conferred by the passage of time. We are now two generations removed from the Holocaust, for example, and there is much that we can see about those terrible times that was difficult to understand or to speak about at the time. Without discounting this important aspect of distance, however, I want to explore another sense in which distance is not simply received, but also constructed. Every history – indeed every representation of the past – has to engage with the problem of positioning its audience in relations of proximity or detachment to the events and experiences represented. Equally, as I have already noted, distance needs to be recognized as an element in all forms of engagement or disengagement. Questions about distance should, therefore, direct themselves to a history's ideological impact as well as to its emotional force, to its cognitive assumptions as well as to its formal arrangements.

Does the historical narrative, I want to ask, encourage the reader to stand back, treating the past as a realm of detached observation, or does it seek instead to make the historical scene as vivid or palpable as possible? Is the past presented as a place of emotional or ideological engagement? Does the history try to sweep us up in its dramas or, more subtly perhaps, does it attract us with opportunities for quieter and more private sympathies? Is the past presented as an intellectual problem? Are impersonal social forces a central feature of analysis? In what proportions and for what reasons does the past appear exotic or inaccessible? If indeed the effort is to make some aspects of the past present to us, how is this achieved, and for what purpose? Alternately, to what extent has the historian kept us from assuming too easy a familiarity? What emotional or intellectual satisfactions come with either detachment or engagement, and what ideological consequences follow? Given the particular history we are reading, what are the political implications of 'taking the long view' or of rejecting it?

So far I have focused on the *writing* of history, but there is no obvious reason to limit the discussion to textual representations. Though they employ a different vocabulary of forms, history painting, photography, documentary film, and museums all raise very similar questions about the role of distance in historical representation. Indeed, museum displays, with their combination of concrete materials and a public setting, present some of the issues in their most tangible and accessible form. Very few people outside of the academy could describe recent shifts in the direction of historical writing, but it takes no special museological awareness to spot large changes that have been taking place in museums. When faced with the varied displays of London's Imperial War Museum, for example, no visitor will have trouble distinguishing between the traditional mahogany and glass cases filled with swords and military uniforms and the newer displays like 'The Trench Experience' or 'The Blitz Experience.' To be sure, new materials and new technologies provide some easily read cues to the age of exhibition, but it is as easy to identify new directions in regard to the question of who and what is represented – an essentially political issue – as it is to spot changes of design.

In most contemporary museums, curators and designers are exploring more participatory forms of display, replacing what are now regarded as the static and overly academic presentations prevalent in an earlier day. While stopping short of full-scale 'disneyfication,' they strive to animate their exhibitions in ways that will give the visitor a sense of the past that is socially more comprehensive and visually more immediate. Once dedicated to the scientific tasks of classification and demonstration, museums now seek to evoke an experience of alternative milieus. Frequently this means freeing the materials from their cases, reducing the separation between viewer and object. Music, voices, and videos animate the displays, while the visual impact of the objects is enhanced by photographic blow-ups, a step that radically alters the visual scale and changes the balance between the viewer and the viewed. Of course, since the works are no longer separated from us by glass and mahogany, other, subtler methods must be used to restrain and protect, but the effect is to promote a sense that we have entered into a space that includes and surrounds us.

The contemporary museum, in short, invites us to imagine the past as a field of experience rather than as an object of study – a program that has evident parallels in the more secluded world of professional historiography. In fact, the Imperial War Museum offers its visitors much the same historiographical choice I offered my students, and it operates on a similar conviction that the contemporary audience will gravitate towards those representations of war that are more democratic in their politics and more immediate in their emotional impact. The War Museum's 'Experience' displays attempt to engage all of our senses, giving us the smell of the trenches, the sounds of voices, and even the shuddering impact of the bombs. At the same time, the social lens is set to a much wider angle than in the past. Thus, the voices that we hear as we walk the replica-trenches or crowd into the simulated shelter are deliberately democratic – the voices of common soldiers, of civilians, of women, of ordinary Londoners – while an effort is made in another new display to include the experience of children as well.

Several aspects of the problem emerge with particular clarity from the example of the museum, where choices about modes of representation, as I have said, take on a very public expression. First, the control of distance evidently involves much more than aesthetic or emotional impact alone. Inevitably, it also carries with it significant ideological implications. In the case of the War Museum, the inclusion of London's civilians in the narrative of war risks very little politically. In fact, the exhibition tends towards the celebratory and the sentimental: this, after all, was their 'finest hour.' In some other well-known recent examples, however, clashes between curators and their publics have placed the politics of distance under a spotlight. Washington's Smithsonian Institution knowingly entered into difficult terrain in its plans to show the *Enola Gay* in the context of an exhibition that would also include the effect of the atomic bombing on Japanese civilians. Veterans' organizations, however, made it very clear that they did not want *their* war contextualized in this way and the show had to be cancelled.[7] Similar issues were raised, though by a public that represented a very different location in the political spectrum, by the controversy over 'Into the Heart of Africa' at Toronto's Royal Ontario Museum. The show exhibited primitivist stereotypes of Africans in the service of what was intended as a critical look at the racist attitudes of nineteenth-century missionaries. For Toronto's Caribbean community, however, the images spoke louder – spoke more *directly* – than the words. They read the depictions of powerlessness and backwardness as degrading, whatever the text panels might say. In both cases, it seems, significant portions of the public could not (or would not) adopt the more distantiated perspective assumed by the curators.

Second, there is the issue of changing norms in historical representation. Since distance has never been identified as an important element in constructing the past, it is hardly surprising that we have not thought about the implications of its variability. The tendency, rather, has been to canonize the norms of whatever might be the reigning doctrine and therefore to assume *in*variability. I am not saying, of course, that historians are unaware of changes of direction in their discipline, but they are far more likely to point to new methods or topics – gender history, 'the cultural turn,' environmental history – than to changes in the underlying modes of representation. Even so, it is clear that schools of historical thought have their own characteristic rhetoric, just as they are drawn to particular social issues or ideological positions. I am not suggesting that every product of a particular historiographical school will manifest a single, uniform stance of engagement or detachment. Nonetheless, the parallels I have noted between museum practice and historical writing suggest the idea that the representation of the past, taken in its widest sense, may indeed undergo significant shifts of perspective from time to time. If so, not only would variation in assumptions about distance be an important feature of the way in which readers distinguish the various historical genres (national history, microhistory, memoir, biography), but shifts of this kind may also play a significant role in shaping the development of historiography over time.

Distance and Distances

Every form of historical representation must position its audience in some relationship of closeness to or distance from the events and experiences it describes. Historical distance, in other words, is an issue that is registered in every reading of a historical text, just as it is part of every visit to a historical museum or commemorative monument. But if the problem of establishing distance can be said to be an unavoidable feature of historical representation, it certainly does not follow that there exists a universally privileged distance location. On the contrary, it is essential to recognize that there is no fixed stance, either of detachment or proximity, that is best suited for all contexts, purposes, or genres. Whether we take as our guide the long history of historical writing or the full spectrum of contemporary practice, the range of variation has clearly been considerable. This pattern of variability argues against any attempt to discuss the issue in narrowly prescriptive terms – an important point when viewed against the overly rigid ideas about distance that are implicit in many of our best-known discussions of historical knowledge. At the same time, just because distance is a complex and variable feature of historical representation, an investigation of its vicissitudes may provide us with some useful tools for thinking about differences in styles of historical reasoning as well as changes in historiographical practice.

Some degree of temporal distance is, of course, a given in historical writing, but temporal distance may be enlarged or diminished by other kinds of commitments and responses. Thus historical distance, in the fuller sense I want to give it, refers to much more than the conventional understanding that the outline of events is clarified by the passage of time, or that the historian's perspective necessarily reflects that of his or her generation. It includes political as well as emotional engagement (or disengagement) and is the consequence of cognitive choices as well as formal and aesthetic ones. Equally, our concept of distance, if it is to be helpful, should not be limited to forms of detachment or estrangement; in its wider sense, distance must take in the impulse to establish proximity as well as separation. Distance, to put this another way, should refer to a dimension of our relation to the past, not to one particular location. In this expanded sense, I want to use the term to locate possibilities for making past moments close and pressing – in order to intensify, for example, the emotional or political impact of an event – as well to mark the idea of stepping back from the historical scene – perhaps to emphasize the objectivity, irony, or philosophical sweep of the historian's vision.

Clearly, too, we will need to distinguish between the formal devices that create effects of proximity or distance and the cognitive or ideological ends they serve. After all, very similar formal devices can be put to very different social or political uses. Close description, for example, has often been employed as a way of engaging the reader's sympathies, as Edward Thompson explicitly does in 'seeking to rescue the poor stockinger, the luddite cropper, the "obsolete" hand-loom weaver ... from the enormous condescension of posterity.' Yet detailed narration is not always a strategy for creating sympathy, nor is immediacy always paired with ideological identification. Thus Michel Foucault's grisly description of the dismemberment of Damien the regicide in the opening scene of *Discipline and Punish* is not calculated to spur us to sympathy with efforts of penal reform; on the contrary, this horrific close-up of judicial retribution is intended to shock us into abandoning our comfort with other, much more familiar regimes of punishment. The death spectacle serves as a sort of Brechtian alienation effect, forcing on us the necessary distance to recognize what is at stake in other forms of punishment, specifically in the new, apparently more humane regime of surveillance instituted by the reforms of the Enlightenment.

The historian's effort to establish a distance position cannot, of course, be read as a simple or autonomous act. Both Thompson's gesture of humane inclusion and Foucault's repudiation of any such resort to historical pathos presuppose the norms of historical description from which they dissent. And, as both historians obliquely acknowledge, their work derives some part of its force precisely from its willingness to strain the expected neutrality of academic historical writing, so that both the historian and the reader are pressed into a new relationship to the past. Repositionings of this kind have often made a considerable impact on practice and – as is evident with both of the historians I have mentioned – have helped to set the terms of new historical styles. Remarkably, however, such variations on distance have not done as much as one might expect to change abstract expectations about the ways in which historical knowledge is constituted. Rather, by force of long tradition (albeit modified by these shorter-term fluctuations of style and manner) history has continued for the most part to describe its purposes in a language of impartiality or objectivity. Even the modern professional historian, who is more deeply sceptical about the possibilities of political neutrality or scientific certainty that inspired earlier generations proudly distinguishes his own critical discipline from the merely celebratory or commemorative purposes belonging to less rigorous ways of thinking about the past.

Some Categories of Distance

Clearly we have moved a good way beyond the standard view of distance as a simple reflection of temporality, and as we have done so, distance has come to seem less like something *given* to the historian or his audience than something *constructed* by them in a multitude of ways. One consequence is that, though it will often be convenient to speak of distance in the singular, this must be recognized as a sort of shorthand. When we start to probe the concept, we are brought up against a variety of dimensions of historiographical practice, each of which can produce its own particular forms of distance. On this view, distance seems not so much a single, undifferentiated quality as a complex effect resulting from a tension or balance between a number of different kinds of distance. Though I want to avoid unnecessary elaboration, it seems useful to make distinctions between at least four such kinds. These can be labelled as formal, affective, ideological, and cognitive distances.

By formal distance I refer to the wide variety of textual or other representational devices that shape the reader's experience of the text, or – to change the scene – the visitor's tour of a monument or exhibition. In one sense, this is the dimension of the problem where we have most to draw on, since a number of programs in literary or visual studies have made distance a central term of discussion. Indeed, a central tradition of Western aesthetics, going back most prominently to Kant, has firmly identified aesthetic experience with a distantiated or 'disinterested' relation to objects. Building on this interest in aesthetic distance, literary theorists have investigated 'estrangement' or 'defamiliarization' as an essential element of fictions; rhetorical critics, reception theorists, and narratologists have examined 'point of view,' voice, or 'focalization' as means of controlling distance, while students of the theatre, influenced by Brecht's modernist innovations, have pursued parallel issues in drama. In practice, however, except for an interest in the nuances of authorial voice, historians in general have not shown much interest in these formal issues, while students of literature have seldom occupied themselves with the practical criticism of historiographical texts. One would be very surprised, for example, to find a journal (historical or literary) featuring a discussion of 'focalization' as an aspect of micro-history, or engaging in a debate over 'alienation effects' in the historiography of the Holocaust. Yet beyond such evidence that disciplinary solitudes still prevail, there is a further problem that may be still more difficult to overcome. As I have indicated, much of our literary theory and critical practice reflects a philosophical tradition that specifically identifies aesthetic experience with a relationship of disinterestedness. This means that these bodies of criticism begin with a prior commitment to certain forms of distance, with the result that other distance relationships are viewed in correspondingly hierarchical terms. Among other consequences, this raising of 'disinterest' into a norm of aesthetic life has produced just that division between aesthetic and non-aesthetic writing that, by placing history and literature in opposing camps, has made it hard to read historical works in formal terms.

For historians, both affective and ideological distances point to much more familiar territories. None of us, certainly, would be surprised to be told that a historical narrative might have designs on the emotions of the reader or that history can carry a powerful ideological charge. Indeed, it has been all too common to read histories as essentially political works – as politics pursued by other means. Nonetheless, in a discipline that since classical times has proclaimed the need to proceed *sine ira et studio*, we are hampered by a simplification of possibilities that sets all forms of political or emotional engagement against 'objectivity.' The consequence is a scale of judgment that elides objectivity with political neutrality, making it difficult to characterize the differences between merely partisan work and the kind of considered non-neutrality that results from a deeply held politics. Nor does objectivity seem a useful way to describe histories that aim not so much at neutrality as at more active forms of detachment. The ironies of Machiavelli or of Tocqueville, to cite only the most obvious examples, do not signal aloofness from politics, but politics of a different sort.

Readers of history, it goes without saying, are often attracted to particular works because there is something in their genres or themes that raise expectations of emotional or ideological involvement. Indeed, it is probably safe to say that in every epoch most historical writing has been animated by this sort of sense of engagement, and when it has not, historical research has often been derided as merely 'antiquarian' – a charge frequently laid against academic historiography. Ironically, of course, loyalties to place, party, or profession have exercised an enormous importance in antiquarian enterprises, and one would be foolish to think that academic writing has lacked the same motives. All this is sufficiently obvious, but it does mean that on a simple scale of objectivity it would be difficult to plot the differences between various genres of historical writing. Is biography, for example, inherently less objective than general history? Yet the idea of distance offers us a wider range of positions to work with and a more complex cross-hatching of form, affect, and ideology. For this reason, it offers richer possibilities for addressing questions about the varieties of forms in which history can be told. Nor would I want to limit the question to traditional genres. Today, on the contrary, it seems especially important to extend its scope by a great deal, asking not simply about biography, memoir, or autobiography, but also about the emotional resonances of film, museums, and heritage sites, all of which have become important media for the representation of the past.

The appeal of biography, museums, or film suggests some other dimensions of affective distance beyond those already discussed. It would be useful, for example, to have a way of approaching not only the strong attachments or antipathies that accompany partisan engagement, but also the more intimate sympathies that have been evoked in so much recent study of the past. The contemporary museum, as I have already emphasized, has evolved forms of evocative display that often focus on the most ordinary experiences of life and are designed not so much to give us information about the past as to lend it additional presence. This populist approach to history is taken still further in heritage sites or historical theme parks, but it also has a recognizable continuity with the academic historian's interest in the history of the body or his preference for microhistory over the *longue durée*. In so much of its historical outlook, indeed, ours has been very much an age of sentiment – a time, that is to say, less interested in the great dramas of power that held the attention of earlier generations than in the small evocative details that illuminate ordinary lives and common experience.

These dramatic shifts in historical representation in the second half of the twentieth century can also be used to illustrate my fourth category, which is the idea of a cognitive distance. The 'revival of narrative,' as it was known at the time, announced itself most explicitly in striking new themes of historical research – gender, the body, the emotions, everyday life, and so on. And coupled with these themes went a new politics –

feminism – as well as experimentation with a new historical form – microhistory. These thematic and ideological interests were well articulated in the literature of the time, but they were also accompanied by other, often less articulate changes where matters of understanding and explanation were central. After all, in the space of a very brief period, historical studies shed much of their credence in the grand narratives of Marxist or liberal historiography and embraced the limitations as well as the pleasures of local knowledge.

Among the many changes that made this new direction possible an important part was played by a widespread critique of long-accepted models of knowledge and their replacement by new strategies of investigation that gave validity to what Geertz called 'thick description.' The most spectacular example of this shift is probably the new direction taken by the history of science where (post–Thomas Kuhn) the grandest of all secular narratives – the progress of scientific reason – has given way to studies of the culture of the laboratory and a deep commitment to understanding the workings of tacit knowledge.[8] An equally self-conscious redirection – more influential perhaps for the majority of historians – was the work of the Italian microhistorians, whose argument for the microhistorical point of view was as much cognitive as ideological. 'The unifying principle of all microhistorical research,' wrote Giovanni Levi, 'is the belief that microscopic observation will reveal factors previously unobserved.'[9] Most notably, the microscopic framework gives us the ability to observe what Levi calls 'the irreducibility of individual persons to the rules of large-scale systems.'[10] Ginzburg, similarly, argued for the exhaustive analysis of the individual document as a counter to the Annales school's stress on long-lasting and repetitive phenomena ('serial history'). 'To select as a cognitive object,' he wrote, 'only what is repetitive, and therefore capable of being serialized, signifies paying a very high price in cognitive terms.'[11] For the historian of popular culture especially, the anomalous document, the one that does not seem to fit the series, is the one that most repays attention.

The shift in historical studies I have been describing was very broad in its scope and was paralleled across a number of academic disciplines as well as other, more public forms of historical representation. Such changes are not easy to name, though a number of useful attempts have been made – including the revival of narrative, the cultural turn, and the academic postmodern. In proposing the idea of a shift in historical distance (incorporating all the sub-categories of distance I have briefly explored) I am not hoping so much to find a comprehensive label for recent events as I am attempting to present more recent changes in terms that suggest possibilities for comparison with parallel shifts in earlier periods. This is not the first time, after all, that we have seen dramatic changes in styles of historical reasoning and representation, and both logic and evidence point to the fact that it will not be the last. In the perspective of the new historiographies of the next few decades, the admired models of the last generation may well look like a sentimental interlude between two more ambitious eras in historical knowledge in which first Marxist and then Darwinian grand narratives predominated.

Notes

1 I am grateful to Professors Peter Burke, John Burrow, April London, and Edward Hundert for many discussions regarding the subject of this essay. For earlier analysis of some of the issues I raise here, see my *Society and Sentiment: Genres of Historiography in Britain, 1740–1820* (Princeton, NJ: Princeton University Press, 2000); 'Historical Distance and the Historiography of Eighteenth-century Britain,' in S. Collini, R. Whatmore, and B. Young, eds, *History, Religion, and Culture* (Cambridge: Cambridge University Press, 2000), 31–47; 'Hume and Historical Distance,' *Lumen* 21 (2003); and 'Distance and Historical Representation,' *History Workshop Journal* 57 (2004): 123–41.

2 I use the phrase 'styles of historical reasoning' by analogy to Ian Hacking's parallel phrase for scientific reasoning. Unlike Hacking (or Crombie, whom he follows), however, I am not arguing that such styles acquire a permanence in the history of practice. See Ian Hacking, 'Style for Historians and Philosophers,' *Studies in the History and Philosophy of Science* 23 (1992): 1–20.

3 *The Memoir of Marco Parenti* (Princeton, NJ: Princeton University Press, 1987; repr. Peterborough, ON: Broadview, 2000).

4 Pierre Nora, *Realms of Memory* (New York: Columbia University Press, 1996), 3.

5 David Lowenthal, *Possessed by the Past: The Heritage Crusade and the Spoils of History* (New York: Free Press, 1996), xi.

6 Peter Novick, *The Holocaust in American Life* (Boston: Houghton Mifflin, 1999), 3–4.

7 See H. Riegl, 'Into the Heart of Irony: Ethnographic Exhibitions and the Politics of Difference,' in S. Macdonald and G. Fyfe, eds, *Theorizing Museums: Representing Identity and Diversity in a Changing World* (Oxford: Blackwell,

1996); and Edward Linenthal and Tom Engelhardt, eds, *History Wars: The Enola Gay and Other Battles for the American Past* (New York: Metropolitan Books, 1996).

8 On this shift, see especially Jan Golinski, *Making Natural Knowledge: Constructivism and the History of Science* (Cambridge: Cambridge University Press, 1998).

9 Giovanni Levi, 'On Microhistory,' in Peter Burke, ed., *New Perspectives on Historical Writing* (Cambridge, UK: Polity Press, 1991), 95.

10 Ibid., 94–5. 'The question is, therefore, how to define the margins – however narrow they may be – of the freedom granted an individual by the interstices and contradictions of the normative systems which govern him. In other words, an enquiry into the extent and nature of free will within the general structure of human society.'

11 Carlo Ginzburg, 'Microhistory: Two or Three Things I Know about It,' *Critical Inquiry* 20 (1993), 10–35.

PART II

History Education and Historical Consciousness

The study of collective memory per se emphasizes the cultural and historical specificity of forms and institutions of memory. Issues of policy, which speak to real and pressing social and political needs in the present, are generally absent. While there may be an underlying nostalgia in Nora, or a critique of the field of memory studies as regressive nostalgia in Klein and Spiegel, one can study collective memory without an explicit normative stance. The goal is to understand how institutions of memory worked in the historical circumstances in which they were constructed and maintained. This normative agnosticism is not possible as we confront issues of cultural policy in our own time, ones that demand our intentional engagement in shaping the future. Collective memory studies may help to shape and contextualize the decisions we make, but we cannot study our own situation in the present with the same relative detachment.

How do we carry forward from here: what is needed, in this culture, in this time, in the way of understandings of the past? There are many institutions where decisions about how to study, remember, and use the past are made. Those whose work has an impact on the next generation have particular weight in considering the future of the past. Furthermore, those whose activities are governed by the broadest collective policy decisions (as opposed, for example, to market-based decisions) are most subject to the question: what is to be done? Thus history education, particularly as it takes place in schools, assumes a central theoretical position.

Evidence that a lot, perhaps most, of collective memory is shaped outside of schools does not diminish this centrality. It has, however, contributed to a key feature of the new and growing body of history-education research. Scholars in this field have, in the past two decades, emphasized the importance of studying students' ideas as they come into the classroom. This focus is not merely on what factual data young people have at their disposal, but on the shapes of their narratives, the sense they make of them, and the tools they have (or fail to have) for assessing their truth and significance. In this sense, the new studies share something very important with the collective-memory studies: they are another kind of examination of how 'everyperson,' beyond professional historians, constructs and uses history. But unlike the memory studies, history-education literature struggles, with more or less determination, towards normative notions of development.[1]

The intersection of collective memory, history education, and disciplinary history receives a paradigmatic explication in the contribution of Jocelyn Létourneau and Sabrina Moisan, who return us to the case of Quebec. Despite the existence of a rich, recent historiography that has moved beyond the conventional narrative of 'Quebec's tragedy,' they found that the Quebec history told by francophone students appears to be just that. Létourneau and Moisan place responsibility in neither the textbooks nor the curriculum, but in pressures on underequipped teachers to offer an interpretative scheme that fits most easily with conventional and thus easily communicated views of Quebec's past. They see this process of schooling as one instance of a more general phenomenon where the construction of powerful, core historical narratives, 'rooted in metaphoric simplicity,' resist contradictory or complicating evidence and details. Readers will think here of the enduring power of Wertsch's notion of schematic narrative templates. In the face of an entrenched narrative resistant to the new historiography, Létourneau and Moisan recommend, not the inculcation of a new narrative, but rather teaching students a critical historical methodology, so that they can compare conflicting accounts, and construct complex narratives that take the world's 'ambivalences and paradoxes, ambiguities and dissonances into account.' A historical consciousness incorporating these qualities is not inconsistent with Rüsen's genetic type, but it does enumerate qualities and characteristics that lie beyond his definition. At the same time, Létourneau and Moisan share with Rüsen (and, indeed, with all those concerned with history didactics) the normative question 'What is to be done?'

British history-education research, in which the work of Peter Lee has been highly influential, also has a strong and explicit notion of development. 'Progression,' as it is called in the British work, takes place in individuals through a to-be-investigated combination of cognitive maturation and purposeful instruction. In contrast to Rüsen, the British have been less interested in the meaning of young people's narratives for practical life, and more interested in 'second-order concepts' like cause, explanation, and accounts, which relate students' historical thinking to that in the discipline. Second-order concepts, Lee explains, are not what history is about, but what shape people's abilities to do history. The British work has influenced numerous North American studies, which share the focus on second-order concepts. The notions of progression draw from disciplinary historiographic notions, in that progression and advancement tend to bring students more towards the practices of historians. Lee justifies this starting point by noting that disciplinary tools – more readily than alternatives – allow people to surmount epistemological and methodological dead ends. Beyond this theoretically derived starting point, Lee's stages of development are resolutely empirical, derived and refined through close analysis of students' talk and writing on historical problems. Nevertheless, the notion of progression is closely tied, conceptually, to modern practices of the discipline of history.

As a result of the symposium in August 2001 that gave rise to this volume, the question of whether Lee's (and the British) notion of progression can be subsumed under, is complementary to, or is fundamentally incompatible with Rüsen's scheme became a driving question, and Lee takes this up in his chapter. What is the relationship between advancement in Rüsen's types and the critical practices of historians? Christian Laville delivers a resounding verdict on this question. As a long-time proponent of history education in the service of critical, participatory citizenship, he fears that the notion of 'historical consciousness' is no more than a dressed-up version of the nineteenth-century nation-building, collective memory-enhancing indoctrination, refitted to the needs of twenty-first century 'European consciousness.' If this is indeed the case – and his examination of the roots of the term lend support to his argument – then school history curricula focused on building historical consciousness will not pay particular attention to history's disciplinary tools and dispositions, and he would see such curricula as a retrograde step. But Lee, himself, is less dismissive. He draws on Rüsen's work to explore the connection between mastering disciplinary history and 'advancement' in historical consciousness.

Roger Simon and his colleagues come to this conversation from a different starting point that, while pedagogical in nature, has clear commitments neither to the disciplinary history of professional historians nor to enhanced collective memory. They are searching for new forms of remembrance, with questions about what and how we in the present owe to the people of the past, as we encounter fragmentary and inadequate traces of profound victimization under oppressive regimes. Simon uses material from the Holocaust to develop and analyse a 'historiographic poetics, the writing of which is itself a practice of remembrance.' Despite the fact that this is a profoundly pedagogical project, Simon has not (like Lee or Rüsen) articulated a hierarchical scheme against which to measure readers' responses to these traces. Yet he does articulate a normative notion of 'attentiveness' to suffering and injustice. And one might posit a scale of responses, ranging from indifference, through emotional reaction, to suffering as spectacle, to one that fundamentally alters the narratives with which the reader orients her commitments and social relations in the present. With such a scheme, the project appears to bear something more in common, at least in form, with Rüsen's definition of historical consciousness.[2] Simon and Rüsen attempted to clarify the differences and commonalities between their approaches in a discussion at the August 2001 symposium. Kent den Heyer has edited a transcript of that discussion and it is included here in order to provide a sense of what was at stake.

By setting broad questions of policy in history education against a backdrop of the study of collective memory and disciplinary history, as the notion of 'historical consciousness' demands, researchers stand to gain a huge amount. Heretofore, the role of historians in history education has been conceived largely in terms of developing the 'governing narratives' that serve as standards against which the narratives of teaching should be measured. Laville, Létourneau and Moisan, Lee, Rüsen, and Simon all move beyond this conception, with a much more active role for students of history. Laville, Létourneau and Moisan, and Lee embrace pedagogical visions of students able to use critical, disciplinary tools of historians in order to engage actively in constructing, interpreting, and adjudicating narrative interpretations of the past. In this conception, historians' practices rather than their products become standards by which to judge history education. Laville, more explicitly than Lee, articulates the role that such capacities enable in regards to participatory citizenship. Rüsen and Simon, for their part, understand the most powerful and successful history pedagogies as generating profound transformations in life orientation.

Notes

1 Important volumes in recent history-education research include Sam Wineburg, *Historical Thinking and Other Unnatural Acts: Charting the Future of Teaching the Past* (Philadelphia: Temple University Press, 2001); Peter Stearns, Peter
Seixas, and Sam Wineburg, eds, *Knowing, Teaching, and Learning History:
National and International Perspectives* (New York and London: New York
University Press, 2000); Bruce VanSledright, *In Search of America's Past: Learn-
ing to Read History in Elementary School* (New York: Teachers College Press,
2002); Linda S. Levstik and Keith C. Barton, *Doing History: Investigating with
Children in Elementary and Middle Schools,* 2nd ed. (Mahwah, NJ: Lawrence
Erlbaum, 2001); Bogumil Jewsiewicki and Jocelyn Létourneau, eds, *Les jeunes
à l'ère de la mondialisation: Quête identitaire et conscience historique* (Sillery, QC:
Septentrion [with the assistance of Irène Hermann], 1998); James F. Voss and
Mario Carretero, eds, *Learning and Reasoning in History* (London: Woburn
Press, 1998).
2 At the symposium where these two theorists met, however, Simon attempted
to define the differences between his approach and Rüsen's, while the latter
argued that Simon's might be subsumed under his own.

Young People's Assimilation of a Collective Historical Memory: A Case Study of Quebeckers of French-Canadian Heritage

JOCELYN LÉTOURNEAU AND SABRINA MOISAN

When young, fifteen- to twenty-five-year-old Quebeckers of French-Canadian heritage attending secondary school, college, or university are asked, without prior warning, to tell the history of Quebec since its beginnings, this is, broadly, what they all write:

- In the beginning, there were people who had come from France. They lived a fairly rudimentary, but peaceful, life, in a world they were building together in French. They suffered under the twin annoyances of a colonial regime and a mercantile system, but felt no need to rebel against the mother country. They traded with the indigenous people, and gradually became aware of the considerable economic potential of the patch of America they inhabited. They suffered few internal conflicts, continued to be dominated by French interests, but did not have to fight to preserve their rights or their tongue.
- Then came the Great Upheaval, touched off by the 1759 Conquest of New France by the British. Thus began the francophones' history of unending struggle to emancipate and liberate themselves from continual attempts at assimilation, whether warlike or underhanded, inflicted on them by the anglophones. From the Quebec Act (1774) to the Quiet Revolution (1960), the dynamics of conflict frames all the milestones of Quebec history, with one side seeking to assert itself and the other ruling with a carrot or a stick.
- The 1960s brought the newly invigorated Quebeckers' collective Great Awakening. They plunged steadfastly into modern life and put

a healthy distance between themselves and their former perceived identity and ways of being, readily summed up under a triple caption: agriculturalism, messianism, and anti-democratism. They opened their doors to the world, shook off the English yoke, freed themselves from a federal government that had been a preferred instrument of control ever since the war, and set about taking back their collective destiny. Jean Lesage, and particularly René Lévesque, are seen as key players in this shift, facilitating collective action and redeeming the group's shared history.[1]

– For various reasons, particularly because the people of Quebec are divided over their future and because there are forces, particularly the federal government, that are frustrating its advent, this future burgeoned during the Quiet Revolution (the liberation of the people of Quebec and the sovereignty of Quebec) only to be stymied by the 1980 and 1995 referendums.[2] Then came a period of uncertainty, the search for a gateway into the future, and maybe even a stab, albeit ambiguous, at redefining Quebeckers' self-identity.

This is the dominant storyline that young Quebeckers of French-Canadian heritage tell of the historical experience of the Quebec community. The amazing thing about this story is how nostalgic and melancholic these young people's memory of the historic course of Quebec and its people is. Their representation of the past seems to be built around three narrative clusters: 'what unfortunately befell a community,' 'what that community might have become if only ...,' 'what that community might yet become if only ...,' all of which point to an unhappy representation of Quebec's place in history.

However, it is hard to understand, or even justify, this representation, in light of advances in historical research over the last twenty-five years – which have managed to afford a much more positive, exciting representation of the experience of Quebec[3] – and of contemporary Quebec's rather enviable overall situation. Whence the inevitable, relevant question, in this case: why does this historical memory persist in young people when conditions have been in place for some time for it to fade away?

Programs and Textbooks

The first hypothesis that leaps to mind, when trying to grasp the origins of this particular memory of the Quebec historical experience, lies in the Ministère de l'Éducation du Quebec's (MEQ) history programs, as well as in the textbooks approved by the Ministry and used in the classroom.[4] Could young people's memory, embodied here in a forceful narrative about the history of Quebec and its people, possibly just be a pared-down version, retelling or reproducing the implicit tendencies and explicit content of those programs and textbooks?

In spite of what one might be led to believe, it is not easy to do a clear-cut assessment of where those programs tend or what those textbooks contain.

A quick overview of the current secondary history program, on the one hand, and the college Social Studies program, on the other, shows a series of perfectly reasonable objectives, focuses, learning paths, and content, with regard to advances in contemporary historical research methods and disciplinary practices, to the intellectual maturity of young people at this particular stage in their lives, and to the purposes served by a history focusing on the Quebec historical experience.[5] Let us assume, as members of the task force on the teaching of history[6] have done, that these programs – particularly the secondary program – should be revised to give more weight to the role played in Quebec's historical experience by indigenous peoples and ethnic communities. It would be overdoing things, however, to start again from scratch to satisfy certain critics who claim these programs are 'chock full of nationalism.'[7] In fact, everything leads us to believe that, were existing programs followed to the letter or covered in all their complexities and openness, they would foster the acquisition of a nuanced, polyvalent representation of the historical experience of Quebec.

This said, let us not forget, while maintaining a hypercritical, 'suspicious' stance concerning the Quebec Ministry of Education's (MEQ) educational endeavours, that the secondary level IV program includes among its final outcome objectives 'explaining the Conquest, its causes and its immediate effects,' 'describing the events of 1837–1838 and the early days of the union of the two Canadas,' 'analysing the clash between traditionalism and changes in Quebec society during the Duplessis era,' and 'characterizing the Quiet Revolution and its consequences.'[8] It is perfectly legitimate to believe that this program may have influenced the structure of the story told by the young people, as it is backed up to a greater or lesser extent by particular foregrounded components of the program (the Conquest, the Rebellions, the Quiet Revolution). In this case, it would not be outrageous to postulate a *transfer relationship* between the learning objectives of the MEQ's programs and 'the history of

Quebec as told by young people.' This said – and this point should be stressed – neither the secondary IV history program nor the college level Social Studies program *explicitly, readily, or easily nurtures* the representation that young people have of Quebec's past or the story they tell in synthesizing it.

Our assessment of the textbooks closely approximates the one we have just made of the programs. It would be a mistake to assert that textbooks approved by the MEQ, at least for the secondary level IV history program, narrate Quebec's historical experience by focusing closely on a sectarian or unitary concept of things. A study of the content of textbooks available on the Quebec market during the mid-1990s does show that their storyline is not narrowly nationalistic, even though the issue of nationalism is at the heart of the narrative told to young Quebeckers.[9] The narrative in these textbooks does not present francophones as either the unfortunate victims of the British or the dupes of Canadian endeavour. Nor are francophones depicted as bearing a cross. The textbooks are patriotic not only towards Quebec, but also towards Canada – or at least they were until recently. In fact, according to the authors of these textbooks, the historical experience of Quebec must be seen and appreciated from the perspective of the various, persistently present, levels of ambivalence surrounding politics and identity. On a socio-economic level, Quebec's situation, particularly for francophones, cannot be boiled down to a single tangible mode of being, that of the dregs of society. In fact, Quebec has always been at the centre of North American and international migrations, social change, and economic processes. This is how its evolution became intimately linked to the dynamics of both the Atlantic system and the North American system.

The foregoing leads to a major observation: there are significant differences between these young people's history of Quebec and the story told in their textbooks. While young people's comments are on the whole pessimistic and melancholy, even anguished and distressed, textbook content is by and large optimistic and hopeful. Similarly, the textbooks' narrative is both many-voiced and ambivalent, while the young people's story is one-sided and unvarying. It would be an exaggeration to claim that the content of the textbooks confirms the whining, nostalgic representation the young people have of the Quebec experience or that it directly nurtures their obvious disappointment in their history. Nonetheless – and this is why we are putting a damper on our statements – we have to concede that textbook content *can* accommodate *this* representation and nurture *this* feeling to the extent that these textbooks contain material for constructing a victimization-based narrative of the people of Quebec, which is pretty much what is on the minds of young French Quebeckers of French-Canadian heritage when they tell about their collective past (see appendix, pp. 123–4, for examples).

Hence, the following concern leaps to mind: how can it be, given the relative abundance of notions and stories of Quebec's past found in the MEQ's programs and in readily available history textbooks, that the image that sticks in the minds of these young people is of a 'people that is pushed around, reclusive, always getting back on its feet, but also fearful of seeking fulfilment'?

To answer to this question it is necessary to follow a touchy path focusing directly on the heart of the classroom process and on the instructional dynamics established between teachers and their students.

At the Heart of the Classroom

While it is true that the classroom is only one among many places for acquiring historical knowledge, it is nonetheless an intensive, organized learning place, as evidenced by the vast store of knowledge that secondary school students acquire about New France and Canada-Quebec in general. Now, teachers are at the centre of the overall student learning process. Teachers can either establish themselves a priori or gradually as the primary classroom source of credible information.[10] There is research showing that students have a natural tendency to consider their teachers to be intellectually honest and responsible people. Even when, in certain cases, students do not approve of particular teachers' personalities or teaching abilities, their sense that those teachers are sincere, straightforward, and open in their teaching is in no way diminished.[11]

Considering the status and role that teachers enjoy in the overall learning process, it is obvious that their influence can be a determining factor in the representation that students develop of historical experiences, such as Quebec's. In fact, teachers have full run of their classes: their presentations always win out over textbook content;[12] they are the ones bringing a program's objectives and content into focus; they also guide and prepare their students, according to the particular knowledge they consider essential to testing, satisfying the objectives they have set, or meeting certain educational requirements specific to the institutions where they work. Above and beyond any other source of information – with the possible exception of an unusually credible family member –

teachers, while not their students' only source of information, are or do become their most authoritative reference.

This, it would appear, is where things get sticky. Some studies, making use of polite, restrained formulas, have indeed shown that history teaching at the secondary level – in an environment where particular *basic* historical concepts, interpretations, or narratives, including the history of Canada-Quebec, are formed and consolidated – is often deficient, due to the staff's limited competence in the area of factual knowledge and historiographic debate.[13] Several observers have found that the problem was so serious and widespread that it needed to be rectified promptly.[14] What was at issue here was not so much teachers' ability to 'manage their classrooms,' arouse their students' interest, or use appropriate teaching strategies, as it was their capacity to provide young people with nuanced concepts, representations, and interpretations based on adequate, up-to-date knowledge of the subject matter being taught.

Indeed, a great many teachers, in spite of their immense enthusiasm and excellent teaching skills, may still impart outdated or obsolete notions and interpretations about the past to their students. Although they teach from a store of incontrovertible raw data, particularly from textbooks, they may form their notions and interpretations by combining that set of data on the past with an overview based on earlier research or on a paradigm that is not always as systematic as it might be.

In practice, a particular teacher's issues or referential paradigm can quite easily overdetermine the storyline presented or told to young people. Teachers juxtapose their own history against history proper all the more readily when, lacking adequate factual knowledge, interpretive skills, or intellectual courage to support an unconventional or eccentric version of Quebec's historical experience, they tend to use, implicitly or explicitly, a socially accepted and legitimized storyline, making it safe and reassuring to display their knowledge and incorporate information gleaned elsewhere into their views.[15]

Although this practice is problematic, it would be a mistake to condemn it out of hand. It should instead be seen as a normal, logical approach for people without all the desirable skills in an area of knowledge, working in a system with pressure from above (the administration) and below (the students) and seeking to compensate for their deficiencies, to forestall any future teaching failures, and to help everyone, including a system that spurns deviations and failures, feel safe.

In the context of a compensatory solution, the use of a conventional historic register and narrative scheme (for example, the story of 'Quebec's tragedy') is probably the most immediate, efficient defence mechanism available to a teacher. That a storyline with so much overall structural coherence and power imposes itself in the public arena is proof of its credibility for many teachers, or is at least a fundamental basis for confidently asserting historic truth. This situation also provides a supportive base for transmitting content to which students may be more receptive. As is well known, any message, even a scholarly one, is easier to accept if it reinforces or confirms previously held notions.[16] It is of course perfectly reasonable to believe that the conventional binaries, French/English, Quebec/Canada, and nationalism/federalism, while more or less mastered by incoming secondary (level IV) students, lay safe, credible foundations on which to erect a coherent, cohesive, plausible, engaging, linear, progressive, predictable, and desirable, history of Quebec's experience. These discursive conventions, which may give rise to a teacher-student community of thought, are indeed widespread in Quebec. They are the custodians of a sanctioned concept of Quebec's history, and constitute significant parameters of the public doxa. These narrative schemes continue to be played out with antagonistic characters in cut-and-dried, more or less fictional or realistic tableaux, on television and film.[17] They even serve as the interpretive infrastructure of some of the most popular syntheses of Quebec history.[18] For a great many teachers, using them as the basic storyline recounting Quebec's historical experience then becomes a way to keep young audiences in familiar territory. One has to be relatively well equipped – that is, factually and interpretively competent and intellectually undauntable – to deviate from an established narrative scheme, or even to criticize it. Even if certain teachers were uncomfortable with the existing narrative scheme – which, one might suppose, is not likely to be the case for most school history staff – it would be very risky to take an iconoclastic approach. There are three main reasons for this:

- Such teachers might indeed put their students at risk of not doing well on the Ministry's standardized exam.[19]
- Without as strong a conceptual framework as the one being challenged, those teachers could be depriving their students of the chance to make sense out of the components provided, leaving them to flounder in an interpretive morass, frustrated and incapable of combining those elements into a satisfying whole or wishing to investigate further.
- As iconoclasts, teachers could finally lead their students – who might

be willing to accompany them in their narrative explorations because they would trust their intellectual prowess – across the divide to stunted memory, to the 'unthinkable' history of Quebec, and the wastelands of collective experience, all places where they must tread with extreme caution, lest they become marooned or lost.

Under these circumstances, it is understandable that history teachers would rather stick to a socially sanctioned narrative scheme of Quebec's historical experience. This would definitely be the case at the secondary level, and largely so, it appears, at the college level. At university, the constraints of a narrative scheme no longer come into play. It is accepted that university-level instruction, nurtured by the faculty's basic research, pushes back the frontiers of knowledge and favours criticism of existing interpretations. It is safe to assume that this is an important process within the institution, but not necessarily the predominant one. This said, students attending universities do not arrive as virgin territory, or devoid of historical knowledge and interpretations about the past. Rather, they acquire or develop their new concepts based on the original, basic ones that they held before even taking their first secondary-level (IV) history course on Canada-Quebec. Our research leads us to believe that the representation of Quebec history held and assimilated by entering university students fits well within the conventional narrative scheme of Quebec's historical experience.[20]

How do their views change over the course of three years of university study? To answer this objectively, we need to compare their B.A. entering and exit answer sheets. However, a series of courses, each reinforcing the previous one's interpretive content, would appear to be necessary to accomplish the task of deconstructing this basic representation of Quebec history in order to shake the pillars of an already assimilated narrative scheme. There are at least two reasons why universities, unfortunately, afford very few such opportunities. First, since the faculty has full control over the content of their courses, what they teach is by and large up to them. Furthermore, no research group in Quebec is currently trying to gain a following for an alternative narrative scheme: in practice, there is only a slim chance that students might gain access to a different narrative register. The situation may be even more formidable for students enrolled in teacher training programs. These programs deliberately focus on teaching introductory or survey courses rather than specialized ones.[21] They give students almost no means to delve into a subject at greater depth. As a result, aspiring teachers are in a weak, rather than a strong position when it comes to acquiring content and interpretations, a situation they themselves deplore.[22]

The college situation is different. A number of instructors hold master's or PhD degrees, implying fairly advanced learning. There is reason to believe that many of them are theoretically capable of discarding the conventional narrative scheme when offering the two optional college-level history courses that deal with Canada-Quebec history. Whether or not they actually do depends on considerations linked not necessarily to their levels of competency or knowledge, but rather to personal motives (adherence to a given narrative scheme), to how well prepared they are (level of competency), or to student expectations (implicit demand for a particular narrative).

It is clear that, in light of the preceding discussion, teachers are capable of fundamentally mediating the development of a specific historical memory in their students. This is the first explanation we have for the basis of young people's particular historical memory. But we cannot stop here in our quest to understand how this memory is formed (and assimilated). We need to take into account another conditioning factor, the social environments of young people's memory.

Collective Historical Memory

In trying to understand what gives rise to the particular version that young people tell of Quebec's historical experience, it would be a mistake to focus exclusively on 'classroom teaching,' on its constraints and limitations, and on teachers' limited competencies. In fact, this is a far more complex problem. It relates to Quebec's strong, publicly held historical memory, which inspires a whole set of references on the part of Quebeckers of French-Canadian heritage to their past. This memory is less about grudges than it is about a melancholy, nostalgic awareness centring on the idea, the concept, of a conquered, reclusive people, abused by others and always fearful of reclaiming their destiny.

We have no intention here of describing at great length the contents that form the basis of this historical memory. The task of description, to which we have contributed,[23] is already partially done. The fact that Quebeckers of French-Canadian heritage have their own historical memory – whether or not individual members of the group hold that memory or stick to it – is not contested by these researchers. The debate has more to do with how to go about updating or modifying this memory as Quebec society marches into the future.[24] Since this issue goes beyond the purpose of this text, we will omit any further discussion here. We simply wish to point out that, in terms of its overall content and focus, 'our' young people's story repeats a great many of the components of the collective historical memory belonging to the group of French Quebeckers of French-Canadian heritage. The correspondence is obvious in their overall storyline when they narrate the Quebec historical experience. It is confirmed as well by the characters and events they include in their narratives. We wish to stress that we had already discovered the main components of this general narrative of the Quebec experience in other speakers, belonging subjectively to the same group and expressing themselves under other circumstances.[25]

In the case of those belonging to, claiming to belong to, or familiar with the set of references proper to the group of French Quebeckers of French-Canadian heritage, there appears to be an expressive relationship and interpretive proximity related to narrating the history of Quebec's past.

This raises the following issue: How do young people learn about, become familiar with, acquire, and master the history peculiar to Quebec's past – one of the vehicles and driving forces of the collective memory belonging to French Quebeckers of French-Canadian heritage?

At this stage in our work, it is very hard to give a concrete answer to this question. However, the speed and intensity of the process for acquiring this story varies by individual, depending on the conditions and the social learning and educational environments under which their development takes place. It appears to happen in this way:[26]

1. Childhood

Young people spend their childhood, particularly in elementary school and through their family circle, casually learning and absorbing a set of historical facts about Quebec, Canada, and the world. These facts vary in their reliability and truthfulness. Children absorb nascent representations, structured as metaphor (e.g.: the 'losing' French and the 'victorious' British), of their immediate surroundings and far beyond. These disconnected, piecemeal facts become engraved on their minds more or less forcefully, depending on where and how often they hear or encounter them. They take form gradually, clustering around the original narrative core, which constitutes a basic matrix to which these young minds attach additional facts as they receive and collect them. The contours of a 'space of the acceptable and thinkable' (that which is logically consis-

tent with an initial 'coherent notional structure,' so it can be incorporated into this concept) are soon traced, along with a 'space of the
incongruous and unthinkable' (that which is incoherent with respect to
this notional structure and which, therefore, cannot be integrated into
the concept).

Regarding the story about the Quebec historical experience, with its
attendant dominant historical and political statements about Quebec,
children quickly come under the sway of such forceful, conventional
declaratory terms as Quebec and Canada, French and English, nationalism and federalism, and so forth. These terms are usually assembled
within a more or less oppositional discourse that children do not comprehend very well, although they can guess or grasp its importance.
They form the solid narrative cores around which the new knowledge
that children cannot help but acquire over time orbits. Obviously, little
ones will inevitably add complexities to their representation of things as
they continue to increase their store of knowledge: they add details here,
correct inaccuracies there, and record further notions there. But their
original narrative cores, their basic matrix and general notional structure, are not challenged unless their families or teachers forcefully
intervene to replace the children's world representation with another
representation – equally strong, probably just as simplistic, and most
likely structured metaphorically. Failing this kind of massive intervention, or an alternative forceful representation, all new knowledge, even
when it is incompatible with the previous concept, will be inexorably
sucked into and swallowed by the initial basic matrix, which behaves like
a black hole and, thanks to its density and attraction, literally absorbs
everything around it. Children's basic matrices expand by adding layers
of shading, while remaining generally unmodified in their foundations
and structures.

2. Secondary-School Years

This is how things generally proceed until young people take their first
World History course (secondary level II), then their Canada-Quebec
one (secondary level IV). For the first time in their lives, their representations of history are challenged by norm-referenced, systematically
organized knowledge. In theory, students might have their own depictions shaken when thus confronted, since they are usually in an intellectually vulnerable position when faced with other knowledge that is vastly
more solid and self-assured than their own. In practice, however, this

happens only rarely. First, the forcefulness of young people's concepts is rooted in metaphoric simplicity. Their narrative cores and basic matrices behave like decoders and encoders of any new knowledge they may encounter, objectively sheltering them, at least at the outset, from any 'alienating' learning. When any new knowledge is catalysed by these cores and matrices, it will simply be rejected, be absorbed by the initial concept, or be rerouted towards it, thus strengthening it. In other words, the only facts that will be accepted or recuperated are those 'recognizable' by students' original, metaphoric, notional structures, including any discursive conventions they may have consciously or unconsciously adopted. In the dynamic interaction between 'former' and 'later' knowledge, the three above-mentioned oppositional binaries that secondary students have *more or less* mastered when entering secondary level IV will serve as devices for decoding and encoding their newly acquired knowledge. Any transmitted historical material will tend to pass through, or orbit around them. This grants the past a clarity of meaning not necessarily present in 'that which has been.' Such clarity is actively sought by students working to develop a coherent understanding of change in order to insert themselves as historical subjects relative to a prior time (where do I come from?), a present time (where am I?), and a future time (where am I going?). This particular link between later knowledge and the basic notion is all the more plausible since the course of Quebec's past makes it possible to nurture the story revolving around the binaries that students already have or acquire. The fact that this is not the most felicitous story for explaining all the richness and complexity of Quebec's experience is of lesser concern here. When students can reinforce their own established ideas about the past with new ones they encounter, and especially when that material also provides a coherent representation about the history of the world or their home community, they can complete a virtuous circle of learning. In this fashion, the past in their own stories is validated, thereby, in turn, validating that past. What more could they possibly need or seek? In addition to the effect of mutual transfer between the past and its telling, the reinforcement of a socially sanctioned narrative of the Quebec experience, history programs, textbooks, teachers, and classroom processes are all contributing factors. There is a good chance that students at secondary level IV are at a stage in their lives where the narrative about Quebec's past that they assimilate will remain central to their awareness of history, and structurally inhabit their collective identities for a long time to come.

This is not to say, however, that it will condition or determine their political behaviour.

3. College Years

Between the secondary level and college, the previously acquired narrative appears to undergo minimal change, merely widening and complicating its structure and content. Evidently, the original basic cores and matrices around which young people structure their representations are only open to letting new knowledge build up in sedimentary layers on top of the older ones, reinforcing, ipso facto, the narrative's truth system rather than modifying it. At this stage in assimilating a history of the Quebec historical experience, it does, indeed, become difficult to refocus a narrative about the past when it is already firmly seated and structured around assorted raw data, nurtured by a great many social discourses, and inserted within a narrative intertextuality that also includes works by learned historians.

4. University

While it is extremely hard to swim against the stream, young people's original narrative cores, discursive conventions, basic matrices, metaphors, and structures for decoding and encoding will eventually be brought into question at university, as their initial concepts gradually split apart and dissolve, opening the way to new *narrative possibilities*. Other conditions must be met, however, if any such narrative change or reworking of historical awareness is to take place. First, students must be intellectually inclined towards detaching themselves from their initial story if they are to be receptive to any new material they are provided or discover. Next, students must be open to taking several courses that both cover a variety of historical and historiographic topics and reinforce one another in presenting an alternative concept of the Quebec historical experience. Finally, students must demonstrate the ability to think and use their imaginations actively in structuring a story about Quebec's past that overcomes or removes the conventional boundaries between Quebec's 'thinkable' and 'unthinkable' history. It is obviously difficult in practice to achieve or assemble all these conditions *at once*. As a result, any chance of overcoming or transforming a historical narrative is very slim, especially since most university students are not particularly interested in conceptualizing or reworking their studies to take into account the issue of great collective narratives or in gainsaying any historical knowledge that already appears to be established or secure.

Conclusion

This chapter has examined the degree of complexity in the process whereby young people acquire a historical memory. While it is obvious that history classes, where teachers play a privileged role as information providers and orchestrators, are the source par excellence for acquiring that memory, it is also obvious that the prevalent, general flow of social discourse, which is both more muffled and perhaps more influential, also contributes to the assimilation of this memory.

This observation has three consequences for the history education of young people:

1. When planning course objectives, teachers – to the extent that they can situate themselves in a *different* memory and history regime – should accept that young people become repositories, at a relatively young age, of a stock of historical knowledge and a generalized concept of history. This is why teachers, rather than focusing their teaching on transmitting empirical facts, should concentrate on deconstructing specific basic matrices of understanding or on helping young people to grasp the conceptual limitations proper to those matrices. This approach will eventually disrupt the reinforcement dynamic of these matrices and, in the process, counter the perpetuation of a historical memory with many factual discrepancies.

2. Since society as a whole generates memory, teachers should also do as much as they can to help young people evaluate various historical platitudes present in social discourse. They should either have them compare discourses against one other or apply the principles of historical methodology, two precepts of which are the rejection of anachronism and of teleology. This approach helps students hone their critical skills relative to particular social platitudes and particular memory and history discourses.

3. Finally, teachers should provide their students with the factual and interpretive means to construct a story of the past that takes the world's complexities, ambivalences and paradoxes, ambiguities and dissonances into account. They should not, however, leave them prey to a kind of

confusion of meaning that might render them intellectually 'impotent' when faced with abusive, ideologically slanted efforts to reconstruct the past.

Appendix

Fragments of Victimization Narratives in Young French Quebeckers of French-Canadian Heritage

[After the Conquest] England attends to its new colony. It institutes its laws and ideas. The Canadians are discontented. Right from the start, the British try to assimilate them. They are still trying to assimilate us now. All those constitutional changes were made for that purpose! Assimilating us, turning us into a minority group and treating us like an inferior race ...

(University student)

After some political shenanigans, France gives up and hands the colony over to the British forces. And they start trying to assimilate us. Present-day Quebec's true face, with all its power relationships and tensions, starts to take shape. The blows are too numerous to list; fixed elections, economic alienation of the Francophones ...

(University student)

The people of Quebec have often resisted being assimilated into Anglophone culture. This gave rise to a separatist movement leading up to several events: The *Patriotes*, the October crisis, the two Referendums ...

(College student)

From 1608 to 1665, New France is kind of 'shitty,' in the sense of nothing happening in the colony allowing it to make its mark as a major presence on the world map. When Louis XIV (finally) decided to allow New France to develop a local economy, everything was going great in the best of all possible worlds. 1760 unfortunately, the evil-minded British took hold of New France, which, in my opinion, amounts to their taking hold of the truly magnificent future New France would have known under the French government.

(Secondary level V student)

After many a confrontation, the French lost their territory to the British (note that I am writing the French and not the Canadians; we are the ones who suffered the defeat of the French). After that, all the constitutions we were ever given were always designed to assimilate us or keep us quiet.

(University student)

The greatest conflicts began at the time of the British Conquest of 1759. Ever since then, we have been fighting for our survival as a people.

(University student)

The massive influx and settlement of British in Montreal was done to assimilate us. Later on, they (the King of England) decided to separate the two Canadas: Lower Canada and Upper Canada. Lower Canada became Quebec. Because of the false democracy the British instituted, the French Canadians, who became the people of Quebec later on, rebelled and became *Patriotes*.

(Secondary level V student)

Ever since, the wound left from this defeat (1759) has reopened every time ideological and cultural differences between the French and the British have been felt. Ex.: conscription, the First World War, ... Francophones used as cannon fodder during the Second World War, etc.

(University student)

This business of the Conquest still isn't settled, because Quebec has definitely shown, in two referendums, that it still feels [wronged] by the 'invader.' Later on, the people of Quebec became identified with a distinct society within Canada, which takes us down to the present.

(Secondary level V student)

Notes

This chapter, translated by Yolanda Broad, is a revised version of an article published in *Canadian Historical Review* 85, no. 2 (2004): 325–56. It is based on data collected from a survey we ran between 1998 and 2001 among 403 young people enrolled in educational institutions in the Quebec City urban area. Of that group, 237 were university students, 62 attended academic and vocational colleges (CEGEP), 51 were enrolled at secondary level V (12th year) and 53 at secondary level IV (11th year). The following task was assigned to these young people, to stimulate their memories and generate history narratives: 'Present or narrate the history of Quebec since its beginnings, as you perceive it, know about it, or remember it.' It should be mentioned that the respondents' identities were neither requested nor desired; that the subjects were given about 45 minutes to elaborate; that the exercise took place in the classroom, with their instructor or teacher present, but not, however, providing the class with any input. It should also be pointed out that the young people were told that the compendium of their work would only be used for academic research, that there were no right or wrong answers, and that they should perform the task as carefully and well as they possibly could. To the extent that almost all of our respondents mentioned that their ethnic origins were French Canadian, our analyses are only valid – and this must be stressed – for young French Quebeckers of French-Canadian heritage. This is what the subtitle of our article is meant to indicate.

1 Jean Lesage was premier of Quebec from 1960 to 1966. René Lévesque, who played a major part in nationalizing Quebec's hydroelectric power companies from 1962 on, was, in the latter half of the 1960s, and up until his death in 1987, one of the main figures in Quebec's sovereigntist movement. He was premier of the province from 1976 to 1985, and presided over the first referendum on the sovereignty of Quebec in 1980.

2 Two provincial referendums on Quebec's political future were held, in 1980 and 1995. In both cases, the sovereigntist option was defeated, but in 1995, it was only by a 50.6% to 49.4% margin.

3 J. Létourneau, 'The Current Great Narrative of Québécois Identity,' *South Atlantic Quarterly* 94, no. 4 (autumn, 1995): 1039–54.

4 It should be noted that Quebec's educational system requires a minimum number of history courses in the school curriculum. During the elementary cycle, in the francophone schools (things are often slightly different in anglophone schools), students are given a very general introduction – and it would appear that most teachers don't push it very hard – to social studies, with history tossed into the general mix. At the secondary level, students take two required history courses: one survey of history course at secondary level II and one history course on Quebec and Canada at secondary level IV. They may also take an optional contemporary world-history course at secondary level V. In practice, about 3% of young people take that course. During CEGEP (general and vocational college), students may opt for the history program if they wish. Theoretically, there are five history courses available, including two national history courses. Very, very few young people take those courses. At university, enrolment in history courses or

programs depends on students' individual choice of vocational track. In sum, the vast majority of young Quebeckers are satisfied with the training in Canadian-Quebec history they received during their required secondary level IV course. This is scant indeed. A new system was recently approved, requiring a history course during every year of the secondary cycle and at least one required history course at the college level.

5   In spite of various minor modifications made over the years, the history program introduced in 1982 is still in place today in Quebec's secondary schools.

6   *Se souvenir et devenir: Rapport du Groupe de travail sur l'enseignement de l'histoire* (Quebec: Ministère de l'Éducation, 1996).

7   Monique Nemni, 'Quand le Canada se perd à l'école québécoise,' *Cité Libre* (June–July 1998), 63–74.

8   Ministère de l'Éducation du Québec, 'Direction générale du développement pédagogique, Programme d'études, histoire du Québec et du Canada, 4e secondaire, formation générale et professionnelle' (Quebec, 1982), 18.

9   J. Létourneau, 'Nous-Autres les Québécois: La voix des manuels d'histoire,' *International Textbook Research* 18, no. 3 (1996): 269–87.

10   See Jean-François Cardin, 'Le Programme d'histoire et les manuels: Réplique à MM. Jedwab et Anderson,' *Bulletin d'histoire politique* 5, no. 2 (Winter, 1997), 115–19.

11   Roy Rosenzweig, 'How Americans Use and Think about the Past: Implications from a National Survey for the Teaching and Learning of History,' in Peter N. Stearns, Peter Seixas, and Sam Wineburg, eds, *Knowing, Teaching and Learning History: National and International Perspectives* (New York: New York University Press, 2000), 262–83.

12   Several experts do not believe that classroom teachers, who prefer using workbooks, are currently using their textbooks either amply or methodically enough. See Robert Martineau, 'Les Cahiers d'exercices ... un cheval de Troie dans la classe d'histoire?' *Bulletin de liaison de la Société des professeurs d'histoire du Quebec* 23, no. 6 (1985): 20–5.

13   *Se souvenir et devenir*, chap. 4.

14   On this topic, see Robert Martineau, *L'Histoire à l'école, matière à penser* (Montréal, Paris: L'Harmattan, 1999). See also Jean Gould, 'La Formation des maîtres au secondaire ou comment avancer en arrière,' in Gilles Gagné, ed., *Main basse sur l'éducation* (Quebec City: Nota Bene, 1999), 121–65.

15   Note that it is equally likely that a large number of teachers feel that the 'tragic tale' of the Quebec historical experience is the one that best represents the course of Quebec's history.

16   See Rainer Riemenschneider, 'La Confrontation internationale des

manuels: Contribution au problème des rapports entre manuels et mémoire collective,' in Henri Moniot, ed., *Enseigner l'histoire : Des manuels à la mémoire* (Bern: Peter Lang, 1984), 127–40).

17 Films and television series focusing on the history of Quebec are a major genre and enjoy very large audiences.

18 In this respect, the works of Jacques Lacoursière, probably the most widely read Quebec historian in the province, are still the primary source for a great many teachers in the field of history.

19 It is well known that the MEQ's standardized examinations, which are rather traditional, are geared towards controlling the acquisition of basic learning by students, much more than towards helping them develop their critical thinking about historical narrative. See *Se souvenir et devenir*, 50–1. See also Martineau, *L'Histoire à l'école*.

20 The basic structure of university student narratives is fairly similar to those of secondary or college students (see appendix to this chapter).

21 The same knowledge gaps are also found in the United States. See Linda S. Levstik, 'Articulating the Silences. Teachers' and Adolescents' Conceptions of Historical Significance,' in Sterns, Seixas, and Wineburg, eds, *Knowing, Teaching and Learning History,* 284–305.

22 See Laurent Moreau, Patrick Bérubé, Michel Arsenault, and François Turgeon (bachelor in history candidates at Université Laval), 'L'Enseigne-ment de l'histoire au secondaire: Former un corps professoral compétent pour nourrir la pensée critique du futur citoyen,' mémoire présenté au Groupe de travail sur l'enseignement de l'histoire, Quebec City (December 1995).

23 It is not within the scope of the present article to list exhaustively all the work done on this subject. See especially Jacques Mathieu, ed., *Étude de la construction de la mémoire collective des Québécois : Approches multidisciplinaires* (Quebec City: CELAT, 1986); and Jacques Mathieu and Jacques Lacoursière, *Les Mémoires québécoises* (Quebec: Presses de l'Université Laval, 1991). For an overview of our work, see J. Létourneau, 'Digging into Historical Conscious-ness, Individual and Collective: Overview of a Research Trajectory,' at www.cshc.ubc.ca/pwias/papers.php.

24 On this subject, see Gérard Bouchard, *La Nation au futur et au passé* (Mon-treal: VLB, 1999); Robert Comeau and Bernard Dionne, eds, *À propos de l'histoire nationale* (Quebec City: Septentrion, 1998); J. Létourneau, *A History for the Future: Rewriting Memory and Identity in Quebec Today* (Montreal, King-ston: McGill-Queen's University Press, 2004); and Joseph-Yvon Thériault, *Critique de l'américanité: Mémoire et démocratie au Québec* (Montreal: Québec-Amérique, 2002).

25 J. Létourneau and Jacinthe Ruel, 'Nous-Autres les Québécois: Topiques du discours franco-québécois sur Soi et sur l'Autre dans les mémoires déposés devant la Commission sur l'avenir politique et constitutionnel du Québec (1990),' in Khadiyatoulah Fall, Georges Vignaux, et Daniel Simeoni, eds, *Mots, représentations: Enjeux dans les contacts interethniques et interculturels* (Ottawa: Presses de l'université d'Ottawa, 1994), 283–307.
26 Note that the following paragraphs are not intended as a statement of general theory on how young people acquire their historical awareness.

Understanding History

PETER LEE

Understanding History and Understanding the Past

Learning History

History education is often thought of as a relatively straightforward matter: it is learning what happened in the past. Everyone admits to some difficulties, of course. Students of all ages will have to come to grips with more or less specialized concepts belonging to the past activities that historians discuss (for example, in economics, art, diplomacy, or politics). Youngsters will have to face the complexities of an adult world. But the world of history is 'recognizably "ordinary," requiring no special concepts of description or explanation other than those commonly appropriate to the subject matter.'[1] Learning history is a matter of knowing the story, albeit with a leaven of common sense and worldly experience.

There are several reasons why this view of history education will not do, and two of them are central to this chapter. The first and most obvious reason for saying this is that 'learning what happened' is not so easily taken care of. There is not one true story about the past, but a multiplicity of complementary, competing, or clashing stories. (This, of course, raises questions – beyond the scope of this chapter – about how far we can talk of stories being true.)[2] Alternative stories are encountered not just in school or university, but outside in the wider world. Such stories do not come only in written texts purporting to tell us about the past, but in a variety of other ways too. Nor are they confined to the media, although film and television have much to say about the past.

The sources of what is sometimes called collective memory are multifarious and often indirect, hinting at shared stories even in the words we use to talk about politics and society or to think of possible futures. Buildings, monuments, and signposts for tourists all whisper of 'memories.' 'Learning what happened' cannot be an adequate account of history education, because 'what happened' is never a given, and even where there is consensus among historians, students will meet rival versions outside school or college.

The second reason for rejecting claims that history education is straightforward is that research evidence increasingly suggests that history is not 'ordinary' or merely a matter of common sense. The burden of this chapter is that students learning history have to learn ideas that are to some degree counter-intuitive, and it is precisely because of this that learning any single version of the past cannot provide a viable, let alone a valid, history education.

Before we address the central issues, however, one or two preliminaries must be disposed of. There is some truth in the idea that the working concepts from the past that historians customarily deal with, like *money, law, king*, and even *predestination* and *providence* are 'ordinary' from a philosophical point of view. They are concepts from practical life, as opposed to notions like *mass, electron, carbon*, or *gene*, which fit into more or less tightly articulated theories.[3] But such a view cannot be made to yield easy consequences for history education, because the concepts that are part of the substance of historical accounts may not be our practical concepts, and this is, of course, a well-recognized difficulty for students.

Moreover, there are concepts of a very different kind in history: contested, colligatory concepts, like Renaissance, English Revolution, Enlightenment, or Industrial Revolution, that behave more like names than concepts.[4] Their status in history is the subject of considerable philosophical argument, and these arguments relate to the question we shelved earlier, about the sense in which historical accounts can be 'true.' Whatever we say about them, they are not 'ordinary' in the same way that *money* or *law* or *king* are ordinary. At the very least, then, the assumption that history deals only with 'ordinary,' 'common sense,' or 'everyday' concepts already demands qualification on these well-known grounds.

There are philosophical questions in plenty here, and any move we might want to make can all too easily become entangled in a web of begged questions. If I cannot cut through the web with a quotation, perhaps I may be allowed to use one to bypass it.

Now, the word 'history' denotes an engagement of enquiry, which has emerged without premonition from the indiscriminate gropings of human intelligence and has come to acquire recognizable shape. Like other such engagements, its shape is somewhat indistinct. Its practitioners are notoriously generous; they have been apt to keep open house to all who have seemingly similar concerns, to welcome and accommodate a miscellany of intellectual enterprises, and to find virtue in their variety. Nevertheless, taken at this level, and even when it is recognized merely in terms of the directions of enquiry followed by writers commonly alleged to be historians, it is not an entirely indiscriminate engagement. It has some identifying marks, some characteristic organizing ideas and a vocabulary of expressions to which it has given specialized meanings: 'past,' 'happening,' 'situation,' 'event,' 'cause,' 'change' and so on. As they come to us, these marks of identity are often obscure and ambiguous. Nevertheless, to recognize them is to make our first groping attempt to distinguish and take hold of a current manner of enquiry.[5]

We do not have to agree with the whole of Oakeshott's position to find this an acceptable summary of something important. History may be diverse, but it may have 'some characteristic organizing ideas.' We need to make some distinctions (initially very crude) between the substantive concepts that are part of the content that historians explore and the metahistorical or second-order concepts that are central to the discipline of history itself.[6] Historians write histories of things that go on in the world and passages of the past (the Renaissance, the French Revolution, or the history of the Ming dynasty). Although they give their readers explanations, use evidence, and write accounts, they do not write *about* the idea of explanation, or the notion of evidence, or what kind of thing a historical account is. These latter *metahistorical*, 'organizing ideas' give meaning and structure to our ideas of the discipline of history. Our ideas about the nature and status of *historical accounts, evidence, understanding* and *explanation, time* and *change* frame the way in which we make sense of the past. They should, perhaps, be thought of as an important part of our historical consciousness.[7]

If we want to understand the way in which children's and adolescents' ideas about history may be developed, we need to pay attention to their metahistorical ideas as well as to their substantive knowledge. The three year eight (age 13) students in the excerpt below are discussing why the Second World War started, and whether it could have been avoided. Their school history so far extends only to the First World War, *not* the

Second, although it is very likely that they have encountered the latter at home and in the media.

> ANGELA: I think Hitler was a madman, and I think that's what, um ...
>
> SUSAN: He was ... a complete nutter, he should have been put in a ... er ... um ...
>
> ANGELA: He wanted a super-race of blond, blue-eyed people to rule the world.
>
> SUSAN: Yeah – that followed him ...
>
> ANGELA: I mean, but he was a short, fat, dark-haired sort of person.
>
> KATIE: Yeah.
>
> SUSAN: ... little person.
>
> KATIE: Could it be avoided? I don't think it could of.
>
> ANGELA: No
>
> KATIE: If Hitler hadn't started ... I mean I can't blame it on him, but if he hadn't started that and provoked ... you know ... us ... if, to say, you know, that's wrong ...
>
> SUSAN: It would have been [avoided] ...
>
> KATIE: Yeah, it would have been, but it wasn't ...
>
> SUSAN: Yeah, if you think about it, every war could've been avoided.
>
> ANGELA: I reckon if Hitler hadn't come on the scene that would never have happened.
>
> KATIE: Oh yeah, yes, yes ...
>
> ANGELA: There must've been other underlying things, like [in] World War One we found out there was lots of underlying causes, not only ...
>
> SUSAN: ... um ...
>
> ANGELA: Franz Ferdinand being shot ...
>
> SUSAN: Yeah ...
>
> KATIE: ... um ...
>
> ANGELA: ... but loads of other stuff as well.
>
> KATIE: Oh yeah, I don't think he was so far ...
>
> ANGELA: Yeah, there must've been a few other main currents ...
>
> KATIE: But, like that Franz Ferdinand, he didn't get, that was the main starting point for it all, that really blew it up ...
>
> ANGELA: But I don't know whether ... because we don't know any underlying causes. If Hitler hadn't been there, I don't know whether it could've been avoided or not.
>
> SUSAN: Yeah but most wars can be avoided anyway, I mean if you think about it we could've avoided the First World War and any war ...

KATIE: ... by discussing it.
SUSAN: Exactly.
KATIE: Yeah, you can avoid it, but I don't think ...
ANGELA: Yeah but not everybody's willing to discuss.[8]

These girls are employing two different kinds of knowledge about history: knowledge of what happened, of the *content* or *substance* of history, on the one hand, and knowledge about the *discipline* of history itself, on the other. Their knowledge of the events of the First World War seems to tell them that if people negotiate in a reasonable way 'most wars can be avoided.' Susan and probably Katie have learned a 'lesson' from their study of one passage of the past and try to apply it to another. Sadly, the lesson is not valid. In contrast, Angela is cautious about her friends' lesson, because her earlier study of the First World War has equipped her with a different kind of knowledge. After initially talking in the same way as they do, she begins a new line of thought: 'There must've been other *underlying* things, like [in] World War One we found out there was lots of underlying causes, not only Franz Ferdinand being shot ... But I don't know whether [*pause*], because we don't know any underlying causes. If Hitler *hadn't* been there, I don't know whether it could've been avoided or not.'

Historical consciousness, as orientation in time, encompasses different elements here. Both Susan and Angela are drawing lessons from the past, but they are drawing on different kinds of understanding as means of orientation.[9] Angela understands that a historical explanation is likely to require more than a single immediate cause, and that 'underlying causes' may also be at work. So, even if Hitler had not existed, we need to know more before we can say that the Second World War could have been avoided. In this case, both Angela and Susan have similar content knowledge of the First World War, but Angela's knowledge of historical explanation gives her a more powerful way of thinking than is available to Susan.

This brings us back at last to the problem about the 'ordinary' and common-sense nature of history that drives the research discussed in this chapter. Whatever we say about the concepts we employ in our explorations and narratives of the past, there is mounting evidence that key concepts operating in the discipline of history are counter-intuitive, at least for school students (and probably for many adults). Even if the *substantive past* is 'ordinary,' the *discipline* of history is not.

History and Everyday Ideas

Students approach history, in school or outside, with their own ideas. These will include tacit knowledge and assumptions as to how the world works, what motivates people, what 'wealth' or 'science' might be, and so on, but will also include ideas about what we can know about the past and how we can know it. School students are generally taught a good deal of substantive history, but very little about the ideas that make the discipline of history what it is. They are somehow expected to understand what history is by picking up metahistorical ideas as they go along, and in these circumstances it is hardly surprising that students assimilate 'doing history' to the everyday life they already know. Research gives us two important reasons for taking students' ideas about history seriously. First, it seems to be suggesting that key ideas central to history as a discipline are counter-intuitive.[10] Second, it provides evidence that some of the working assumptions about history used by students are much more powerful than others.[11]

To say that history is 'counter-intuitive' is to say that the 'intuitions' students bring to history lessons are those that they use to make sense of everyday life (and which usually work very well for that). But people doing history are looking at things rather differently from the way we treat them in daily practical life. One example of this is the way our assumptions about the past function in everyday life and in history. The kind of situation in which children learn what counts as 'telling the truth' is one in which the past is treated as given, and, in some sense, known. A child breaks a window, and later, on discovering the damage, Mom asks how it happened. The child has a choice between 'telling the truth' and 'telling lies.' From her point of view there is a fixed past, which she knows only too well because she did the deed in question, and there is a large measure of agreement about the conventions for reporting such actions. The only issue is whether she tells it 'like it was.' The child and the adult can both treat the past as unproblematic, and in that sense it can function as a touchstone: it is as if what is said can be held up against the (experienced and known) past to see if it matches up. But history isn't like this, and an idea that works perfectly well in everyday life is likely to become very misleading when applied to history.

'The past' in history is not 'given,' and cannot play any direct methodological role, although it remains as a central regulatory idea. None of the ways in which we have to go about (re-)constructing history involves direct access to the past.[12] The inferential discipline of history has evolved precisely because the real past cannot play any direct role. Even when it is a recent enough past for someone to remember, historians' questions about it are rarely the sort that can be answered by appeal to memory, however reliable.[13] In any case, memories cannot have privileged status: *evidence* has to come in, and with it inference and judgment. So the historical past, unlike the past in the everyday world of children, can never be treated as given, or as something 'there' against which historians can test their claims.

The consequences of ideas like this are revealed when students confront conflicting (or apparently conflicting) accounts of the past. Consider these typical (written) responses from students, asked why two stories each gave different dates for the end of the Roman Empire. (See Appendix 2 and the second part of this chapter, where the research is discussed in more detail.)

CLAIRE (year 6)
Why are there different dates?
Because no-one knows. Nobody alive today was there so nobody knows when it ended.
How could you decide when the Empire ended?
I do not think we could.[14]

NICOLA (year 7)
How could you decide when the Empire ended?
We can't unless we found someone who lived at that time.

OLIVER (year 6)
Why are there different dates?
Because one story must be wrong. They can't both be right.
How could you decide when the Empire ended?
I don't think we could.

For Claire the past is unknowable because no one was there. She is sure that if historians read the same things, dig up the same things, and are honest, 'there will be no important differences' between their stories, and when asked if she agrees or disagrees that there can only be one proper story about the end of the Roman Empire, she firmly agrees: 'That is right.' Nicola shares the same basic stance, and even extends it to an impossible hypothetical. She thinks that 'if the stories are different one must be telling lies,' and insists that 'only one thing happened but we don't know which is correct.' Oliver also thinks it is impossible to decide, although he does not say why. He believes that if there are two accounts, one of them must be wrong. He thinks that historians reading and finding the same things will not necessarily tell the same story, because 'they don't really know the real answer,' but asserts that 'there can only be one true story' about the end of the Roman Empire. Everyday ideas are apparent in these responses, but they do not help the students solve the problems they face.

It is as though the everyday situation is still governing their thoughts, but this time it is not like the case where Mom is confronting a child about what they both know she did, but more like a case where someone did something unobserved and without leaving any clear traces. In the everyday world we are likely to say that we will never know what 'really' happened, and often have to accept that this is probably the only possible answer, because the kind of answer we need is a practical one. Allison, another year 6 student, puts it very clearly: 'You cannot really decide unless you were there.' But if you think like this, history becomes impossible. If there is only one 'right' story, and knowing it depends on having seen it (or better still, having done it), we can never say anything worthwhile about the past. Many students stop there, wondering what the point of history is.

Other students understand that the past has to be reconstructed, that a historical account is not fixed by the past, but something that historians have to work at, deciding on what time scale and theme they will deal with. So the problem of the date of the end of the Roman Empire is not a matter of knowing the right answer, but of deciding what, within the parameters of a particular account, is to count as the end. The problem ceases to be simply a factual one, and becomes criterial.

ALAN (year 9)

Why are there different dates?

Because it depends whether you consider or what you consider to be the end of an empire.

How could you decide when the Empire ended?

We would first have consider what we think was the end, whether it was the split in the Empire, the Barbarians coming, the capture of Romans or the Capture of Constantinople.

LARA (year 9)

Why are there different dates?

Because there is no definite way of telling when it ended. Some think it is when its city was captured or when it was first invaded or some other time.
How could you decide when the Empire ended?
By setting a fixed thing what happened for example when its capitals were taken, or when it was totally annihilated or something and then finding the date.

Some Ideas Are More Powerful than Others: Progression in History

This takes us to the second point raised by research: whereas some working assumptions make history seem to students a dubious or even futile activity, others allow it to go forward. In the example above, Oliver does not even raise the question of how we could know about the past, and Claire and Nicola raise it only to despair of finding an answer. Other youngsters, only too well aware of the difficulty, can nevertheless envisage connections between past and present.

JENNY (year 7)
Why are there different dates?
No one knows when it ended. If two people put down two different dates then no-one knows and they just guessed.
How could you decide when the Empire ended?
I think no-one knows unless someone wrote it on a bit of paper and someone found it.

The problem of the end of the Empire remains a factual one, but there is at least some possibility of finding the answer. Perhaps someone told it like it was, wrote it down, and we could find it. As Samantha (year 6) put it, 'If you found an old diary or something it might help.' This view remains very limiting, because it still sees the past as fixed, but it does make history possible. If we have true reports, historians are in business. Of course, many students see that truthful testimony may not be easy to come by. They are very well aware that people have reasons for saying what they say and the way they say it. As Brian (year 9) remarks, 'I don't think we could find out definitely [when the Empire ended] because there is only biased stories left.'

Students who think history depends on true reports, but that bias rules out reliance on these, are once again faced with history coming to a halt. It is only when students go beyond dependence on eyewitnesses or agents and begin to think in terms of *evidence* that history once more becomes possible. The idea that historians can ask questions about historical sources that those sources were not designed to answer, and that much of the evidence used by historians was not intended to report anything, frees history from dependence on truthful testimony.

If history is a 'common sense' subject, in which students acquire knowledge of more and more passages of the past, it is hard to conceive of a 'progression' of ideas of the kind that takes place in different ways in science, mathematics, and, perhaps, modern languages. But if we ask how far students understand what the discipline of history involves, 'progression' makes more sense. Changes in metahistorical ideas allow us to talk sensibly about 'progression' in students' understanding of history as a discipline. For example, research suggests a pattern of progression of ideas about 'evidence' running from less to more powerful ideas:

- a 'given' past where questions about how we can know do not arise
- a notion of 'testimony' that provokes questions about how truthful a report may be
- a concept of 'evidence' allowing questions to be asked that no one was intending to answer (even records can be treated as relics; battle orders and railway timetables were not constructed to fool historians)

Research carried out in the United Kingdom and elsewhere over the past three decades has begun to produce more elaborated models of progression in students' metahistorical concepts.[15] These are generalizations about what students' prior ideas are likely to be. As such, they do not predict individual learning paths, but give some idea at the group level of what students may do. They are like the trails left by sheep on a mountainside, which show us the way most of the sheep happen to go, not the paths they *must* take.[16] Just as a sheepdog can make important changes in the routes taken by the sheep, so teaching can change the way in which students' ideas develop. Nor are models of this kind to be thought of as resembling ladders, where one step must be mounted before the next, or stages through which it is *necessary* to pass. Some students, once their existing ideas have been disturbed, will make a rapid leap to much more sophisticated understandings. Others will move only slowly. Progression models suggest what teachers might expect, and what they might need to look out for. Awareness of patterns of this kind enables us to see how students' understandings can gradually be extended, either by breaking down prior (mis-)conceptions or by building on existing ideas. Teachers can help students develop more powerful ideas that make history an intelligible task, even when they must confront multiple histories bringing with them disagreement and uncertainty.

Some Caveats

It is important to clarify at this juncture what is *not* being said. First, it should be clear that insisting on the importance of developing students' understanding of history need not imply grandiose claims. What is at stake is not the training of mini-historians, but changing students' understanding of history. If this seems to imply absurdly pretentious implications and impossibly difficult tasks for young students, it must be emphasized that metahistorical understandings of the kind we are talking about are not all-or-nothing matters. Many historians have learned some science at school or college, but it is unlikely that their understanding of science is in the same league as that of a professional physicist. This does not make it useless, let alone reduce it to equivalence with a seven year old's understanding. Once this is accepted, it is easier to see why there is nothing impossibly difficult about our task. Moreover, we should be careful not to assume that metahistorical ideas of the kind at issue are automatically more difficult than the substantive ideas routinely tackled (or assumed) in dealing with the content of history. Is the idea that (for example) history depends on evidence obviously more difficult than the notion of feudalism? The point is that both may be understood at different levels, but it makes little sense to say that one is just harder than the other.[17]

The second caveat is that learning to understand the discipline does *not* replace the goal of understanding particular passages of the past. The point of learning history is that students can make sense of the past, and that means knowing some content. Moreover, understanding history implies some grasp of how and why some passages or aspects of history, in particular enquiries or accounts, may be claimed to be more important than others. Students need to know about the past, or the whole exercise becomes pointless. But understanding the discipline allows more serious engagement with the substantive history that students study, and enables them to *do* things with their historical knowledge. Here we can make a connection with Jörn Rüsen's wider notion of historical consciousness.

Historical Consciousness and Historical Understanding

Rüsen offers us a model of the 'disciplinary matrix' of historical studies that elucidates the relationships by means of which five elements of historical studies 'organize historical knowledge into a cognitive process.'[18] This is not the place to do justice to Rüsen's extensive and complex theory of historical consciousness, even if I were equipped to do so (and regrettably little of it is so far available in English). However, a glance at figure 1 suggests that, while practical interests drive our orientation needs, our thinking about the past is filtered (nowadays) through the theories and methods of history (as they exist at any moment in time).

Rüsen has much of interest to say about these matters, but here I have space only to comment on the importance of what is above his notional line in the disciplinary matrix. For Rüsen, the acquisition of factual knowledge involved in history education must not remain inert: it must 'play a role in the mental household' of a student.[19] It is possible to conceive of this happening without the involvement of anything 'above the line' – that is, without the discipline of history playing any role at all (and maybe this would be something like Oakeshott's 'practical past').[20] In our present state of historical consciousness, however, history education usually claims at least to take its representations from above the line, and if what students learn is indeed to play a role in their mental furniture, it is hard to see how we can sensibly treat such representations as 'given.' (The arguments offered above about the counter-intuitive character of metahistorical understandings press strongly in the same direction.) The line dividing the diagram cannot become a barrier to a different world, permeable only in one direction, unless we intend to leave students as consumers of stories handed down from higher regions, either to be accepted in awe or tested only against the direct demands of practical life. Rüsen's insistence that history education 'increases the competency to find meaning,' his treatment of perspectives and their status in history, together with his remarks on their increasing flexibility and movement away from dogmatism all suggest that history education must go above the line if students' historical consciousness is to be adequately developed.[21]

Rüsen's a priori typology of the development of historical consciousness postulates a development from *traditional* historical consciousness, in which traditional narratives are pre-given and furnish us with the

Figure 1   Jörn Rüsen's disciplinary matrix

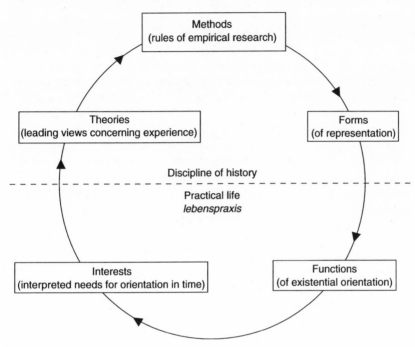

origins of our values and our form of life, through *exemplary* historical consciousness, where the past embodies rules of change and human conduct that remain valid for all times, to *critical* historical consciousness, which challenges traditional narratives and draws attention to deviations from exemplary rules, and finally to *genetic* historical consciousness, in which change is central to the past, and gives history its meaning. In this last category differing standpoints are accepted by being integrated in a perspective of temporal change, and permanence and continuity are themselves temporalized: people and things survive by, as well as through, change.[22]

For the purposes of this chapter, two points arise from the typology. First, the genetic category at least may imply rather complex understanding of *some* elements above the line: metahistorical ideas that make history the discipline it currently is.[23] Second, a typology of this kind is unlikely to be able to account for all the metahistorical ideas involved in the development of students' understanding of the discipline of history. Rüsen's typology is designed to deal more directly with some questions (about orientation in terms of substantive ideas about the past and our relation to it) than with others (about changes in metahistorical ideas). This is not a defect in Rüsen's ontogenetic typology, but a normal feature of any set of categories for interpreting human beliefs: the interpretative schema will vary with the questions we are asking (something that also applies in history itself).

Rüsen makes it quite clear that it is possible for more than one of his categories to coexist in any particular encounter with the past. This suggests that we should not expect the typology to be directly applicable to particular changes in metahistorical understandings. For example, let us assume for the moment that we try to operationalize Rüsen's typology and provide, for a given task, indicators for each type of historical consciousness. If a student's orientation, as evidenced by responses on particular tasks, seems to fall under the category of (say) 'exemplary,' then we will still not know whether he or she understands claims about the past involved in this orientation as information, or as guaranteed by testimony, or as inferred from evidence.[24] Even a student whose responses are categorized as 'genetic' may either be thinking of accounts of the past as copies of that past, or alternatively may conceive them as constructions more akin to theories than to copies. The subtly different ways in which different kinds of claims relate to evidence may elude a student who nevertheless 'prefers to represent experience of past actuality as transformational events, in which alien cultural and life-patterns evolve into more positive "modern" configurations.'[25] Recent research suggests that students' metahistorical ideas do not develop at the same rate, and we therefore should not assume that ideas about (say) historical *evidence* will change in step with ideas about *explanation* or about *change*.[26]

Historical consciousness is a valuable concept because it offers the prospect of integrating the wide range of ways in which human beings position themselves in time and take account of their past.[27] Rüsen's theory is clearly integrative, providing an account of history within a wider theory of historical consciousness. It is natural in these circumstances for Rüsen's ontogenetic typology to join the substantive and the metahistorical under the aegis of *orientation*, which is his central interest and the basis of his integrative theory. But if we are to provide an evidentially supported account of the development of students' historical consciousness, we will have to make distinctions – at least initially –

between the stances students take towards (their conception of) the substantive past and the metahistorical assumptions they make. This is because, although there may be a priori reasons for arguing that Rüsen's typology does not allow those located within any particular category to hold any assumptions whatsoever about (say) *change* or *evidence*, it does leave a great deal open. We have no grounds for believing that developments in orientation of the kind set out by Rüsen account for all the important changes in metahistorical understanding. Given the relation of interpretative typologies of this kind to our questions, it may well prove impossible to come up with one that encompasses all aspects of the development of historical consciousness in a single progressive schema; however, this is not a matter than can be decided a priori.

For the purposes of this chapter, then, I will assume that Rüsen's theory of historical consciousness, in relating the elements above and below the line in his disciplinary matrix, licenses the assertion that history education must include the development of ideas about the (current) discipline of history, metahistorical understandings about *historical evidence*, *historical explanation*, the nature of *historical accounts*, and *change*.[28] However, for the reasons already advanced, I will not work directly with Rüsen's typology, but report research on one particular strand in the development of students' ideas about history, and offer a tentative schema for just this strand, which may serve as one possible starting point for further explorations.[29]

Understanding History: Historical Accounts

Project Chata

The remainder of this chapter will focus on a research project that investigated children's and adolescents' second-order ideas about history. The project is only one example of work in this area that goes back at least to the early 1970s. Early research was largely confined to the United Kingdom, where it was part of a much wider change in approaches to history education, but work in the field now flourishes in North America and in parts of Europe, and is beginning to develop in South America and Taiwan.[30]

Concepts of History and Teaching Approaches 7–14 (Chata) was funded by the Economic and Social Research Council. Its central task was to map changes in students' ideas about history between the ages of seven and fourteen years. The project focused on metahistorical or

Table 1   Phase 1 schools

School	Phase and type	Intake	Y3	Y6	Y7	Y9
A	Primary	urban	17	29		
B	Primary	small town	16	18		
C	Primary	rural	22	28		
D	Secondary comprehensive	urban			24	24
E	secondary comprehensive	suburban			24	25
F	secondary comprehensive	urban			23	
G	secondary comprehensive	small town				10
H	secondary selective (girls)	urban +			14	16
I	secondary selective (boys)	suburban +			15	15
Total			55	75	100	90
					(N = 320)	

Notes
+ indicates a wide catchment area drawing students from beyond the locality.
Mean age of year groups: Y3, 8 years 1 month; Y6, 11 yrs 2 mos; Y7, 12 yrs 1 mo;
Y9, 14 yrs 1 mo.

second-order disciplinary understandings like *evidence, accounts, cause,* and *rational understanding* (the latter meaning understanding of action in terms of reasons, or of social practices in terms of beliefs and values). In the first phase of the investigation reported here, pencil-and-paper responses were collected from 320 children between the ages of seven and fourteen, across three task sets, on three separate occasions.[31] The task sets were self-standing, providing children with the material necessary for the tasks. Each addressed different historical content from the English National Curriculum. Follow-up interviews were conducted with 122 students on all three task sets. All the youngest were interviewed, and their interviews were analysed along with written responses; for the remainder, interviews were used only to check that the written responses were not seriously misleading.

The written tasks took the form of four slim booklets and a colour-printed clue sheet. The children were asked to complete these by writing, ticking boxes, ordering statements, or drawing arrows. The three task-sets were given over a period of three weeks for secondary, and slightly longer for primary, children. For the twelve- and fourteen-year-olds around ninety minutes was available for a task set, but the younger children had a full day: most eleven-year-olds finished within half a day. The eight-year-olds were read the background information, and were then taken through the tasks by a research officer with considerable experience as a primary deputy head; they worked for short spells alternating with games in the playground.

Researching Students' Ideas about Historical Accounts

Students were given pairs of stories running vertically side-by-side down the page.[32] The form of the stories remained the same on each task set, but their content differed. For all three pairs of stories we asked what differences there were between the stories, and why those differences existed.

Each pair of stories differed in theme, tone, and time scale. In task set one, dealing with the Romans in Britain, one story emphasized material life and the other culture and ideas. The first stressed the benefits to the Britons of improvements in material life and the peace brought by the Romans. The second emphasized British achievement before the conquest, and the imposition of a Roman way of life. The first story ended with the (relatively) short-term deleterious consequences for material life in Britain of Roman withdrawal, but the second took the account through the beginnings of a unified kingdom to end with the survival of Roman ideas in the present. (Each 'chapter' in the version for the youngest students was slightly shortened.)

In addition to the questions common to all task sets, we also asked students whether they agreed or disagreed with the claim 'If two historians read the same things and dig up the same things and do not lie, there will be no important differences between the stories they each write,' and why they thought as they did. (In order to avoid lengthy repetition this 'evidence determination claim' will be abbreviated in the following discussion as 'the EDC.')

The stories in the second task set dealt with the end of the Roman Empire.[33] Emphasis in the first was on barbarian incursions, and the story ended with the claim that the 'real end of the Roman Empire' was in 476, when the last western emperor was overthrown. Its partner story focused on internal problems, and gave the 'real end' of the Empire as 1453, when the Turks captured Constantinople. The students were asked whether this meant that no one knows when the Roman Empire ended, or that it is just a matter of opinion, or that there was no single time when it ended, or that one of the stories must be wrong about when it ended, and they were asked to explain their views. They were also asked how we could decide when the Roman Empire ended, and if there were other possible times we could say it ended.

The stories in task set three were about the Saxon settlement of Britain. The first concentrated on the details of the coming of the Saxons, and the second dealt with the longer period of settlement, through to the establishment of a unified English kingdom. In addition to the questions asked in all task sets, students were asked to put in order of importance six sentences offering reasons why historians' stories might differ. They were also asked if they agreed or disagreed with the statement *History really happened, and it only happened one way, so there can only be one proper story about the Saxons in Britain,* and to explain their decision. (This 'single story claim' will be abbreviated as 'the SSC' in the following discussion. Appendix 2 gives the stories in all three task sets.)

Explaining How There Can Be Two Different Stories

Students' responses on the three task sets to the question why there could be 'two different stories about the same bit of history' allow the construction of a model of the development of ideas about historical accounts. However, this model is a first approximation, and more work is needed on how changes in student ideas about historical accounts relate to increasing sophistication in their wider understanding of the nature of historical knowledge.

Analysis of responses across all three task sets indicates a broad shift with age from the idea that stories are ready-made and simply retold (labelled as 'Telling' in figure 2), through the idea that historians find, compile, and collate information ('Knowing' in figure 2), to ideas about historians actively producing their stories ('Author' in figure 2), whether by distorting them for their own ends or legitimately selecting in response to a choice of theme.[34] A small proportion of (mainly) year 7 and year 9 students showed signs of recognizing that accounts could not be complete, and had to fit different questions, themes, and time scales. They were beginning to understand that it was in the nature of historical accounts to differ ('Nature' in figure 2).

1. Differences in accounts are in the telling.
There was a marked tendency among year 3 children to say that both stories were 'the same,' and that any differences were 'just the words.' The main problem here is to understand what 'the same' meant to

Figure 2   Ideas about differences in accounts: percentages of year groups

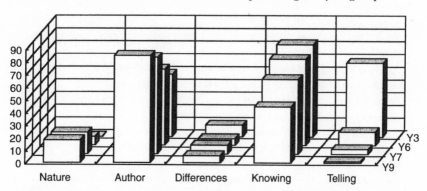

Note: This figure only registers an idea if it appeared on any given student's response on at least two of the three task sets. For 3.75% of the sample, a total of 12 cases, no ideas appeared more than once, so single occurrences were used, at the risk of a reduction in reliability.

Categories: Nature – It is in the *nature of accounts* to be different from one another; Author – Differences occur because accounts are written by *different authors*; Differences – The stories differ because they are about *different things, times or places*; Knowing – Accounts differ because of problems in obtaining *knowledge* of the past; Telling – Any differences are only in *how the stories are told*; the accounts are the *same*.

children making the claim. Nicola, year 3, said in all three task sets that there were no differences between the stories, and was succinct at the interview.

You said there were no differences, are they both exactly the same then?
NICOLA: They're in different words but they both mean the same thing.

It is possible that some of these responses signified an inability to hold two stories in mind at once, but in the majority of cases there seemed to be much more at stake. Notions of 'saying the same thing' or being 'about the same thing' clearly need more exploration: they may indicate the dominance of content in history, or may suggest something more complex and subtle.[35] Similarly, caution is required in interpreting 'different words.'

Some of the children who said the stories were the same also said they were just told in different ways. Samantha, year 3, wrote in task set 1: 'I do think they are both the same.' But there could be different stories about the same bit of history, 'because 2 different people can tell the same stories in their own words.' She expanded this in talking to the interviewer.

> SAM: There isn't any difference because they are just the same stories but they are put into different words.
> *So they are saying the same thing but just the words are different. OK then ... how can there be two different stories about the same bit of history then?*
> SAM: Two different people can tell the same story, but they can tell it in different words from each other.
> *So they say the same thing but they just use different words, so if you told one story and I told the other story would we say exactly the same thing?*
> SAM: Well, if it was a story about the same thing like, say, we had to write a story about the snow, and we wrote the same story in different words.

Samantha's model here seems to be the familiar task of taking information from a teacher or a book, and writing it down in her own words: it is the *same information*, but it has to be in *different words*. In task set 2 Samantha wrote, 'There is no difference,' and in task set 3, 'There is no difference apart from the ending at story 2.' She recognizes a difference (one story mentioned the Vikings, the other did not) but it was as though it counted for nothing.

The idea that there were no differences between the stories, or that any differences were in the words, or in the way they were said, was also present among some older children. Joe, year 7, having recognized differences in the stories, wrote, 'Both stories only have little bits different from one another. So it is possible to have 2 stories from one time.' The implication is that greater differences would forbid more than one ('proper') story. Lizzie, also year 7, in disagreeing with the EDC, said, 'Just because they dug up the same information they are still going to · word it differently.'

2. Differences in accounts are a knowledge problem.
As might be expected from the discussion in the first part of this chapter, younger children tended to make much more than older ones of the fact that the past is not open to direct inspection. Daniel, year 6, put it straightforwardly: 'No-one from them days is alive today.' The same kind of ideas were to be found in year 7 and year 9. Christopher, year 7, wrote in task set 2, 'No-one was there when the Empire ended so nobody really knows.' Stuart, year 9, agreed with the SSC, 'because none of us was there when all this happened.'

Reference to the impossibility of direct observation did not always appear on its own or only in unsophisticated responses. It continued, though rather infrequently, to show up in more subtle forms in the responses of older pupils. Emily, year 9, was almost able to reconcile this problem with her more sophisticated ideas about history. She disagreed with the SSC:

> Different historians have different ideas about what really happened, and so there are lots of different stories. Just because one person's idea is different to another person's idea it doesn't mean it is wrong – it just means it is different. Nobody alive today was there more than 120 years ago and so people have to base ideas on what they find and on what they read. Archaeologists dig things up to try to piece together information but as nobody really knows it is impossible to say whether one story is correct and one story is wrong. It is true that history only ever happened one way but as nobody knows then new ideas and new theories help other people to realize what did really happen that long ago.

Another 'knowledge-problem' explanation for differences in accounts was that they occur because historians just happen to come across different books, or dig up different objects, and these fix what can be said. Many year 3 children (and some in years 6, 7, and 9) gave this explanation.

A smaller but still substantial proportion of students mentioned gaps in what historians knew as a likely reason for differences in accounts. Kate, year 6, said, 'Stories may be different as different bits may be left out,' and Nathan, year 7, explained, 'It is difficult for historians to find everything.' While some students were aware that there might be problems with sources, they tended to see these more as defects in the material than as necessitating interpretation: transmission errors, mistakes, or inaccuracy in the sources were picked out. There was also reference to lies or bias, and differences in the thinking or viewpoint of the sources themselves. In this category respondents saw problems such as bias in the sources as defeating historians: if the sources were wrong, historians would get their accounts wrong too.

A few students were aware that sources need interpretation. Rosalyn, year 7, disagreed with the EDC:

> They will use their imagination to some extent. Their brains will think about different things, for example. One might think that something they dig up is a spoon, another might think it is made for digging.

In responses of this kind authors had an active role, not yet in the construction of accounts, but at least in the use they make of sources. The problem remains a knowledge matter, but ideas like this are nevertheless more sophisticated than some found at the lower end of the range in (4) below.

3. The differences were in the 'real past.'
A relatively small group of students from all age groups appealed to reality to explain differences in accounts; they accepted the differences and tried to show them as stemming from differences in the 'real past.' Oliver, year 6, invoked differences in time in task set 1: 'The first story happened before the second story.' Alison, year 6, explained the different dates for the end of the Roman Empire in task set 2 by differences in location: 'Because for the West the Roman Empire finished at one time and for the East it finished at another.' The small numbers and rather even age distribution for this category suggests that it requires further investigation.

4. Differences in accounts are an author problem.
Many students mentioned the role of authors in their most direct relation to knowledge issues: authors could make mistakes. Some children took a hard line with different accounts: either or both were obviously mistaken. Tony, year 7, was unhappy with both dates for the end of the Roman Empire, but his reasons were slightly unexpected: 'Well the calendar couldn't be right from the start so they both may be wrong.' In responses of this kind the role of the author is at best implicit, and the issue may be just as much a problem about knowledge, but others more explicitly treated mistakes as the responsibility of the author. Emma, year 7, when asked if differences in history stories mattered, replied, 'Because they happened and the writers should tell the truth.' She agreed with the SSC, 'because you can have 2 stories but only one is right.'

When we turn to ideas invoking author problems that clearly leave knowledge issues behind, the most frequent explanation for differences in the pairs of stories was that people have different opinions or views. Emma, year 7, explained differences in accounts by reference to the writers: 'because they both have different opinions.' She did not think this mattered, 'because people can think what they like.' Richard, year 9, explained in task set 1, 'There can be 2 different stories about the same bit of history because they can be written from different views.' In task set 2, discussing the end of the Roman Empire, he again stressed opinion:

One story says it ended in AD 476 – that was his opinion.
One story says it ended in AD 1453 – that was his opinion.
It is just a matter of opinion.

Asked how one could decide when the Empire ended, he wrote, 'You couldn't. The answer you come up with is just your own opinion.' The difference in stories did not matter, 'because they are both opinions and no-one really knows what happened even if they do have what they think is proof.' Personal opinion seems to float freely here.

Opinion covered a range of ideas, but children often treated it as if it were an entirely personal matter, with no procedures for weighing up or testing claims, however tentatively. People's opinions belonged to them, and were held as a matter of personal right: it was almost as if to challenge another's opinions was to undermine or debase that person's status. A minority of older children talked about historians having different viewpoints, rather than simply different views or opinions, implying that sets of presuppositions and values might influence accounts, but there was little to distinguish such remarks from those who treated views as if they were just arbitrary opinions historians happened to hold. Few responses showed signs of thinking in terms of social standpoints influencing accounts, except in terms of crude bias or partisanship. (See Appendix 1 for a breakdown of the kinds of ideas that students seem to be employing within the general category of 'opinion.')

There was a steep increase with age in references to bias, side-taking, and partisanship in responses to the three task sets. Chris, year 9, wrote in task set 1, 'There can be two different sides to the story both biased for a different cause.' Different dates for the end of the Roman Empire were explained in terms of opinion: 'Because different people think in different ways and have different opinions etc.' We could decide about the date, but there were conditions to be met: 'When a primary source from a strong Roman influence states that the Empire is over (it should be unbiased).' Finally, Chris disagreed with the SSC, 'because, one thing that happens in history can be caused by several different stories all biased against each other; from this you can draw the truth.' Despite – or perhaps because of – the omnipresence of bias, the historian can reach the truth.

Not all students were so optimistic. Most responses citing bias seemed to appeal to partisanship and straightforward, conscious side-taking; it appears that historians are not to be trusted even to make real efforts to be impartial. Bruce, year 9, was more specific in his references to the sources of bias than most students. He wrote in the first task set, '2 biased historians have written these stories in favour of their country.' He disagreed with the SSC, 'because people are biased about their explanations, perhaps because they wish to favour their own race, culture, or country.'

A few students talked about selection, about attributions of importance, and about the authors having a legitimate viewpoint or having theories about what happened. (The latter were seen as something personal to the author: students thinking like this did not treat accounts themselves as though they are theories, or see importance as something having some structural relation to accounts.) Rachel, year 6, thought differences between accounts in task set 1 could happen 'quite easily.' 'The storyteller might aim it at one subject another storyteller would aim it at something else.' Debbie, year 9, wrote of the stories in the first task set: 'The first story is about the housing. The second story is about working and education. They are the same bit of history, but about different things.'

She disagreed with EDC:

> There would be important differences, as they could each have their views on things. They might say more about one thing than another. They might not put every bit of information in, so they could have different information, which could change the meaning of a story.

Selection here is not yet clearly an intrinsic feature of any account, and seems to be linked to differences in the views held by authors. But it is not based on bias, or even on generalized 'opinion.'

5. It is in the nature of accounts to differ.

A relatively small proportion of children, increasing with age, made very sophisticated points about the nature of accounts themselves in explaining how there could be different stories. Some of these ideas remained implicit, particularly in the case of responses to the problem concerning the end of the Roman Empire. Peter, year 9, from a school with a difficult student population and low achievement in public examinations, wrote, 'I don't think there could be an exact time. There was no time when someone stood up and said "The Empire's ended."' It is possible that this carries an implicit reference to differences in criteria that are built into accounts. Peter's responses in task sets 1 and 3 support the view that he is thinking of intrinsic features in the nature of all historical accounts as explaining differences between the examples confronting him. He characterized differences between the last chapters of the two stories on task set 1 in a startlingly sophisticated way: 'because the first ... is concerned with the physical changes and 2 is about cultural reproduction.' In task set 3 he referred to the way accounts will differ in response to different questions. 'Historians answer different questions in a story. If what they are trying to find out is different then the answers may also be different, even if they are about the same thing.'

Some children explicitly pursued the idea that historical accounts operate with different criteria. David, year 9, made the point in personal terms: 'Because it depends on whether you think the Empire in the east really was still a Roman Empire as it now had many races in it and much of the old way of life had been lost.' He was sure that there are other possible times for the end of the Empire: 'Because it depends on how you think. I personally think it could of ended at a different time. I think this time is when Latin was no longer used much or when the countries separated up.' But asked how we could decide when the Empire ended, he went beyond the personal: 'See when the last Roman Emperor died and a new Barbarian leader took over. You could also see around when most of the people in the Empire were Romans or when Latin is no longer used.'

Natasha, year 9, explaining the different ending times given for the Roman Empire, was elegant as well as precise:

> Because it all depends on your opinion and whether you are thinking about the Empire physically ending or mentally ending. If people still thought about the Empire and talked about it in 1453 then it hadn't ended until then, mentally. I think different bits of it ended at different times, i.e. it ended physically before it ended mentally. The Empire ended physically when it was all no longer governed by the same person, mentally, when it was no longer thought about and spiritually when there was no longer a shadow of it in people's lives, we still use Latin derivatives now so the Empire's influences still haven't ended now.

Responses like Natasha's and David's display an awareness of key features of historical accounts, over and above defects in the quantity or quality of knowledge, or the defects or partialities of authors. They are beginning to see accounts as answering questions, as operating with criteria appropriate to such questions, and as necessarily 'incomplete.' There is some sign of the idea that accounts are constructions, not just conjunctions of facts, and that they might have different tasks to per-

Table 2   Progression in students' ideas about accounts and their relation to the past

---

- The past as given
  Stories are about the same thing: the story is equivalent to something 'out there.'

- The past as inaccessible
  We can't know – we weren't there. Nothing can be *known*.
  Differences in accounts are a result of lack of direct access to the past.

- The past as determining stories
  Stories are fixed by the information available: there is a one-to-one correspondence.
  Differences in accounts are a result of gaps in information and mistakes.

- The past as reported in a more or less biased way
  Shift of focus from the *story* and *reports* to the *author* as active contributor. Differences in accounts are a result of distortion (in the form of lies, bias exaggeration, dogmatism); the problem is not just a lack of information.

- The past as selected and organized from a viewpoint
  Stories are written (perhaps necessarily) from a legitimate position held by the author. Differences in accounts are a result of selection. Stories are not copies of the past.

- The past as (re-)constructed in answer to questions in accordance with criteria
  Shift of focus from the author's position and choice to the nature of accounts as such. It is in the nature of accounts to differ.

---

form for different audiences. These are powerful ideas, which do not leave their owners helpless in the face of alternative accounts, shrugging their shoulders at a multiplicity of opinions.

Table 2 gives a summary of changes in students' ideas about historical accounts, but the relation between ideas about problems of knowledge and problems of authorship needs further work. Although the shift from authors as reporters and compilers to a more active role seems to go hand in hand with older students' increasing awareness of partisanship, individual students may treat knowledge and author problems as running parallel in explaining differences between stories. These students seem to be beginning to develop a more sophisticated and inclusive notion of 'knowledge.'

Conclusion

If it is not to pre-empt precisely the questions its chief virtue is to raise, 'historical consciousness' must be an inclusive notion. But whatever it does include, space has to be found for the ideas that people have about the nature and status of historical claims and accounts. Any attempt to give substance to a concept of historical consciousness through typologies that 'can be arranged according to a certain logical order' implies an interest in 'the ontogenetical development of historical consciousness.'[36] In most (perhaps all) societies students will acquire some sort of historical consciousness with or without schooling. They will learn particular stories, and with them tacit understandings as to what sort of entities those stories are. It is only in formal education that they are likely to have an opportunity to reflect on their tacit understandings and confront the historical construction developed over the past couple of centuries to deal 'historically' with the past: the discipline of history.

Research suggests that students do not find it easy to understand the ways in which history approaches the past. Nevertheless, when they are taught with the aim of enabling them to make sense of history, as well as the past, there is evidence that they can acquire powerful ideas. While politicians insist on students learning the 'right' stories, some fourteen-year-olds already know that historical accounts are not copies of the past. They expect to meet competing narratives, but are not entirely helpless when they do so. Whatever else it does by way of acquainting them with different kinds of past, history education in schools should give students an intellectual apparatus for handling history. No one else will.

Appendix 1

The following represents a schematic pattern of progression in concepts of 'opinion' used to explain differences in historical accounts, resting on qualitative analysis of different usage; quantitative analysis of distribution by age has not yet been performed.

Opinion as knowledge deficit

1 'Opinion' fills in for inevitable lack of knowledge (qua information), because of our lack of access to the past; or
2 'Opinion' fills in for contingent lack of knowledge, because there are gaps in our information.
3 'Opinion' is a tentative substitute for properly established knowledge.

Opinion as point of view

4 'Opinion' is what we have when we take sides: it is a partisan viewpoint, which distorts the past, and in that sense at least is illegitimate; but it is also inevitable (and it may be our duty to exercise it).
5 'Opinion' is a consequence of everyone thinking differently: it is a legitimate viewpoint.
6 'Opinion' is a judgment made on the basis of some sort of criteria, whether implicit or explicit, which in turn set the parameters necessary for the production of any story whatsoever.

Appendix 2

Task set 1

FIRST STORY

Chapter 1

Before the Romans came the Britons lived in wooden huts. They had no towns. Almost no-one could read. The Britons often fought each other.

Chapter 2

The Romans went to Britain and took most of it over. They made Britain peaceful.

The Romans built towns and cities. Some houses had central heating. Many Britons lived more comfortably. Some Britons learned to read.

Chapter 3

Much later, invaders attacked the Romans. The Roman armies went off to protect their other lands. The Anglo-Saxons took over England.

Towns and cities fell into ruins. It was as if the Romans had never been in Britain. It was ages before people in Britain lived as comfortably as they did when the Romans were there.

SECOND STORY

Chapter 1

Before the Romans came the Britons had their own way of life. They were good at making jewellery and tools. Almost no-one could read.

Chapter 2

The Romans took Britain over. They beat the Britons who tried to stop them.

The Romans made Britain like other countries they lived in. Britons copied the Roman way of life. Some learned to read.

Chapter 3

Much later, invaders attacked the Romans. The Roman armies went off to protect their other lands. The Anglo-Saxons took over England.

Once the Romans left, Britain gradually became one country, with a mixture of Britons and Anglo-Saxons. After a time people remembered Roman ideas. Some Roman ideas are still used now.

Appendix 2 (*continued*)

Task set 2

FIRST STORY

Chapter 1

The Roman Empire got very big. It was hard to protect. Barbarians raided it, burning towns and farms and killing people. It cost a lot to keep up big Roman armies.

Chapter 2

After a time the Empire was split into two halves, east and west, to make it easier to run. But Emperors had trouble finding money to pay for the army. When lots of people were killed by disease, there were fewer people to be soldiers, especially in the western half of the Empire. Barbarians were allowed to join the army. Before long, even many army leaders were barbarians.

Chapter 3

An Emperor who lived in the eastern Empire allowed barbarians to settle in the western Empire. But still the western Empire couldn't protect itself. In 410 and again 455 the city of Rome was captured by barbarians. In 476 the last western Emperor in Rome was overthrown. That was the real end of the Roman Empire, even though in the east an Empire of some kind managed to last for a time.

SECOND STORY

Chapter 1

The Roman Empire got very big. That made it hard to look after and keep in order. It cost a lot to run the Empire. Emperors had trouble finding enough money.

Chapter 2

After a time, the Empire was split into two halves, east and west, to make it easier to run. Each half had its own capital city: Rome in the west and Constantinople in the east. Sometimes each half of the Empire had its own Emperor, sometimes one Emperor ran both halves. The east was richer than the west. Emperors often preferred to live in Constantinople in the east rather than in Rome in the west.

Chapter 3

Barbarians attacked the Empire. The west was too poor to protect itself properly. The city of Rome was captured by barbarians. The eastern half managed to keep the barbarians out. It lasted a long time, but was soon very different from how the old Empire had been. The real end of the Roman Empire came nearly 1000 years later when Constantinople was captured by the Turks in 1453.

Appendix 2 (*concluded*)

Task set 3

FIRST STORY

Chapter 1

When the Roman army left, the Britons started quarrelling The Picts from Scotland attacked the Britons. The Picts did terrible damage. King Vortigern, king of the Britons, asked the Saxons from across the sea for help.

Chapter 2

Three shiploads of Saxons came. They were given some land in Britain, and in return they beat the Picts in battle. But really the Saxons wanted to conquer Britain themselves. When the Saxons across the sea heard what good farmland there was in Britain, and how weak the Britons were, more and more Saxons came.

Chapter 3

The Saxons joined up with the Picts. They destroyed cities, burned crops, and killed many people. Many Britons were made slaves. Some Britons hid in the mountains.

After many years the Britons got together and fought back. They stopped the Saxons taking over Britain for a long time. But then the Britons began to quarrel again, and the Saxons took over most of what we now call England.

SECOND STORY

Chapter 1

After the Roman army left, the Britons started quarrelling. They were attacked by the Picts. The Britons let some Saxons stay in Britain to help beat the Picts. But the Saxons soon brought friends from across the sea.

Chapter 2

The Saxons attacked the Britons. They took over almost all of what we now call England. At first England was not one country. Saxon kings set up separate countries. The Saxons made their own laws. They cut down forests to make farm land. Some Saxons learned to read and write. They were good at art.

Chapter 3

Much later the Vikings from Norway and Denmark began to attack England. For a time it seemed that the Saxons would never be able to stop them. Vikings settled in England and took part of it over.

But the Saxons fought back, and took control of the whole of England. Five hundred years after the Roman army had left Britain, England had become one country.

Notes

1 M.C. Lemon, *The Discipline of History and the History of Thought* (London: Routledge, 1995), 9–10.
2 This is clearly an important matter for education, but too large to pursue directly here. See C. Lorenz, 'Can Histories Be True? Narrativism, Positivism, and the "Metaphorical Turn,"' *History and Theory* 37, no. 3 (1998): 309–29; and, on the implications for history education, P. Seixas, 'Schweigen! Die Kinder! Or, Does Post-modern History Have a Place in Schools?' in P.N. Stearns, P. Seixas, and S. Wineburg, eds, *Knowing, Teaching and Learning History* (New York: New York University Press, 2000).
3 Of course history of science may cause special problems for the idea that history deals with common sense or everyday concepts, even if we assume that historical concepts are borrowed from the human activities historians seek to explore.
4 A follower of Ankersmit might want to say that such names pick out the metaphorical 'narrative substances' that are at the heart of historical narratives, but such a characterization would commit me to an argument I would prefer to leave to more qualified scholars, and to theoretical baggage that I do not want to carry.
5 M. Oakeshott, *On History* (Oxford: Basil Blackwell, 1983), 6.
6 There is a problem about terminology here. In the United Kingdom it has been common to use 'second-order' ideas to refer to ideas that children, adolescents, lay adults, and professional historians employ in thinking about the nature of our access to the past, the historical claims we make, and the historical accounts we give. In this chapter I have used 'metahistorical' for such ideas, perhaps at the risk of hinting at wider philosophical agendas I do not intend to raise. Whereas 'second-order' could apply to higher-order substantive concepts, 'metahistorical' unambiguously goes beyond the substantive.
7 Patient readers may be willing to forgive a long – if still insufficient – note at this point, on the grounds that more needs to be said about the notion of metahistorical ideas, but that introducing caveats into the main text will interrupt what is, after all, an avowedly introductory argument. First, the distinction between substantive and metahistorical ideas is not marked by a rigid demarcation line. The idea of change, for example, might be thought to be substantive rather than metahistorical: surely it is a matter of understanding what substantive patterns of change there have been in the past. There is truth in this, but the difficulty is that youngsters often see change as equivalent to events. This makes accounts of change the same as narra-

tives of events, and students cannot distinguish between (borrowing Shemilt's distinction) 'what happens' and 'what is going on.' Looked at from this perspective, the concept of change can be thought of as a metahistorical understanding, while people's knowledge of patterns of change in the past is substantive knowledge. The latter may inform the former, but certain tacit assumptions in the former may prevent students from making any sense of the latter. The distinction between substantive and metahistorical ideas is thus an approximate working distinction, based on the difference between the questions that historians pursue in doing history and the ideas that play a role in characterizing and helping students understand the kind of activity that history (the discipline) is.

Second, talk of 'ideas' here is clearly loose, and conceals a more complex picture. At the very least we need to recognize that some of the metahistorical 'ideas' may (for some purposes) be thought of more as dispositions than concepts. An important issue for students' understanding of history is likely to be whether they tend to look for links between wider beliefs and values and particular actions. Do they write off strange actions or social practices, or do they work with a presumption – however defeasible – that people in the past did things for reasons? Other ideas about the past may be thought of as more like principles or generalizations than concepts (but, of course, that begs the question as to how we are to understand concepts). Such principles as 'Peoples' choices are both enabled and constrained by the choices of others,' 'Actions have unintended consequences,' or 'People's reasons do not always give a complete explanation of what happens to them' may be crutches for beginners, but form an important part of what students need to learn about the past. For discussion of theories of the nature of concepts, see E. Margolis and S. Laurence, 'Concepts and Cognitive Science,' in S. Laurence and E. Margolis, eds, *Concepts: Core Readings* (Cambridge, MA: MIT Press, 1999), 3–81.

8 P.J. Lee and R. Ashby, unpublished research at the University of London Institute of Education.

9 One possibility here is to say that both these students are – at least at this point in their discussion – showing evidence of what Rüsen would call exemplary historical consciousness. However, it is difficult to see how Jörn Rüsen's categories for the development of historical consciousness, at least in the forms they take in English translation, can be made to take account of the crucial metahistorical differences involved. (See below, in the section 'Historical Consciousness and Historical Understanding,' further discussion of and references to Rüsen's publications available in English.)

10 See, e.g., D. Shemilt, 'The Devils' Locomotive,' *History and Theory* 22, no. 4

(1983): 1–18 (implicitly) and (explicitly) P.J. Lee and R. Ashby, 'Empathy, Perspective Taking, and Rational Understanding,' in O.L. Davis Jr, S. Foster, and E. Yeager, eds, *Historical Empathy and Perspective Taking in the Social Studies* (Boulder, CO: Rowman and Littlefield, 2001), 21–50.

11 D. Shemilt, *Evaluation Study* (Edinburgh: Holmes McDougall, 1980); P.J. Lee, R. Ashby, and A.K. Dickinson, 'Progression in Children's Ideas about History,' in M. Hughes, ed., *Progression in Learning*, BERA Dialogue (Clevedon, Bristol, PA, and Adelaide: Multilingual Matters, 1996), esp. 61–4; P.J. Lee and R. Ashby, 'Progression in Historical Understanding among Students Ages 7–14,' in Seixas, Stearns, and Wineburg, eds, *Teaching, Learning and Knowing History*, 199–222.

12 L.J. Goldstein, *Historical Knowing* (Austin: University of Texas Press, 1976).

13 R.F. Atkinson, *Knowledge and Explanation in History* (London: Macmillan, 1978).

14 This and the other examples in this section are from Project Chata (Concepts of History and Teaching Approaches 7–14), funded by the Economic and Social Research Council.

15 See, e.g., the works in note 11; R. Ashby and P.J. Lee, 'Children's Concepts of Empathy and Understanding in History,' in C. Portal, ed., *The History Curriculum for Teachers* (Lewes: Falmer Press, 1987), 62–88; P.J. Lee, R. Ashby, and A.K. Dickinson, 'Just Another Emperor: Understanding Action in the Past,' *International Journal of Educational Research* 27, no. 3, ed. J. Voss (1997): 233–44; D. Shemilt, 'Beauty and the Philosopher: Empathy in History and Classroom,' in A.K. Dickinson, P.J. Lee, and P.J. Rogers, eds, *Learning History* (London: Heinemann Educational Books, 1984), 39–84; and D. Shemilt, 'Adolescent Ideas about Evidence and Methodology,' in Portal, ed., *The History Curriculum for Teachers*, 39–61.

16 This is Denis Shemilt's analogy.

17 It is possible that ideas about evidence may clash with more tenaciously held tacit understandings than ideas about feudalism, but that is not the same as saying that the former is 'harder' than the latter, let alone that it is 'too difficult' for school students.

18 J. Rüsen, 'Paradigm Shift and Theoretical Reflection in Western German Historical Studies,' in P. Duvenage, ed., *Studies in Metahistory* (Pretoria: Human Sciences Research Council, 1993), 162.

19 J. Rüsen, 'Experience, Interpretation, Orientation: Three Dimensions of Historical Learning,' in Duvenage, ed., *Studies in Metahistory*, 87.

20 M. Oakeshott, 'The Activity of Being an Historian,' in *Rationalism in Politics* (London: Methuen, 1962), 137–67.

21 J. Rüsen, 'Experience, Interpretation, Orientation,' 89–90.

22 For the typology, see Rüsen's chapter in this volume and also the collection of his papers in Duvenage, ed., *Studies in Metahistory*, in particular 'Historical Narration: Foundation, Types, Reason' (pp. 3–14), 'What Is Theory in History?' (15–47), 'The Development of Narrative Competence in Historical Learning: An Ontogenetical Hypothesis concerning Moral Consciousness' (63–84), and 'Experience, Interpretation, Orientation: Three Dimensions of Historical Learning' (85–93).

23 See P. Seixas, 'Historical Consciousness: A Scheme of Progress in Knowledge for a Post-progressive Age,' in Jürgen Straub, ed., *Narrative, Identity and Historical Consciousness: On the Psychological Construction of Time and History* (Cambridge: Berghahn Books, in press).

24 Lee, Ashby, and Dickinson, 'Progression in Children's Ideas about History,' esp. 61–4.

25 J. Rüsen, 'The Development of Narrative Competence in Historical Learning,' in P. Duvenage, ed., *Studies in Metahistory*, 75.

26 Lee and Ashby, 'Progression in historical understanding.'

27 The chapters in this collection give some indication of the range and scope of what is potentially included in a theory of historical consciousness.

28 But see also note 7 for some elaborations and qualifications.

29 Although work on students' ideas about historical accounts is still relatively sparse, there is a considerable body of work examining the development of other strands of students' metahistorical ideas. See above, notes 10, 11, and 15. Talk of 'strands' here is not meant to imply that students' ideas are necessarily clustered in the particular strands picked out, but that this is one defensible way of looking at those ideas. Once again, the kinds of question we ask will influence the ways in which we interpret the ideas we seek to understand. It would be perfectly possible to construct typologies based on different questions, working with different interpretative constructs, and hence different 'strands.'

30 The most influential publication was Denis Shemilt's *Evaluation Study*.

31 In subsequent phases a further sample of 92 students were interviewed at the beginning of the spring and the end of the summer term, and then the 23 year 3 children from this sample were followed through years 4 and 5, using the same questions and interview schedule structure, but different content.

32 'Accounts' is used in this chapter to cover both narratives and developmental accounts of change, and is intended to avoid dichotomies between 'mere narrative' and 'explanatory narrative.' 'Story' will be used interchangeably with 'account,' because when talking with young children, 'story' is the nearest available intelligible equivalent.

33 The status of colligations like 'the Fall of the Roman Empire' is of course much discussed in recent philosophy of history; see F.R. Ankersmit, *Narrative Logic: A Semantic Analysis of the Historian's Language* (The Hague: Martinus Nijhoff, 1983), esp. chap. 6, and C. Behan McCullagh, *The Truth of History* (London: Routledge, 1998), esp. chap. 2. We hope that, despite our use of a concretized simplification, 'the end of the Roman Empire,' none of the central issues was closed down for students.

34 The examples given here are organized in terms of a conflated inductive category set used in the later stages of analysis. For the initial categories, see P.J. Lee, '"None of us was there": Children's Ideas about Why Historical Accounts Differ,' in S. Ahonen et al., eds, *Historiedidaktik*, Norden 6, Nordisk Konferens om Historiedidaktik, Tampere 1996, (Copenhagen: Danmarks Laererhøjskole, 1997), 23–58. For a more precise picture of the proportions of students using ideas in the subcategories referred to below, see Lee and Ashby, 'Progression in Historical Understanding.'

35 Elsewhere in the Chata analysis we have been driven to use the neologism 'aboutness' to pick out the tendency of children to centre on overt content – what something is 'about.' (The Piagetian resonances of 'centre' are intended here.) Two sources, for example, are the same if they are 'about the same thing.' There is much to be pursued here, but no space to do so in this chapter; in any case more investigation is required.

36 Rüsen, 'Historical Narration,' in *Studies in Metahistory*, 12.

Historical Consciousness and Historical Education: What to Expect from the First for the Second

CHRISTIAN LAVILLE

Recently, Eric Hobsbawm, like many before him, urged vigilance and prudence on his fellow historians, an injunction repeated thousands of times over since Paul Valéry's famous aphorism, 'History is the most dangerous product the chemistry of the brain has ever created.' Hobsbawm, reminding historians that they are 'the primary producers of the raw material that is turned into propaganda and mythology,' warned them about the possible misuse or abuse of the information they provide to the public: 'It is quite essential,' he insisted, 'that historians should constantly remember this. The crops we cultivate in our fields may end up as some version of the opium of the people.'[1] Bearing Hobsbawm's warning in mind, we have chosen to examine a trend – historical consciousness – that has become more and more popular of late.

In recent years, the concept of historical consciousness has been discussed with increasing interest in the scholarly literature. This approach, though not new in itself, has given rise to new forms of investigation and research by serious historians. Now we see its influence growing in the field of history education. Because of the important role the teaching of history plays – and will continue to play – in our society, it seems appropriate and even necessary to consider, from a pedagogical point of view, the possible advantages to be gained from this new approach.

This interest in historical consciousness first reached the field of history teaching in the 1970s[2] via German (and other culturally related) historians motivated by didactic concerns. If the concept was current elsewhere in the world, it failed to elicit discussion at that time. A survey conducted in the early eighties by the Dutch professor Piet Fontaine, who interviewed thirty historical pedagogues in twenty different countries, bears this out.[3] However, when we note the broad interest it arouses in historical education circles today, we are forced to ask, Why now? What is the substance of the idea? And where will it take us? These are the questions we will address in this chapter.

We will begin by reviewing the current state of history teaching, after which we will discuss the historical consciousness trend, its origins, its character, and the possible uses to be made of it.

The Current State of History Education

Today, most of us see the goal of historical education as the formation of the citizen – someone who is well informed, ideally, and able to think critically, and ready to participate in democratic society, as the fundamental principles of democracy require. This, however, has not always been the case. In earlier times, the teaching of history was geared instead to the creation and development of the nation-state; its goal was to foster in the citizen a sense of inclusion and respect for established order. Such an attitude now seems to have been definitively cast aside and, with it, its principal pedagogical tool, the official version of a shared historical past – the story of the nation's birth – used to teach future citizens what they should know and even, by extension, what they should think and feel.

Rather than teaching an official version of the past, today we prefer pedagogy based on what we call 'historical thinking.' Such an approach encourages the development of those intellectual and affective qualities that students will need in the exercise of their civic responsibilities. It calls upon the critical faculties common to historians – their ability to isolate a problem, analyse its component parts, and offer an interpretation – as well as their qualities of curiosity, empathy, and so forth, all of them built upon a solid foundation of analytical reasoning. Two further points should be made about historical thinking.

First, our students as adults will rarely be called upon to bring these faculties to bear upon versions of prefabricated history, but more often upon the great variety of issues, most of them unforeseeable, that will constitute their social reality. And, second, the conceptual and methodological tools they acquire or develop in our schools must be as durable as possible, preferably for lifelong use. In short, we must not forget that these pupils we are preparing in class will be less likely, as adults, to deal with history texts than to use their skills as citizens in the identification of social problems, the analysis of areas of conflict, the rational calculation of risks and rewards, and the weighing of competing interests, and in their personal decisions on the issues of the day.[4]

Such is the official line in historical education at this time, as we see it expressed in curricula, directives, and pronouncements, and no doubt in classroom practices as well. Not everyone, however, accepts it. In many parts of the world, we hear authorities, both public and private, argue for a return to the traditional didactic history with its manageable curriculum and prepackaged values. We have observed such a trend in the former socialist states, for example, as well as in the United States, with their National Standards controversy, in Great Britain, in discussions of the National Curriculum, and in France, earlier, in calls for curricular reform.[5] We have seen it (and continue to do so) in Canada as well, which is one of the reasons why I have been drawn to examine this new interest in historical consciousness.

At this point we come back to our earlier question, formulated more precisely: *What should we understand of the historical consciousness trend and what can it contribute to historical education?* Note that we pose the question with reference to the fundamental principles of democracy and liberalism, that is, in the context of the individual's freedom of thought and freedom of personal choice in society.

Consciousness, Memory, Identity: What Do They Mean?

If we have taken a detour to arrive at the historical consciousness question, it may be because the concept itself is hard to pin down. It is even less clear what role it might play in relation to the teaching of history. What exactly does the concept entail, and what potential pedagogical benefit does it hold out to us?

The concept of historical consciousness shares the contemporary stage with two other related concepts, namely, memory and identity. In the background – behind the scenes, so to speak – we can perceive the relevance they share to the education of the citizen.

On the scholarly level, these fields have only recently begun to attract attention. Their underlying concepts, however, are decades old. The French sociologist Maurice Halbwachs raised the subject of collective memory in the 1920s,[6] but failed to excite further discussion. Dan Ben-Amos confirmed this fact when he wrote that the concept experienced 'fifty years of hibernation in the archives of ideas and on the library shelves.'[7] In the last twenty years, however, studies of collective memory have multiplied, as the catalogue of any university library or any data bank in history or the social sciences will testify. For example, if you search under 'collective memory' or 'mémoire collective' in the 'Titles' index of the library catalogue of Laval University, you will find that twenty of the twenty-four titles containing these words were published within the two last decades. The same is true for thirty-seven of the forty-seven titles containing 'historical memory' or 'mémoire historique.'[8] The same applies to references to 'identity,' which pop up all around us, sprinkled liberally in the scientific literature, but also in public discussion and in the media. We meet 'identity' also in the area of education, where it has inspired new curricula, such as the new national history course in the province of Ontario, entitled 'Canada: History, Identity and Culture.'[9]

We have seen that historical consciousness, as a field of study, has been a focus for some time for German experts in history education; German philosophers, Hegel and Dilthey notably, discussed it even earlier. More recently, in 1958, Hans-Georg Gadamer delivered a long lecture on the topic, which was brought out in book form three years later by the press of the University of Louvain.[10] The delay in publication would indicate that, in the early sixties at least, historical consciousness was far from being a burning issue for most scholars. Note that all the aforementioned authors are German philosophers. In effect, until recently interest in historical consciousness was centred in German culture and more in the field of philosophy of history than in that of history itself. Francophone historians showed no interest at all in it until quite recently. The historian of modern French culture François Bédarida was unable to find any mention of 'memory' or 'historical consciousness' in any of the three volumes of Jacques Le Goff and Pierre Nora's *Faire de l'histoire* (1974),[11] though that magisterial work discussed in great detail the perspectives and practices of contemporary historians.[12] By the same token, neither *(L'Encyclopédie de) La Nouvelle histoire*, published under the editorship of Le Goff in 1978,[13] nor the *Dictionnaire des sciences historiques*, brought out by André Burguière in 1986,[14] made reference to 'historical consciousness.'

In the world of Anglo-Saxon culture, the situation was not very different. John Lukacs published his *Historical Consciousness: Or, the Remembered Past*[15] in 1968, a pioneering book in the field, as we now see it, although at the time it had relatively little impact. Its re-editions appeared only much later, in 1985 and 1994. As for anthropologists, David Sutton has pointed out that it was only in the mid-eighties that a noticeable interest in historical consciousness could be detected among them.[16]

Why, then, is it that questions of historical consciousness, memory, and identity have occupied such a central place in historiography in recent years? Some explanations for this phenomenon have already been suggested, and others can easily be imagined. We will advance some possible explanations, keeping foremost in our minds the possible impact of this new field for historical education.

Crisis, Globalization, Historical Consciousness

François Dosse, a specialist in the evolution of historiography, dates the appearance[17] of memory in the field of history to the 1970s, when the paradigm of history in the service of the nation was finally abandoned. 'The breakdown in the seventies of the linear, monolithic notion of history as the collective memory of the Nation-state,' he writes, 'has given rise to a profusion of diverse memories, each insisting upon its own uniqueness, and with them has come a richness which had long been surpressed.'[18] According to this view, the state, through the agency of the schools, lost control over the concept of history as national memory, thus allowing a new conception of history, involving multiple memories, to reach the public. Other scholars support Dosse's dating of this change. Henry Rousso and François Bédarida – close observers of our age through their work at the French Institut du Temps Présent, have suggested that the preoccupation, first with memory, and later with commemorations and historical consciousness, coincides with the economic crisis that began in the seventies.[19] With the postwar boom at an end, the crisis seemed to call into question the march of progress itself;[20] horizons appeared clouded, the future uncertain. Soon the fall of the Berlin Wall, followed by an acceleration of the globalization movement, would bring into question the viability of great social or political projects. There would be talk of an 'end of ideology' and even of an 'end of history.' With no clear future before them, people fell back upon the present. And in searching for the roots of the present, in seeking to give it legitimacy, they looked to their pasts, individual and collective. The idea of 'heritage' now embraced anything in the past that had left a trace in the present. Historical roots of any and all kinds had value for what they told us about the present.[21] The seven large volumes assembled by Pierre Nora on French 'places of memory'[22] and other related works no doubt have their origin in this way of thinking. Furthermore, given the importance of the past in this philosophy, it becomes imperative to have a sufficiently deep knowledge of it: thus, probably, the reforms in the teaching of history[23] that have been observed in most Western countries in the course of the last fifteen years. Furthermore, as a result of the complexity of modern society and the demands it makes of the citizen – and, more especially, because of the many different communities and minorities, established or recently arrived, that coexist in our populations – we have seen the reintroduction of civics as an adjunct to history education.

The uncertainty of the future, reflected in an uncertainty about the direction and the values of the present, has led not only to an interest in the preservation of the past, but also to a reappraisal of those versions of the past that call the present into question. According to Michel Wieviorka, as it happens, 'the emergence of a greater and more diverse number of memories in the public domain coincides with the pressure of groups who are collectively demanding, among other things, the recognition of their past sufferings.'[24] No one really believes that we can go backward in time and rewrite history. However, certain modern states, seeking perhaps to keep peace at home or simply to project an impression of openness, have more and more often agreed to proffer, in reply to these accusations from the past, official apologies. In recent years, we have seen a succession of such public declarations, in which Western powers confess their past errors.[25] The Vatican has apologized for the condition of women, Canada for the sufferings of its Japanese citizens during the Second World War, Poland for its behaviour toward the Jews, the Western countries for their colonial pasts, and so on. 'Memory has, thus, begun to quarrel and compete with history,'[26] as Wieviorka puts it. Some militant groups have even successfully forced governments and historians to agree to observe the 'duty of memory,' a kind of prohibition against forgetting certain historical episodes. Thus, by this sort of agreement, we allow the past to impose conditions upon the present.

History, the Historian, and Postmodernism

Meanwhile, historians have also allowed these concepts, memory and historical consciousness, into their professional domain. Their craft has always been one of scientific production based on research, usually invisible to consumers; what the latter see instead is the product of the historian's labours, namely, historical narrative. However, in recent years, traditional historical narrative has found itself seriously challenged by rival forms and new intellectual alternatives. For whatever reason – to protect their turf, perhaps, or out of personal conviction – some historians have sought to adapt their philosophy and practices to this new set of circumstances.

Already, in the field of education, the historian had been losing influence: the transition from a pedagogy of texts to be mastered to a pedagogy of apprenticeship in historical thinking gave less value to the role of the historian-as-editor. At the same time, the historian no longer enjoyed the status he had had for over a century as the author of textbook narratives. These had become tools of apprenticeship now more often left to schoolteachers and pedagogues. While these changes were occurring in history education, some historians appear not to have been aware of them. They have not noticed that history teaching is no longer based upon the communication of a pre-constructed 'story,' but instead aims at the development of certain intellectual abilities that can be used, for example, for independent historical inquiry. Fortunately, some other historians do understand the changes that have taken place and welcome them. For instance, Chad Gaffield, a specialist in Canadian studies, writes in his introduction to an article on this evolution: 'The scholarly rethinking of the history curriculum in recent years has been redefining course objectives. Rather than designing the history curriculum for the purpose of transmitting to students the interpretations of leading historians, educators are now exploring how courses can help students discover the past for themselves.'[27]

The historian's world view was even more threatened by the arrival of postmodernism. By simplifying only a little, we can say that, for the postmodernist, all knowledge is a form of narrative – a simple text, if you will – and that any one text has the value of any other text. But the historian, as we observed earlier, is, first and foremost, a producer of texts, texts we generally call narratives. These are constructed according to strict rules and procedures, without which, in the eyes of the historian, the text would have no validity whatsoever. When, however, the postmodernist says that any text is valid, without regard to its nature, its goal, and, above all, its mode of construction – when objectivity is seen as totalitarian – the historian feels the ground shake under her feet. And not only is she destabilized. She is, to some extent, dispossessed, for she suddenly sees her former domain invaded by a crowd of literary types, linguists, philosophers, anthropologists, psychologists, and specialists in 'cultural studies.' These new arrivals in his field of expertise may take no notice of her at all; sometimes they even try to elbow her out of the way. For example, the anthropologist Dan Ben-Amos sums up his collaborators in the volume on collective memory of which he is co-editor thus: 'None of the contributors to this volume is a historian. They are scholars of folklore, literature, communication, and culture. A glimpse at the selected bibliography reveals that collective memory is a viable concept in sociology, anthropology, political science, as well as history.'[28]

If society no longer looks to the historian's traditional expertise for guidance on present problems or future choices, then, in order to maintain their professional standing, some historians choose to broaden their perspectives and their methodology. New practitioners may prefer to sift the past for phenomena that, more or less consciously, they say, shape our understanding of the present. Still, the historian need not cede this new field entirely to them. Instead, historians themselves can also delve into memory and historical consciousness. They will no longer search for realities in the past with an eye to understanding and explaining it and to interpreting its impact on the present. Instead, they will focus on the perceptions held in the present day, accurate or not. The search for perception thus replaces the search for the true and verifiable, or, in the formulation of François Bédarida, the history of facts gives way to a history of the collective imagination (*l'imaginaire social*).[29] It is this kind of professional adaptation that Michael Confino criticizes when he writes: 'Abandoning the realm of the historian's craft and imitating literary scholars and anthropologists, these imperialistic approaches tend to define their task as one of interpretation and, instead of seeking causes, try to "understand meanings."'[30]

Ironically, less than twenty-five years ago, the historian Pierre Nora asserted that the function of the science of history – and therefore of the historian – was not to collect memories but to protect people against them through the application of 'instructive reason,' that is, through the analytical and critical activity of the historian, debunker of myth and of all other obstacles to our proper understanding of reality.[31]

Thinking 'Historically' and Teaching History

The same embarrassment in the minds of historians, which has led some of them to modify their conception of their discipline, has been echoed in the teaching profession. When, in the seventies and eighties, teaching students to 'think historically' became one of the principal goals of history education, many teachers were in favour of this view. Few, however, have experienced how to put this new pedagogy into practice. After a few years, a general sense of failure developed, and some teachers began looking back nostalgically to the comfort (or the security) of the traditional pedagogy based on telling a story.

Research in didactics has brought little help to these embattled teachers. There has been much research done in the West in those years, particularly in Great Britain, into the ways in which students learn to think 'historically.' The results of much of this research, however, suggested that historical thought was particularly difficult to get across, and that students could only begin to employ it in the later grades. In point of fact, much of this research, and its methodology notably, had serious shortcomings,[32] which, had they been corrected, would have given quite different results. Subsequent studies, including those by Robert Martineau,[33] have borne this out. These pessimistic conclusions, however, were both consoling and reassuring to those teachers who were either having difficulties in the classroom with the new pedagogy or who simply remained attached to the traditional way of teaching.[34]

Despite the discouraging problems they encountered, researchers have not abandoned their goal of teaching historical thinking. They have simply applied a kind of postmodernist solution: relying on the proximity of two words, they have redefined that goal: historical 'thinking' has become historical 'understanding.' From history as a form of reasoning, they have passed to history as text – from the process to the product. As we noted earlier, historical thinking is a set of thought processes and attitudes that, taken together, recreate the intellectual apparatus of the historian. Historical understanding, however, is the process of searching for meaning embedded by an author in a given text, of attempting to understand the author's intentions and presuppositions. Some researchers, such as Peter Lee and his associates, would couple this with a working knowledge of certain important historical concepts known as 'second-order ideas,' such as 'evidence,' 'explanation,' and 'change.'[35] Familiarity with these concepts serves, no doubt, as a valuable apprenticeship. However, these skills alone do not adequately equip the student for independent historical reasoning. In Lee's system, they are accompanied, moreover, by a return to the pre-established narrative as the centre of historical education. Incidentally, looking at the number of scholars from outside the field of history education taking part in this reorientation of research, one can suspect an influence of postmodernism similar to the one observed earlier in history writing. Among the researchers, once again, we note the prevalence and influence of linguists and teachers of reading – the sciences of discourse – as well as of cognitive psychologists. One example of this tendency can be observed in the second volume of the *International Review of History Education*, which bears the title *Learning and Reasoning in History*:[36] though 'history' is its subject, fewer than a third of its authors come from the field of history or history teaching.[37]

Is Historical Consciousness European?

The question of historical consciousness, which, as we have seen, had German origins, seems to be more widely discussed now in Europe than anywhere else, no doubt as a consequence of European unification. The number and variety of publications and projects that have sprung up in this field clearly support this thesis. For example, the large number of articles – a third of the total – devoted to historical consciousness in the sixty-page bibliography of *Looking Back–Looking Forward: Understanding History in Europe*, and the recent date of most of them, constitute a case in point.[38] Europe also gave rise to the vast research project *Youth and History*, subtitled 'A Comparative European Survey on Historical Consciousness and Political Attitudes among Adolescents.'[39] Here the context and the goals of the enterprise are clearly spelled out: 'This purpose is of great political interest as well, in order to get information about the readiness for European integration and the outlook concerning intra-European conflicts.'[40]

In effect, many of these works seem to be devoted, in varying degrees, to the construction of a new historical consciousness, European in nature[41] and therefore supranational. The first in a collection created to this end entitled 'Eustory Series: Shaping European History' states their objective frankly: the *construction* of a common historical consciousness.[42] This shared consciousness would serve as a tool for the 'active shaping of present development,' according to one of the authors of the study.[43] Indeed, the intention of the volume was very clear even without its being spelled out in so many words. Take, for example, the chapter by Jörn Rüsen, the German philosopher of history who, incidentally, was one of the first to use the concept of historical consciousness in the teaching of history.[44] Rüsen's chapter is devoted in its entirety to the argument that what European unification needs in order to succeed, in addition to the Euro, is a common historical consciousness, which Rüsen likens to a common cultural currency. This concept, in fact, gives the title for his chapter: '"Cultural Currency": The Nature of Historical

Consciousness in Europe.'[45] This cultural currency, he explains, is urgently needed for economic and political unification: 'There is a need for the common currency to be accompanied by a corresponding "cultural currency" that could help the European nations and their citizens to identify culturally in the already existent economic area, so that they can treat it as their own.' He makes it clear that 'such a cultural currency cannot be introduced, prescribed, and pushed through the same way as has been done with the "Euro."'[46] How is this then to be done? Principally through the schools and their history curricula, with fact-based content presented in the form of narrative. 'What matters is concrete historical knowledge about aspects which define Europe historically,'[47] he explains, before launching into a long list of what the building blocks of such a concrete knowledge should be.

What, then, has become of the history-teaching model described in the first part of this essay? The scale – now covering all of Europe – may be greater, but isn't history still serving the same ends here as it did earlier for individual nations? We will take up this question again in our conclusion.

But first, let us note the paradoxical appearance at the same time – in Europe especially, but not only there – of public commemorations of a national nature. This refocusing on the nation seems to run counter to the supranational trend we have seen.[48] As Patrick Garcia[49] has observed, France is far and away the leader in this regard, having staged great public ceremonies to commemorate the bicentenary of the Revolution, the conversion of Clovis, and so forth. At the same time, the French have taken to celebrating what Pierre Nora has called 'places of memory,'[50] that is, monuments, institutions, symbols, or social practices whose character is, or seems to be, typically French. Should we see these types of celebration or commemoration as representing a certain resistance to the imposition of a supranational historical consciousness? Is this apparent reawakening in the French of a sense of their own history a counterweight to the idea of Europe? *Mutatis mutandis*, might we ask the same question of other countries with similar practices? Canada, incidentally, comes to mind, with its local heritage fairs subsidized in recent years by the wealthy, private Historica Foundation.

Conclusion: What Does the Future Hold?

Finally, what should we understand of the historical consciousness trend and what can it contribute to historical education? That question was our point of departure in this essay.

Having posed it, we began with a review of the present state of historical education. We then discussed some of the factors leading to the introduction and spread of the historical consciousness trend in the field of history.

We have discussed the transition from a history pedagogy devoted to the nation-state to a pedagogy in the service of democracy, whose aim is the formation of independent-minded, rational citizens, capable of critical thinking. Rather than the imposition of a ready-made historical narrative, our present goal is to equip students with those intellectual tools that, taken together, constitute what we call 'historical thinking.'

Can 'historical thinking' collaborate successfully with the historical consciousness trend in the teaching of history?

'Practical orientation and identity–building are the decisive functions of historical consciousness,' Jörn Rüsen explained in his article cited above.[51] We have found nothing in our overview of the trend to contradict this assertion. A disturbing question remains: will students be free to use these functions independently, orienting themselves as they like?

We have cited several examples of efforts to redirect historical consciousness toward European unity. One could find many other examples, in many different countries, of such efforts on a national level. Take, for example, this reflection by a French historian: 'Would a version of our history which brought us together by asking tough questions instead of edifying and moralizing help us to reconstruct our national life, to recreate a common polity in which newcomers would want to participate?'[52] Another French author, concerned about the painful legacy left by French colonial wars, declares: 'At the crossroads of a new century, the reinvention of French identity is taking place through the creation of a "unifying sense of shared memory."'[53] Similar opinions (which have contributed in no small way to our interest in this subject) have been expressed in Canada. For example, in Quebec, Gérard Bouchard, in his proposal for historiographical reform, has called for a national history that would bring all Quebeckers together, a version that would 'consolidate and, if possible, reconcile opposing visions.'[54] Elsewhere, Jocelyn Létourneau calls for 'the great collective history on which the country's vision of itself will be based.'[55] Similarly, in English Canada, Jack Granatstein, in a recent broadside, has railed against all forms of history teaching other than the traditional unifying shared narrative.[56] And Rudyard Griffiths, in the name of the Dominion Institute, calls for a single and unified history of Canada for use in the schools, because 'the men and women who wrestled the country's identity from the political morass of pre-Confederation Canada and the battlefields of Europe and North America deserve nothing less.'[57] We could mention many other examples, in Canada and elsewhere.[58]

Are we not witnessing a return here, in a somewhat modernized form, to the unifying and legitimating historical discourse of years past?

Let it be said that such a discourse may, on occasion, recommend itself by the nature of its goals, which, like some of those we have cited earlier, may be valid and even desirable from a social point of view. Furthermore, it would be naive to imagine that a history curriculum mandated by a public authority would not harbour some degree of intent at social orientation and, explicitly or not, offer the great themes of a common historical narrative for the awakening of historical consciousnesses of its youth.

Should we not, then, accept this dual pedagogical reality – of history teaching, on the one hand, that furthers the creation of a common historical consciousness and, on the other, of historical education aimed at the acquisition or development of historical 'thinking.' Let us keep in mind, however, that the latter alone will hold the key to independence of thought and freedom of choice. It will also function, to some extent, as an antidote for those who would want to resist the imposition by others of an alien historical consciousness and choose instead to create their own.[59]

Notes

Translated by Susan Darnton.

1 In *On History* (New York: The New Press, 1997), 275.

2 On this topic, see Jörn Rüsen, 'The Didactics of History in West Germany,' *History and Theory* 24, no. 3 (1987): 275–86.

3 The results of the survey were published in four parts, from vol. 7, no. 2 (1986) to 9, no. 2 (1988) of *Information/Mitteilungen/Communications* (of the International Society for History Didactics).

4 Donald Reid explains it this way: 'The goal of historical literacy is to develop students' skills to construct arguments based on partial and sometimes conflicting evidence of different kinds and to assess the arguments of others rather than succumb to relativism.' In 'Social History Goes to Class,' *History and Theory* 40 (October 2001): 397.

5 I have treated this subject in 'A l'assaut de la mémoire collective: Discours et pratiques de l'histoire scolaire au tournant du XXIe siècle,' *Traces* 38, no. 4

(November–December 2000): 18–26. See also the work of Sirkka Ahonen on the recent use of 'grand narrative' for the purpose of constructing social and political identity, in this case in Estonia, where it has been used in the traditional way, to nurture national consciousness: 'Politics of Identity through History Curriculum,' *Journal of Curriculum Studies* 33, no. 2 (2001): 179–94.

6 See *Les Cadres sociaux de la mémoire* (Paris: Alcan, 1925; re-edited 1952 and 1994); and *La Mémoire collective* (Paris: PUF, 1950; re-edited 1968).

7 'Afterword' in Dan Ben-Amos and Liliane Weisbert, eds, *Cultural Memory and the Construction of Identity* (Detroit: Wayne State University Press, 1999), 297.

8 In France, the historian Henry Rousso, writing about the contemporary period, has stated that 'scarcely twenty years ago, the word "memory" was almost never used by historians, and was never mentioned in course offerings or university textbooks.' 'Réflexions sur l'émergence de la notion de mémoire,' in Martine Verlhac, ed., *Histoire et mémoire* (Grenoble: CRDP de l'académie de Grenoble, 1998), 76.

9 This course has been offered in grade 12 since the beginning of the school year in the autumn of 2002. For another example of the important role that identity plays in the teaching of history nowadays, we could cite the summer school for the teaching of Canadian history sponsored by the Historica Foundation (Montreal, 16 July 2001), whose theme was 'Exploring Our Identities.'

10 *Le Problème de la conscience historique* (Louvain: Publications universitaires de Louvain, 1963). This lecture was first published in English only in 1975, in a New School for Social Research review; a French reprint, in an edition by Le Seuil, appeared only in 1996.

11 Paris: Gallimard.

12 See 'Mémoire et conscience historique dans la France contemporaine,' in Verlhac, ed., *Histoire et mémoire*, 90.

13 Paris: Retz-CEPL.

14 Paris: PUF.

15 New York: Harper and Row, 1968.

16 See *Memory Cast in Stone* (Oxford: Berg, 1998), 1. 'In the mid-1980's,' the author writes, 'the issues of history and historical consciousness had gained a renewed importance in anthropological theorizing.' The connection with history-in-the-making was very apparent at that time. Thus, Berg writes, 'the worldwide growth of nationalism and other forms of identity politics in the late 1980's meant that an understanding of the uses and abuses of the past in service of present purposes was placed high on the agenda for anthropology' (p. 2).

17 The 'reappearance,' one might say, in light of the publications of Halbwachs in the 1920s and again in the 1950s and of a few other works that
failed to generate discussion. In 'On the Emergence of *Memory* in Historical
Discourse,' Kerwin Lee Klein agrees: 'Outside of experimental psychology
and clinical psychoanalysis, few academics paid much attention to memory
until the great swell of popular interest in autobiographical literature,
family genealogy, and museums that marked the seventies.' In *Representations* 69 (Winter 2000): 127.

18 'Entre histoire et mémoire: Une histoire sociale de la mémoire,' *Raison
présente* 128 (1998): 10. In the same spirit, Michel Wieviorka writes, 'Until
the sixties – religious texts and mythology aside – history enjoyed an almost
total monopoly in public discussion of the past. Then memory appeared,
with a new legitimacy and strength derived from the transmission of eye-
witness accounts and actual experience.' In 'Retours de mémoires,' *Le
Monde des débats*, November 2000: 10.

19 For Rousso, see 'Réflexions sur l'émergence de la notion de mémoire'; for
Bédarida, see 'Mémoire et conscience historique dans la France contemporaine'; both of them in Verlhac, ed., *Histoire et mémoire*, 78ff. and 90ff.

20 In his analysis of interest in history and its function, Marc Angenot recently
assessed the idea of progress: *D'où venons-nous? Où allons-nous? La Décomposi-
tion de l'idée de progrès* (Montreal: Trait d'union, 1991).

21 On the pervasiveness and the misuse of the concept of heritage in society,
one might look at David Lowenthal, *The Heritage Crusade and the Spoils of
History* (Cambridge: Cambridge University Press, 1998).

22 Pierre Nora, ed., *Les Lieux de mémoire*, 7 vols (Paris: Gallimard, 1984–93).
An abridged English version exists as well: *Realms of Memory: Rethinking the
French Past*, 3 vols (New York: Columbia University Press, 1996).

23 These reforms in Great Britain, France, and the United States were mentioned earlier in passing. A number of other countries – and many Canadian provinces, notably Quebec – have already instituted similar changes or
are in the process of doing so.

24 'Retours de mémoires,' 10.

25 A discussion of the principle of the redeeming quality of history-as-memory
can be found in John Torpey, '"Making Whole What Has Been Smashed":
Reflections on Reparations,' *Journal of Modern History* 73 (June 2001): 333–
58.

26 'Retours de mémoires,' 10.

27 'Towards the Coach in the History Classroom,' *Canadian Issues / Thèmes
Canadiens*, October–November 2001: 12. Gaffield also notes that 'more and
more professors recognize that changes since the 1960's have undermined

the view of students as containers awaiting content and of history as a Truth to be revealed' (14).

28 'Afterword,' in Ben-Amos and Weisberg, eds, *Cultural Memory and the Construction of Identity*, 297.

29 'Mémoire et conscience historique,' 76.

30 'Some Random Thoughts on History's Recent Past,' *History and Memory* 12, no. 2 (2001): 49.

31 In the article 'Mémoire collective,' *(L'Encyclopédie de) La Nouvelle histoire* (Paris: Retz-CEPL, 1978), 399.

32 In collaboration with Linda Rosenzweig, we have considered some of these in 'Teaching and Learning History: Developmental Dimensions,' chapter 5 of *Developmental Perspectives on the Social Studies* (Washington: National Council for the Social Studies, 1982), 54–66.

33 See *L'Histoire à l'école, matière à penser* (Montreal: L'Harmattan, 1999).

34 We should also mention that, in the eighties, a behaviourist trend appeared that tended to accent the goals of education while neglecting the contents. This also irritated teachers.

35 See Peter Lee and Rosalyn Ashby, 'Progression in Historical Understanding among Students Ages 7–14,' in Peter N. Stearns, Peter Seixas, and Sam Wineburg, eds, *Knowing, Teaching, and Learning History* (New York: New York University Press, 2000), 199–222.

36 James F. Voss and Mario Carretero, eds (London: Woburn Press, 1998).

37 On this topic, see also my 'La Recherche empirique en éducation historique: Mise en perspective et orientations actuelles,' *Perspectives documentaires en éducation* 53 (2001): 69–82. One might also look at Bronwen Swinnerton and Isobel Jenkins, *Secondary School History Teaching in England and Wales: A Review of Empirical Research, 1960–1998* (Centre for Studies in Sciences and Mathematics Education: University of Leeds, 1999).

38 Gabriele Bucher Dinç, ed., *Looking Back–Looking Forward: Understanding History in Europe* (Hamburg: Körber-Stiftung, 2000), 115–76; the bibliographical section is entitled 'Teaching of History, National Identity, and Historical Consciousness.' See also Sharon Macdonald, ed., *Approaches to European Historical Consciousness: Reflexions and Provocations* (Hamburg: Körber-Stiftung, 2000).

39 Magne Angvik and Bodo von Borries, eds, *Youth and History: A Comparative European Survey on Historical Consciousness and Political Attitudes among Adolescents* (Hamburg: Körber-Stiftung, 1997). Vol. A: Description; vol. B: Documentation; a database on CD-ROM is included.

40 Ibid., A:23; see also A:20 and A:22.

41 Some have gone so far as to suggest that the concept itself might be limited

in scope to a specifically European historical consciousness. Thus, in an article devoted to a definition of the term, Katia Fausser writes, 'The English term "European Historical Consciousness" serves as an approximation of the German "Geschichtsbewusstsein."' See 'Historical Consciousness: Dimensions of a Complex Concept,' in Macdonald, ed., *Approaches to European Historical Consciousness*, 43.

42 Macdonald, *Approaches*, 7, 8, and passim. The italics are ours.

43 Fausser, 'Historical Consciousness,' ibid., 43.

44 Among other publications, see his 'The Didactics of History in West Germany,' *History and Theory* 24, no. 3 (1987): 275–86.

45 In MacDonald, *Approaches*, 75–85. I would like to thank Jean-Pierre Charland for bringing the title of this work to my attention.

46 Ibid., 76.

47 Ibid., 77.

48 On this subject, see John R. Gillis, ed., *Commemorations: The Politics of National Identity* (Princeton, NJ: Princeton University Press, 1994).

49 In 'Commémorations: Les enjeux d'une pratique sociale,' *Raison présente* 128 (1998): 25.

50 Nora, *Les Lieux de mémoire*.

51 '"Cultural Currency": The Nature of Historical Consciousness in Europe,' in Macdonald, ed., *Approaches to European Historical Consciousness*, 78.

52 Verlhac, ed., *Histoire et mémoire*, 21.

53 Alain Gresh, 'Inventer une mémoire commune,' *Le Monde diplomatique – Manière de voir* 58 (July–August 2001): 97.

54 'Une Nouvelle perspective pour l'histoire du Québec,' *Spirale*, May–June 2001: 27.

55 In 'L'Avenir du Canada: Par rapport à quelle histoire?' *Canadian Historical Review* 81, no. 2 (Summer 2000): 230.

56 *Who Killed Canadian History* (Toronto: HarperCollins, 1998). See especially chapter 2: 'Teaching Ignorance: History in the Schools.' Among many other critical pieces written in the same spirit, but with more technical expertise, one could cite Bob Davis, *Whatever Happened to High School History?* (Toronto: James Lorimer, 1995).

57 'Mistakes of the Past,' *Globe and Mail*, 18 September 2000: A13.

58 We are thinking, for example, of the major conferences on the teaching of Canadian history organized recently by the McGill Institute for the Study of Canada and by the Association for Canadian Studies, and of the efforts of the Historica Foundation, the Dominion Institute, Canada's National History Society, the CRB Foundation, and of Radio Canada with its *Canada: A People's History*. It is troubling to note, in passing, that several of these

projects were supported – at a cost of millions of dollars – not by educators or even by politicians, though some of them are involved, but by businessmen. Europe has experienced the same phenomenon. For instance, the Körber-Stiftung, which supports the publications in the Eustory Series and other similar projects, is the offspring of the Körber Corporation, a large German mechanical engineering firm. Moreover, the first really school-like textbook on the history of Europe, a collaboration by twelve European historians, was the brainchild of another businessman, Frédéric Delouche (published by Hachette in France and by Weidenfeld and Nicolson in England, in 1992 and 1994, respectively). Such interest in history education on the part of the business world might invite us to overlook Henry Ford's unfortunate pronouncement, 'History is bunk,' but should in no way allow us to forget Eric Hobsbawm's warning against the possible misuses of history, with which we began this chapter.

59 In other words, as Sirkka Ahonen, citing Noam Chomsky, reminds us, '[E]verybody has to go to a school of intellectual self-defense in order not to be manipulated by texts.' In 'The Past, History, and Education,' *Journal of Curriculum Studies* 33, no. 6 (2001): 750.

The Pedagogical Insistence of Public Memory

ROGER I. SIMON

July 13, 1944. Sore Voloshin is approaching the *maline*, the hideout, where the Voloshin and Rudashevski families hid for several weeks after the liquidation of the Vilna Ghetto. Sore had been with the Jewish Partisans since October 1943, when she escaped murder at the hands of the Germans, and now, with the liberation of the city by Soviet troops, she has returned to Vilna. She writes:

> With halting steps I climb the stairs and reach our room. I become short of breath. I glance at the four empty walls and immediately go up to the attic. Without a ladder, with great difficulty, I lift myself up. I reach our *maline*. A shudder goes through me. For here my whole family lived during the liquidation of the ghetto and from here they all went to Ponar ... I begin to dig around in the sand. Perhaps something will turn up? ... In a corner, covered with dirt, lies a notebook ... These are my friend Yitzhok's notes – his Diary of the ghetto ... I started to wipe the dust and sand off each page. After cleaning them, I began to read with bated breath. On each and every page I saw before me what had happened to us, all that had taken place and the great suffering ... I cannot think anymore. I now see only our *maline*, a corner of the attic, where he sat and read a book, still and silent, speaking only infrequently. Now only his diary remains, which tells us so much about his impressions, about what happened to him and all his experiences.[1]

The German army occupied Vilna (Vilnius) on 24 June 1941. At the time there were nearly 70,000 Jews living in the city. During July and August approximately 30,000 Jews were murdered, most shot at the killing fields at Ponar by Germans and their Lithuanian accomplices. On 6 September 1941, Vilna Jewry was driven into a ghetto. Mass *aktions* against the Jews continued until late December 1941. By that time another 20,000 Jewish people had been murdered. During the first months of 1942, a period of relative stability was established for the remaining ghetto population, most of whom worked in factories in support of the German war effort. During these months, under indescribably horrific conditions and constant threat of individual execution and mass annihilation, the Jewish population reorganized itself into a complex and multifaceted community.

Yitskhok Rudashevski, fourteen years old at the time the German army entered Vilna, kept a diary during his incarceration in the ghetto. Its scattered pages found by Sore Voloshin, this text survives as Rudashevski's testament of life in Vilna under Nazi subjugation. In the fall of 1942, he wrote of his participation (with other young students) in a communal effort to chronicle a history of the ghetto:

> Thursday the 5th [Nov. 1942] – Today we also went to [an apartment block] with the questionnaire for investigating the ghetto. We did not get a good reception. And I must sadly admit that they were right. We were reproached for having calm heads. 'You must not probe into another person's wounds, our lives are self-evident.' She is right, but I am not at fault either because I consider everything should be recorded and noted down, even the most gory, because *everything will be taken into account* [italics mine].[2]

Rudashevski predicts that everything will be taken into account; he expects it, anticipates it. Indeed, we presume that he would have demanded it. His diary, as with many other diaries kept by Jews under Nazi subjugation, is written with a doubled address. As an 'act of responsibility that situates the diarist and the diary within a relation to the community and its ebbing way of life,'[3] it is addressed to those to whom it is accountable, the Jews of the Vilna ghetto, the vast majority of whom were murdered before the end of the war. But it is also addressed to those who have yet to come, those yet born, whose gesture of welcome is nonetheless expected. In this sense, Rudashevski wrote into a future that we, if not uniquely, then singularly, inhabit. What has arrived is not only his account, but his expectation, his insistence, his claim that now, in our time, indifference is not an option: 'everything must be taken into account.' But this arrival is problematic, its welcome onerous and awkward. A response is expected; everything must be taken into account.

But how should this be done? Who is required to do it? And for how long must this remain a task?

It is to questions such as these that my colleagues and I in the Testimony and Historical Memory Project at the University of Toronto have devoted ourselves. Our current work is focused on contemporary questions of 'Holocaust Memory' and specifically the challenge of reading, listening to, and responding to the testament of the Jews of the ghettos of Lodz and Vilna; the diaries, memoirs, video testimony, poetry, songs, and visual images that are the traces of what once was. Central to this work is the consideration of the possibilities of learning inherent in a creative form of collective study – rigorously referential and reflexive – a form of historiographic poetics the writing of which is itself a practice of remembrance.[4] Yet while I gesture to that work now, my purpose here is not to detail the practice of this poetics, but rather to speak of its larger pedagogical and ethical design, its memorial impetus, the broad framework of our approach that we believe has considerable generality; something we have called 'the touch of the past.'[5]

The Non-indifference of Learning to Listen

From its inception, our work has been an inquiry into the responsibilities of historical memory initiated by the testament of those subjected to mass violence, particularly as this violence was perpetrated on persons because of their membership in a larger group conceived of in terms of particular common characteristics. In North America, at the dawn of the twenty-first century, we are inundated with the demands for such memory. There is a flood of stories and images that continue to testify to the violence, oppression, and hatred that have wrought so much suffering and death.

What is one to do with all these stories and images? The list is familiar to some, 'news' to others: the genocide of the Armenians at the hands of the Turks, the race wars such as in those Homewood, Florida, and Tulsa, Oklahoma (as just two events that marked the extensive murder and subjugation of African-Americans throughout the United States during the twentieth century), the Nazi genocide of European Jewry, the Nazi genocide of the Roma, the widespread murder and oppression of Poles and Slavs also by the Nazi regime, the rape and murder of Chinese people by Japanese troops in Nanking, the Cambodian genocide initiated by the Pol Pot regime, the massacre of Timorese civilians by the Indonesian army and the militias supported by that army, the 'ethic cleansing' attempted in Bosnia and Kosovo, the slaughter in Rwanda of Tutsis by Hutus, the murderous violence of the apartheid regime in South Africa, the extensive slaughter of indigenous peoples in Guatemala – and this list is by no means exhaustive! Furthermore, such exacting, unbearable, distinct accounts are not confined only to the century just past, but as well hark back to the long periods of colonial expansion, the genocide of indigenous peoples, and the cross-Atlantic slave trade.

As they arrive in the form of books, memoirs, poetry, archives of audio and video testimony, exhibitions, video and film documentaries, newspaper accounts, and Internet websites, a frequent response is, What is being asked of me, as the one (the one that could be anyone) to whom these stories are addressed?[6] Inherent in this response is indeed the realization that the transitive character of these texts and images demands of their readers a logic of accountability. They demand a reckoning; not only a taking in of stories, but a taking of stories into account, the practical working through of a logic of accountability, a non-indifference. And as difficult as it might be for any of us – given our psychic and social limits – to be responsive to such demands, there are various options open to us: memorialization (mark what happened so that it should not be forgotten), historical study (understand why it happened), retribution (people must be held accountable for their actions), apology (acknowledge complicity in what happened), reparation (social and material repair must be made), 'never again' (don't let anything 'similar' happen again), and reconciliation (new possibilities for living together must be initiated).

All of the above forms of non-indifference are significant and consequential, and all constitute difficult but vital questions in regard to the possibilities for justice and a reconstructed human futurity. Our work at the University of Toronto, however, is devoted to a different response, a different form of non-indifference, although one that parallels and complements those above. Our concern is with remembrance as simultaneously an ethical and a pedagogical practice. Thus our overriding question: what practices of response to the arrival of the demands of testament might enable an opening into learning, not just in terms of the acquisition of previously unheard of, unknown facts and stories, but also as an opening of the present in which identities and identifications, the frames of certitude that ground our understandings of existence, and one's responsibilities to history are displaced and rethought. In other words, how might remembrance be understood as a praxis creating the possibilities of new histories and altered subjectivities?[7]

Our interest then is in new memorial spaces, temporal and ontological boundary spaces that advance, encourage, and enable practices of critical learning through which one might explore the fundamental terms of relation with an absent presence that – through the trace of testament – arrives asking, demanding something of us. The endeavour of such spaces is the invigoration of what Derrida calls 'learning to live with ghosts.'[8] The consequence of such learning extends to reworking notions of community, identity, embodiment, and relationship. In effect, this reworking requires us to contemplate a revised notion of the political that supplements conventional questions of power (questions of who gets to decide for whom the privileges, opportunities, and resources that will be made available and withheld within any given community). While never, ever disregarding this dimension of the political, what we are attempting to bring to the fore here is the recognition that remembrance as learning fundamentally reconfigures both a 'politics of relationality' and its associated notion as to what constitutes the character of public life. This is a move toward a critical and risk-laden learning that seeks to accomplish a shift of one's ego boundaries, that displaces engagements with the past and contemporary relations with others out of the narrow, inescapably violent and violative confines of the 'I' to a receptivity to others, to (in Derrida's terms) a 'welcome' of the other's difficult, onerous approach.[9] On such terms remembrance might enact possibilities for an ethical learning that impels us into a confrontation and 'reckoning' not only with stories of the past but also with ourselves as we *are* (historically, existentially, ethically) in the present. Remembrance thus is a reckoning – an accounting – that beckons us to the possibilities of the future, the possibilities of our own learning. What we emphasize is that a politics of relationality is implicated in the examination of how it is each of us reads, listens, learns, and responds to those whose identities, bodies, and memories have been fundamentally impacted by such violence – impacts that cannot ever be reduced to versions of our own troubles and traumas. Thus, we emphasize the importance of remembrance/learning for what it means to live relationally, to live justly and publicly, with others, both living and dead.

On the Touch of the Past

In a recent issue of the journal *Race and Class*, John Berger contemplates the prophetic qualities of Hieronymus Bosch's *Millennium Triptych*.[10]

Focusing in particular on the right-hand panel, which depicts Hell, Berger discusses how the form of the painting prefigures contemporary culture under the threat of globalism. He notes that in Bosch's vision of hell, there is no horizon.

> The world is burning. Every figure is trying to survive by concentrating on his own immediate need and survival. Claustrophobia, at its most extreme, is not caused by overcrowding, but by the lack of any continuity existing between one action and the next which is close enough to be touching it. It is this which is hell. The culture in which we live is perhaps the most claustrophobic that has ever existed.[11]

While Berger goes on to emphasize the lack of an elsewhere or otherwise in this vision of Hell, a condition that reduces 'the given' to an imprisoning actuality justifying self-serving projects and unrelenting greed, it is his diagnosis of a contemporary cultural claustrophobia that I find most evocative. For what Berger is suggesting is a cultural dysfunction actualized by a specific readiness to hand of sound, image, and text that convey the narratives, sentiment, and sensibilities of other people's lives. Brought close through the mediation of book publishing, broadcasting, film and video tape distribution, and Internet web pages, the testaments of people subjected to oppressive circumstances, who have struggled (not always successfully) to survive on historical terms not of their own making, are increasingly evident, present, nearby. Yet these testaments remain fragmented, neither touched by nor touching us.

What would it mean for one to be 'touched' by the testament of another? To be touched by the memories of others is, at first blush, a phrase that brackets a matter of affect. It is commonly used as a synonym for those occasions when one is 'moved,' where one begins to feel a range of possible psychic states in response to another's story: sorrow, shock, elation, rage. There is obviously some form of human connection referenced here. Most commonly characterized as an empathic response to stories and images of other's plight, this is clearly one trajectory through which an archive of narrative and images might be redeemed from its hellish construction as a set of disconnected fragments. But, there are other, less affect-laden possibilities. If 'being touched' amounts to a negation of the fragmentation and isolation of experiences, then also redemptive is the contiguity and causality supplied by the historiographic impulse, which seeks human continuity within historical narratives. Likewise, connectedness of experience is possible in the context of allegorical or emblematic readings wherein one set of experiences is understood through the representation of another. But all these interpretations of the event of 'being touched' limit the force of Berger's observation.

Edith Wyschogrod has suggested that 'touch is not a sense at all; it is in fact a metaphor for the impingement of the world as a whole upon subjectivity ... [T]o touch is to comport oneself not in opposition to the given but in proximity with it.'[12] The proximity she refers to here is not a spatial concept denoting an interval between two points or sectors of space: not a state, a repose, but rather, as Emmanuel Levinas would have it, a restlessness, a movement toward the other in which one draws closer.[13] It is a 'welcome' in which one not only becomes emotionally vulnerable (open to feeling), but also exposes one's self to a possible de-phasing of the ego wherein the cognitive terms on which one makes connection with others is shaken, put up for revision. Thus, more than being moved or being able to integrate the stories of others into the communally established framework ordering one's grasp of the world (past and present), 'being touched' demands taking the stories of others seriously, accepting such stories as matters of 'counsel.'

In his essay 'The Storyteller,' Walter Benjamin referred to counsel as 'less an answer to a question than a proposal concerning the continuation of a story which is just unfolding.'[14] For Benjamin, in order to seek and receive counsel, one would first have to be able to tell this unfolding story. On such terms, for the lives of others to truly matter – beyond what they demand in the way of an immediate, necessary practical solidarity – they must be encountered as counsel, stories that actually might initiate a de-phasing, a potential shifting of our own unfolding stories, particularly in ways that might be unanticipated and not easily accepted. Benjamin was attempting in this essay to reflect on the erosion of the very possibility of the exchange of experience. To him, this exchange was actually being prevented by the proliferation of news reports and the mass dissemination of stories and images that accompanied the meditated transmission of experiences, experiences that he thought were being reduced to a phantasmagoric flow of 'information.' Missing was the 'wisdom' of experience, the possibility that the telling of a story would actually make a difference in the way one's own stories were told, either by opening one's existing narratives to assessment and revision or by influencing one's actions.

Benjamin's diagnosis was that this inability to 'experience' the stories of others (something other than simply being able to read/hear and

recount them) was a historical condition. The etiology of this condition
was to be found not only in the estrangement, forgetting, and dis-
articulation that results from the increasingly rapid flow of images and
words to which the citizen of the modern state is subject, but more
basically in the advance of capitalism as a fundamental logic for the
organization of human sociality. Capitalist relations not only mobilized
and supported an effusion of contemporary re/presentations but, as
well, produced a constriction of what counts as one's own experience,
with the result that the elemental structures of sociality are also increasingly narrowed. But the promise of 'counsel,' the potential for the
experience of others to 'touch' us, is too important to the prospect of
hope, to the possibilities of human futurity, to simply abandon within
the hegemonic prerequisites of a neo-liberal logic. If there is to be a
future – and not just more of the same – central to our present concerns
must be an openness to what Homi Bhabha calls 'translating' cultures
and histories in ways that make it possible to reassess and revise the
stories with which one is most familiar.[15]

Here then is the core of my concern. How might the responsiveness to
the responsibilities of a transitive public memory be enacted as a welcome of 'counsel?' How might the testament of others arrive as something other than the spectacle of suffering – clearly a form of arrival that
might move me emotionally and provoke me into what I hope might be
helpful action, but would not fundamentally alter the stories that orient
my social relations and commitments? While narrated memories are a
sign of civic life, the motivated, authorized character of that *civitas*
immediately raises the issue of how historical memories might construct
a sense of one's connection to those who have gone before us. Public
memory is not just that which contributes to knowledge of the past and/
or underwrites a claim to group or communal membership. Quite diver-
gently, acts of memory must become transitive, actions that 'pass over'
and take effect on another person or persons. This effect is not simply a
coming into knowledge, a causing us to know what we cannot have
known. Rather memory here is literally 'trans-actional,' in its address. It
enacts a claim – providing accounts of the past that may wound, or better
haunt – that may interrupt one's self-sufficiency, demanding an attentiveness to an otherness that cannot be reduced to a version of our own
stories.

It is for this reason that I have become interested in the pedagogical
and political implications of the question of attentiveness.[16] That is, what
form of attentiveness, what mode of sensibility might support the possi-

bility that the memories of others might be accepted as counsel; what would help us to welcome the 'touch of the past' that arrives in the stories – the memories – of other people's lives? And what forms of educative relationships and institutional forms, what elements of new memorial practices, are necessary to sustain such a sensibility, one that might transform lived experience of the inter-human? Much of the current work in Toronto is devoted precisely to these questions. I now want to provide one extended example of what it might mean to concern oneself with questions of attentiveness and their pedagogical consequences.

Listening as a Mode of Thought

Aboriginal communities across North America have been producing written and oral testimony as part of an attempt to contribute to a historical awareness and understanding of the history of Aboriginal–settler relations and the its impact on the lives lived in its wake. A central aspect of this history has been government-initiated removal of native peoples from land they had being living on for centuries. One compelling chronicle of such a forced dispossession and displacement is Ila Bussidor's *Night Spirits: The Story of the Relocation of the Sayisi Dene* (written with the collaboration of Üstün Bilgen-Reinart).[17] In *Night Spirits*, Bussidor provides an account of her people's removal by the Canadian government from their traditional homelands and hunting grounds. On 17 August 1956 the Sayisi Dene were forced from the Caribou country of northwestern Manitoba and taken by a Canso amphibious military aircraft to the barren shores of Hudson Bay near Churchill. Not only does Bussidor write the story of her family as they experienced the relocation and its devastating personal repercussions, she provides as well interview excerpts from various Sayisi Dene who bear witness to the particulars of this shameful event and its tragic, traumatic communal consequences.

Let us listen to some of these words of witness in citations from two accounts that attempt to convey the memories of this event, and then consider what form of attentiveness might be adequate to a responsible response to such testament. First, words from Charlie Kithithee, who was working at Churchill airport the day the aircraft moved the people:

> We were outside, doing casual labour, when the plane landed and the people were unloaded. The plane was a huge aircraft with a round belly. It landed and the people came out one by one. I remember the children

crying and the few dogs yelping to get free. Eventually everything and everyone was unloaded and put on a big truck and driven down into town. They were all taken to the point at Cape Merry. There, the people were dumped to fend for themselves on the shores of Hudson Bay. Winter was closing in. Some of the people set up their tents, and some made makeshift shelters for themselves. One of the tents stood out because you could see the shadows of the people who were sitting inside. Already, the feeling of hopelessness was in the air. There was no laughter, no joy, only dead silence. Even the dogs were not moving. The feeling just hung over the people like death.[18]

Listen now to the words of John Solomon as he describes what happened on 17 August 1956:

The plane came with three white people plus the pilot. They said they came to move the people. The people never replied. We took whatever we could with us, we left behind our traps, our toboggans, our cabins, and we got into that plane. When we got out in Churchill, there were no trees. The wind was blowing sand on everything. We didn't know what to do next. We couldn't do anything there. We couldn't go trapping. We couldn't set a net. There was nothing to hunt. We were in a desperate state. We had nothing to live on.[19]

Testimonial accounts such as those of John Solomon and Charlie Kithithee have the potential to make a transactive claim on Canadian public memory, one with the possibility of shifting the stories that non-Aboriginals tell of themselves and hence of possibly renewing the terms on which to build a redefined relationship between native peoples and Canadians. But what could it mean to listen to such testimonies in order to open oneself to the radical pedagogical and political potential of such memories? What would it mean to attend to these words, welcoming them and thereby opening oneself to the 'touch of the past'?

While accounts such as those of Solomon and Kithithee seem straightforward enough, they can place difficult and serious demands on readers who recognize they are being called to listen to a bearing witness directed toward themselves, a 'telling,' a 'speaking to' of traumatic events that will always exceed the words spoken.

The inevitable limits of the testimonial act mean that narratives and images of historical trauma, such as reported by Solomon and Kithithee, are shot through with absences that, in their silence, solicit questions.

Actively attending to the transitive claims of such testimonies includes more than their simple comprehension, more than registering a few shocking facts that one did not know, more than chalking up more evidence of a history of injustice. Such listening, at the very least, requires an attentiveness to the questions that such accounts solicit, that is, an attentiveness to the compulsion to pose difficult, and at times unanswerable, questions, which nonetheless impulsively press for responses that seemingly (from within one's own entanglement of history and epistemology) promise help in deciphering what is to be heard in a testamentary account.

What is sought in such questions typically is not attached to something within the text but rather to something missing from the text. Rooted not just in textual incompleteness but in one's own insufficiencies, these are not necessarily polite questions. Indeed, it may be troubling to those bearing witness to hear them spoken. Nevertheless, what is crucial to stress is that such questions are affect-laden interrogatives on the part of the listener, marks that the testimony heard is breaking the well-ordered frame that regulates our everyday sense of how human relationships take place. Thus it is that more than one non-Aboriginal reader of *Night Spirits* has asked the question (minimally, to themselves): given the lack of information as to why they should move, the sudden unexpected arrival of the plane in mid-August 1956, the short time they were given to collect belongings (a few hours), the fact that only four white people (the Indian agent, two officials of the Department of Indian Affairs, and the pilot) arrived to initiate the move, and the absence of reports of people being threatened if they resisted being removed, why did the Sayisi Dene get on the plane? Why didn't the people simply refuse to comply with the government agents who told them to do so?

Now we may indeed interpret this question as being not simply impolite or even cruel, but violent and obscene. This obscenity is rooted in at least two possibilities. Given that the testament of mass suffering and subjection is often spoken or written as an attempt to heal oneself and one's community from the disordering of trauma, such witness requires readers and listeners who are supportive, empathetic respondents. Thus, in some instances, questions and critical judgments may actually be experienced as a return of psychic violence. Furthermore, to the extent that a question such as 'Why did they get on the plane' carries an accusation of complicity in the acceptance of government authority, it re-victimizes the Sayisi Dene and works to alleviate government responsibility for the forced removal and its consequences. Indeed, in my view, when the genesis of a question such as this is left unexamined, there is little to redeem this form of 'curiosity.' True, one may take the pedagogical position that no question is inappropriate and that, indeed, such a question can be taken as a teachable moment for the provision of information regarding the long history of the development of British and Canadian state-structured authority as it imposed itself on and became entwined with the lives of Aboriginal peoples. However, the provision of information rarely addresses the generative basis of such a question. If information is provided as authoritative history that cancels the question, it may in fact short-circuit the pedagogical process, which takes as problematic one's practice of listening to others.

It is the possibility of a critical, transformative attentiveness that offers listeners the chance to redeem their obscene questions. This attentiveness begins when we view such questions as *symptomatic* of the difficult knowledge[20] contained in the testimony of the Sayisi Dene, knowledge that places a disruptive claim on its non-Aboriginal listener and requires a degree of self-reflexivity in order to be responsive and responsible to that claim. Testimonies such as those of Solomon and Kithithee often carry a surreal quality for those who find such experiences unimaginable. In this sense, they lead to the query, How can this be so? How could this have happened? Faced by testimony whose texture unhinges one's sense of 'how things happen,' one often seeks a 'shadow text,' an unstated secondary narrative that provides an explanatory set of propositions that could recover and reinscribe a lost sense to a testimonial account.[21] Drawing on taken-for-granted knowledge and beliefs in order to provide workable interpretations that make traumatic events and experiences less incomprehensible, shadow texts may be written not only with partial historical knowledge but, as well, with misconceptions, misinformation, myths, projections, and prejudice. Thus, whether and how the writing of shadow texts is attempted implies much in regard to how the obligations of witnessing are enacted. The work of attempting to provide at least some partial explanation or rationalization that might stabilize our understanding of what happened in the past is an effort to establish a basis on which the memory of a testimony might be claimed. Yet if one is to be open to the transitive claim of historical testament, one must recognize, as Terrance Des Pres suggests, that often 'the figures through which we experience the arrival of such testament are genuine transgressors ... disturber(s) of the peace ... runner(s) of the blockade ... erect[ed] against knowledge of "unspeakable" things.'[22]

Thus a responsible listening to the testimony of the Sayisi Dene may require that we face up to the question of how to hear accounts of Aboriginal-Canadian history that bear witness to displacement, death, and degradation. This is not merely a matter of an individual's readiness to hear such accounts. Certainly, most people read Bussidor's book without experiencing a loss of significance in regard to the social arrangements that inscribe their everyday lives. Perhaps they will be shocked, perhaps they will 'weep' (as a promotional statement for *Night Spirits* suggests), and perhaps they may demand that the government atone for its actions through symbolic and material means. Much more radically, however, we are still left with the question of how are we to hear and remember the stories such as those of Solomon and Kithithee in ways that incorporate them into an intelligible past, while recognizing that there is an insistence in their stories that calls for reopening the present to reconsideration.

It is for this reason that symptomatic obscene questions asked in the face of testimony hold enormous pedagogical potential. To actualize this potential means, however, recognizing that such questions arise from the claim on the listener that testimony initiates and that in order to respond responsibly to this claim we must rethink how to accomplish the act of listening. A responsible listening thus may require a double attentiveness, a listening to the testimony of the one who is speaking and, at the same time, a listening to the questions we find ourselves asking when faced by this testimony. It is then that we might ask ourselves, in hearing a testimonial account, Why are we asking the questions we do? Why do we need to know this? In other words, in order to work through a responsible listening, rather than setting our questions aside or simply posing the questions to (for example) Bussidor and her people, we must pose questions to ourselves about our questions, interrogating why the information and explanations we seek are important and necessary to us.

The first consequence of this reflexive turn to the grounds of our own questions may be the realization of our own insufficiency to hear the testimony of Bussidor, Solomon, and Kithithee – our own inexperience and our own historical ignorance. Surely an initial response to this insufficiency would be learning more about what happened to the Sayisi Dene, collecting as much information as one can in regard to the relocation and its consequences. To this might be added further study of the history of Aboriginal–settler relations and of how this history is implicated in the event and consequences of the relocation. However, as I have been suggesting, simply acquiring more information will never suffice if one is to respond to the force of a testimonial address, a force that, if acknowledged, puts ourselves into question. Thus, we would have to not only try to alleviate our own ignorance but transform the very grounds for its existence in the first place. Crucial here would be the recognition that our insufficiency to hear the testimony of another is in itself a historical insufficiency, one with structural conditions that hold it in place. Thus, too, we are challenged to study our own education and its limits, beginning to understand how the social arrangements of our lives and the investments that they inculcate are not only incomplete, but deficient at least in terms of what we need to know to welcome testament and reconstruct the substance of Aboriginal–non-Aboriginal relations. But such a formulation of the learning inherent in questioning our questions is far too limited. Ignorance is not simply a rationally orga-nized state of affairs, but is, as well, a dynamic, unconscious structure that fosters resistance to knowledge.[23] Thus, an exploration of our own insufficiencies means attending to what presumptions and defences the Sayisi Dene testimony elicits. This would be an attempt to not only learn *about* this testimony, but to learn *from* it by working through the vaguely felt and little understood psychic projections and culturally invested frameworks that order our attention to narratives that speak to past lives and places.

The recognition of insufficiency, however, sets only one half of the learning agenda. The other half requires yet another turn in the prac-tice of critical remembrance. This is an openness to the possibility that our questions are not really questions at all, but rather rhetorical state-ments based on the premise that we really are able to understand what we are being told, that indeed we have heard of similar things happening before, and that we can understand (and judge) testimony on these terms. Thus is set another learning task, defined as a response to the following questions: What other histories are elicited by us when hearing testimony of Solomon and Kithithee? How does this displacement of the relocation of Sayisi Dene on to other histories condense what, in fact, are separate realities? What knowledge and understanding is subjugated in this process of displacement and what perspective might be gained in it? And what is our relation to these 'other' histories, and how is compre-hension of Solomon and Kithithee's testimony filtered through our struggles to understand these other instances, particularly those includ-ing forced population removal, for example, the Nazi attempt to make Europe *Judenrein* or the recent Serbian attempt at 'ethnic cleansing' in Kosovo? It is not that one can ever completely eliminate the practice of judgment in hearing the stories of another (nor would such an elimination be desirable); rather what is at issue is taking full measure of how and why the terms of our judgments are invoked in the practice of listening, and what this prevents us from hearing.

Holding together the doubled moments of attentiveness to testimony, one informational, the other reflexive, is one way to bind together remembrance and learning. If such a practice is brought to a space of public memory, learning could be more than knowledge acquisition and remembering, more than the retrieval, recollection, or recall of something past but now forgotten. It may be objected that the reflexivity I suggest as being necessary to the formation of a public memory is a narcissism that turns an engagement with history toward a concern with oneself rather than the concerns of others. After all, what is important about the Aboriginal testimony is that it makes a claim on us to learn of events hidden to most North Americans, to hear a story of people who suffered and died unnecessarily and as a result of government action, and to work in solidarity with those who are still living the legacy of this event and attempting to recover a viable and dynamic communal life. The fundamental issue is to recognize an injustice and take the measure of what changes must accrue as a result. But what must accrue as a result is not only memorialization of the forced removal and retributive justice for the Sayisi Dene but, as Bussidor and other Dene recognize, a change in the way non-Aboriginals view their shared history with native peoples. For this change to happen, we will have to learn to listen differently, take the measure of our ignorance, and reassess the terms on which we are prepared to hear stories that might trouble the social arrangements on which we presume a collective future.

Education and Public Memory

That which is being given in and through the testimony collected in *Night Spirits* is a memorial inheritance whose importance exceeds the immediacy of one's own personal exposure to these memories. Bussidor's own testimony and the testimonies collected by her make a claim on public memory. This is particularly so if we take public memory as a sphere for developing a historical consciousness – not as an individual awareness and attitude but as a commitment to and participation in a critical practice of remembrance and learning. Such a transitive memory is a move away from a notion of the public sphere as an innocent dream, a consolation, and a conceit that through the mass dissemination of images and stories an informed public will act once it has the relevant information.[24] It is also a move away from a public sphere as a space wherein stories are reiterated in an attempt to secure the permanence of collective affiliations and identifications. Rather than being employed for spatial consolidations, public memory would become a time of interminable and exacting learning not where one is just informed through remembrance but where one learns to remember anew.

On such terms, public memory bears responsibility for the past to the present, reopening the present in terms demanded by a just hearing of the past. Such an interruption underscores the potential radical pedagogical authority of such a public memory in that it may make apparent the poverty of the present, its (and our own) insufficiency and incompleteness, the inadequacy of our experience, and the requirement that we revise not only our own stories but the very presumptions that regulate their coherence and intelligibility. On such terms, public memory has the potential to expand that ensemble of people who count for us, whom we encounter not merely as strangers (deserving compassion, but in the end having little or nothing to do with us), but as 'counsellors,' people who in telling their stories change our own. In regard to the practice of fostering such a public memory, our responsibility would be not only to support the inclusion of forgotten or unknown histories that pertain to our contemporary problems and relationships, but to help constitute public memory as a pedagogical space by making evident and supporting the critical exploration of the questions, uncertainties, ambiguities, and failures that arise in the process of trying to be responsive to the testament that speaks to these forgotten or unknown histories.

If the public means us, us in our exposure to others, then today 'we' cannot be something given in advance, not the sum total of all of us somewhere or sometime, not a pre-existing community or a people; rather we are something that comes after the image/text, something assembled in the possibility of response to an open address. As Tom Keenan suggests, 'the public, we could say in shorthand, is what is hailed or addressed by messages that might not reach their destination.'[25] Keenan's suggestion seems to me quite important for refiguring the notion of how to think the concept of 'the public' within a social practice of remembrance. Public memory is not something given in advance, it is what is at stake in the transitive address, an address that may not reach its destination. The public is not here evoked as an unproblematic 'we' – a we that could incorporate everyone into a homogeneous category of the citizen subject. Rather, it is meant to reflect the idea of a people summoned to the responsibility of responding to the accounts of others.

One cannot, and need not, minimize the importance of personal, local memories for the formation of ourselves and our communities. But when we are called to attend to testament attempting to convey experiences that bear on the possibilities of new and better relationships among diverse members of the political economy we find ourselves within, it is necessary to affirm one's commitment to creating those spaces and conditions within which we might realize the pedagogical possibilities inherent in the transitive character of public memory. Such possibilities are founded in the acceptance of the responsibility to attend to the concerns of those such as the Rudashevski, Solomon, and Kithithee, who arrive facing us; who in speaking and writing to us draw near, demanding – not just apology, memorialization, and reparation – but something of our time, energy, and thought – thought that includes the difficult challenge of rethinking itself. This demand is no mystifying abstraction; it precisely resonates with Benjamin's requirement that to receive counsel one must be able to think one's story as it is unfolding. We must learn how to tell ourselves this story in ways that enable the recognition that those who approach us bearing the burdensome gift of their testament are 'genuine transgressors' whose words refuse to be reduced to the terms of our prevailing categories and, indeed, are necessary for the invention of new forms of social life.

Notes

1 Sore Voloshin in Y. Rudashevski, *The Diary of the Vilna Ghetto*, trans. Percy Matenko (Israel: Beit Lohamei Haghetaot [Ghetto Fighters' House], 1973), app. C, 147–9. This is the first testimony of Sore Voloshin-Kalivatsh on the turn of events leading to her discovery of the diary.

2 Rudashevski, *Diary of the Vilna Ghetto*, 84.

3 D. Patterson, *Along the Edge of Annihilation: The Collapse and Recovery of Life in the Holocaust Diary* (Seattle: University of Washington Press, 1999), 23.

4 Roger I. Simon, M. DiPalantonio, and M. Clamen, 'Remembrance as Praxis and the Ethics of the Inter-human,' *Culture Machine* 4 (February 2002); http://culturemachine.tees.ac.uk.

5 Roger I. Simon, 'The Touch of the Past: The Pedagogical Significance of a Transactional Sphere of Public Memory,' in Peter P. Trifonas, ed., *Revolutionary Pedagogies: Cultural Politics, Instituting Education, and the Discourse of Theory* (New York: Routledge Falmer, 2000).

6 'Left to Our Own Devices: On the Impossibility of Justice,' in Tom Keenan,

ed., *Fables of Responsibility: Aberrations and Predicaments in Ethics and Politics* (Stanford: Stanford University Press, 1997), 7–42.

7 L.J. Frazier, 'Subverted Memories: Countermourning as Political Action in Chile,' in Mieke Bal, J. Crewe, and Leo Spitzer, eds, *Acts of Memory: Cultural Recall in the Present* (Hanover: Dartmouth/University of New England Press, 1999), 103–19.

8 Jacques Derrida, *Specters of Marx: The State of the Debt, the Work of Mourning, and the New International*, trans. Peggy Kamuf (New York: Routledge, 1994).

9 'A Word of Welcome,' in Jacques Derrida, *Adieu: To Emmanuel Levinas* (Stanford: Stanford University Press, 1999), 15–123.

10 J. Berger, 'Against the Great Defeat of the World,' *Race and Class* 40, nos. 2/ 3 (October–March 1998): 1–4.

11 Ibid., 3.

12 Cited in Martin Jay, *Downcast Eyes: The Denigration of Vision in Twentieth-Century French Thought* (Berkeley: University of California Press, 1994), 557. See also Edith Wyschogrod, 'Doing before Hearing: On the Primacy of Touch,' in F. Laruelle, ed., *Textes pour Emmanuel Levinas* (Paris: Jean-Michel Place, 1980), 179–203.

13 See esp. chapters II ('Intentionality and Sensing') and III ('Sensibility and Proximity') of Emmanuel Levinas, *Otherwise than Being or Beyond Essence*, trans. Alphonso Lingis (Pittsburgh: Duquesne University Press, 1998).

14 Walter Benjamin, *Illuminations*, trans. Harry Zohn (New York: Schocken Books, 1969), 86.

15 See esp. 'How Newness Enters the World: Postmodern Space, Postcolonial Times and the Trials of Cultural Translation,' in Homi K. Bhabha, *The Location of Culture* (New York: Routledge, 1994), 212–35.

16 Roger I. Simon, 'The Contribution of Holocaust Audio-Visual Testimony to Remembrance, Learning and Hope,' *International Journal on Audio-Visual Testimony of Victims* 1 (June 1998): 141–52. See also Roger I. Simon, 'Innocence without Naivete, Uprightness without Stupidity: The Pedagogical *Kavannah* of Emmanuel Levinas,' *Studies in the Philosophy and Education* 22, no. 1 (2003): 45–59.

17 Ila Bussidor and Üstün Bilgen-Reinart, *Night Spirits: The Story of the Relocation of the Sayisi Dene* (Winnipeg: University of Manitoba Press 1997).

18 Cited in Bussidor and Bilgen-Reinart, *Night Spirits*, 48.

19 Ibid., 46.

20 For a discussion of the concept of 'difficult knowledge' see Deborah P. Britzman, *Lost Subjects, Contested Objects: Toward a Psychoanalytic Inquiry of Learning* (Albany: State University of New York, 1998). See also Deborah P. Britzman, 'If the Story Cannot End: Deferred Action, Ambivalence, and

Difficult Knowledge,' in Roger I. Simon, Sharon Rosenberg, and C. Eppert, eds, *Between Hope and Despair: Pedagogy and the Remembrance of Historical Trauma* (Lanham, MD: Rowman and Littlefield, 2000).

21 For discussion of the concept of 'shadow text' see Roger I. Simon and W. Armitage-Simon, 'Teaching Risky Stories: Remembering Mass Destruction through Children's Literature,' *English Quarterly* 28, no. 1 (Fall 1995): 27–31. See also Roger I. Simon and C. Eppert, 'Remembering Obligation: Pedagogy and the Witnessing of Testimony of Historical Trauma,' *Canadian Journal of Education* 22, no. 2 (Spring 1997): 175–91.

22 T. Des Pres, *The Survivor: An Anatomy of Life in the Death Camps* (New York: Oxford University Press, 1976): 42–3.

23 For a classic essay on ignorance as unconscious refusal to know see Shoshana Felman, 'Psychoanalysis and Education: Teaching Terminable and Interminable,' *Yale French Studies* 63 (1982).

24 Tom Keenan, 'Publicity and Indifference (Sarajevo on Television),' Shorenstein Center, Harvard University, 30 March 1998, http://www.bard .edu/ hrp/keenan/sarajevo.htm (permission granted for citation).

25 Ibid.

A Dialogue on Narrative and Historical Consciousness

EDITED AND INTRODUCED BY
KENT DEN HEYER

How might historical consciousness be defined for purposes of comparative studies? Does historical consciousness denote a form of human comprehension or a prescription for what ails it? Is historical consciousness primarily positive, in adding to comprehension, or negative, in taking away easy summations of historical others? Who is the subject of the study of historical consciousness, they in the past or we here today? Is it memory, personal, scattered, and torn as consciousness, or the historical, collated and collected according to objective community standards, that is the object of pedagogical intervention?

The following dialogue, initiated by Roger Simon and conducted primarily with Jörn Rüsen, followed the presentation of the first round of papers at the symposium in August 2001. This dialogue incorporated profoundly different approaches to historical consciousness. Including it in this collection provides future readers with a trace of the once lively, direct, and collegial engagement with significant issues at hand.

Both Simon and Rüsen approach historical consciousness as an orientation towards moral reflection and action. Their approaches, however, are distinct and divergent with regard to identity, recognition, and narratives. Simon's work reflects a sceptical French tradition filtered through North American cultural studies. He explores historical consciousness as a sort of existential encounter with the interpretive limits of concepts and narratives used to understand past lives and events. Rüsen's approach, in contrast, reflects a more empirical tradition emphasizing the necessity of conceptual frameworks with which to discuss and measure how the past becomes meaningfully present.

For Simon, a historical consciousness is a moral awareness that traces of the past arrive 'demanding something of us.' Rüsen too recognizes that the past demands something of us, but that something is cognitive coherence and moral action formed through narrative interpretations by the subject in one of four ways (as in his chapter in this volume). Rüsen's premise is that we comprehend the past in the form of narratives. Through 'narrative competence,' Rüsen postulates, historical consciousness informs moral deliberation by connecting past, present, and future into a perceived actuality. Narrative competence brings this actuality into focus along with concomitant moral obligations. By creating a typology of possible narrative interpretations of the past, as his work seeks to do, empirical recearchers may ask questions such as 'What role does historical consciousness play in everyday life, in politics, and in other spheres of life? Are there laws governing its development that are analogous to the laws that govern the development of logical, moral, and other cognitive skills, particularly as they have been outlined by Piaget?' Where Rüsen cools study of historical consciousness through guiding concepts and typologies, Simon heats it up by questioning the institutionalized and ritualized forms of attentiveness to others.

Simon's interests in historical consciousness lie not with the cognitive or empirical realm but in the social performance and poetry of remembrance. As a social practice, commemoration, for example, directly links past to present to create coherence out of 'heteroglossia' and communities from fleeting passions and identifications. In the dialogue below, Simon questions Rüsen's use of narrative, identity, and recognition as the basis of thinking through historical consciousness. From the perspective of those influenced by French psychoanalytic and post-structuralist thinkers, identity and recognition signify fragment, fracture, and palimpsest. As concepts, they are better suited as objects of enquiry rather than grounds for investigation.

As he mentions in the conversation below, *trace* for Simon is not a line connecting past, present, and future, but rather a signifier, always less than that which it signifies. Narratives, he seems to posit, elide this partiality in a fantasy of wholeness between past and present. His work at the University of Toronto explores practices of remembrance premised on the insufficiencies both of the trace and of our means of reception. Through 'historiographic poetics,' historical traces (bits of narrative, photos, extracts from diaries, and other artefacts of the Shoah, for example) are arranged precisely to indicate where the ability to narrate meaningful explanations fails. This incompleteness itself demands new practices of reception.

The topic of how narratives function to shape cognition and demonstrate veracity has received much attention in the humanities and social sciences. It serves as a sort of talisman of scholarly communities. Considered as a form of cognition, narrative is a vehicle to configure significant parts into more comprehensible wholes. As partial and politically invested social performance, narrative holes, rather than wholes, signal where moral lessons begin when that vehicle breaks down.

SIMON: As a response to several people, I'd like to start with raising questions about two things: the sufficiency of identity and recognition as the basis of talking about historical consciousness or memory, and two, the sufficiency of narrative as Jörn talks about it in his paper as an organizing concept for understanding the form of collective memory ... My own feeling is that neither identity or recognition nor narrative - as important as these organizing concepts are for understanding historical consciousness - are sufficient for defining the range of phenomena that we are potentially interested in. I think that how one takes up these particular issues of what is the underlying purpose of memory and what are its potential forms or modes of representation and transmission have a lot to do with questions of how we talk about hope, how we talk about the notion of history's function in how it brings us together or not as human beings. So that's sort of an opening gambit I suppose.

RÜSEN: My question simply is, can you even think of presentation of memory not being a narrative?

SIMON: Yes.

RÜSEN: Give me an example.

SIMON: The first response that we ask from people who are participating in our groups is for a non-narrative response. The argument is that the task of memory is not necessarily to develop a grasp of an understanding of the event that one can transmit through narrative. Rather, the first task of memory is to confront the traces of lives lived in times and places other than one's own and to try to come to grips with the sufficiency or insufficiency of one's self in relationship to the adequacy of responding to those traces. The juxtapatory method is deliberately non-narrative because it attempts to hold, in the very structure of the juxtaposition itself, the breakdowns, the contradictions, and the insufficiencies of narrative form that are basic responses to the historical material that people are asked to wrestle with. What is important about that is found in a slightly edited version at the end of Sam's [Wineburg] paper. This is incredibly important I think. Sam says that

> our inability to perceive the experiences of others is a reason why the study of history is so crucial. Coming to know others, whether they live on the other side of the tracks or the other side of the millennium, requires the education of our sensibilities. This is what history when taught well gives us practice in doing. What allows us to come to know others is our distrust of our capacity to know them, our skepticism towards the extraordinary sense-making abilities that allow us to construct the world around us ...,

our distrust of those abilities ... There is an important point to practices of remembering which aren't sufficiently dealt with simply with the notion of the creation and transmission of narratives that serve the function of identity and recognition. There is another way of constituting the operation of remembering that I think is important for us to talk about and add to the agenda. This is my response.

RÜSEN: What you are saying is very important to us all. Maybe there are trans-narrative elements in this, but we need a concept. What if it is not narrative, if it is not this very specific time or temporal mental structural narrative, what is it then? Because is it simply a description? What I could hear from you is not that they [participants in your groups] refuse narratives; they refuse meaningful narratives! They have the feeling that the established, the culturally established forms of narrating something, have broken down in respect to this very specific event. Even using the word 'event' presupposes a narrative. You speak of traces ... well, that is a metaphor. A trace is a line in a course of time. If you want to understand it, how can you do that without trying to put what the traces stand for into a temporal connection which makes sense under this type of story?

SEIXAS: I think it's a very interesting and important point to follow through. So why don't we have one more contribution to this.

SIMON: Okay. First of all, I'm using the term 'trace' actually in a technical way, not to be a line that goes through the past, but the notion of a difference between a signification and the inability of the signification to fully represent that which it signifies. This is a Derridean/Levinasian notion of the trace. The importance of focusing on any set of documents is to recognize the insufficiency of those documents in relationship to the adequacy of how those documents represent and what it is we can know. Of course, we can only have those documents as a way of accessing lives and other times or places. But to pretend that those documents are adequate to those lives is silly, in a way, and naive. It's important to figure out how one is going to ... engage the possibility of responsibly remembering, given the slippage between the sign and what it is signifying ...

I want to go back to a more basic kind of question because I think it's an issue that our fundamental questions and interests are different in terms of what it is that we are most interested in as a set of issues or phenomena to be theorized. ... The way I understand your work, it's about the way in which historical knowledge gets mediated into historical consciousness; historical knowledge not being the same thing as historical consciousness. Historical consciousness is how, as you put it, people mediate in a variety of complex ways how the past becomes meaningful to them. I am interested in ... *spaces of remembering* that have the possibility for opening up ... ways of engaging representations of the past, significations of the past, open[ing] up the possibilities for thinking about how we are to live our lives as human beings and what prospects for hope ... might exist in the present. They [your concerns and mine] are complementary, but they are not the same ...

I mean that there are other ways of thinking about the notion of historical consciousness that have to do with ... [its] being a property of performance spaces within which we look at the question of how and· why the activity of remembering becomes important to people and what prospects it has for ourselves as individuals, as groups, and as a society as a whole. These are different kinds of activities, different kinds of issues and problems. So, in this sense, I wanted to open up this space of historical consciousness.

SEIXAS: Okay we have a challenge, in a sense, from Roger; that there are two tasks here that are fundamentally different. I would like to see whether other people have comments, concerns, questions, confusions about the dialogue that has just gone on here. I myself am a little puzzled by the notion that there are two different projects here. I hear different sets of terms being brought to bear, but I don't see yet that there are two different projects. So, let me just open it up to that.

LEE: When you were saying that the first reaction of your people is not a narrative one, were you talking in terms of otherness and distance? ... is that the kind of initial reaction?

SIMON: The initial reaction, as you would predict, if you ask people to talk about or construct in a meaningful way a set of archival materials, is a narrative because that is the way people talk to each other about the meaning of history ... absolutely. Take Sam's position as an alternative point. He says what is important is our insufficiency to understand the lives of others or the education of our sensibilities in terms of having some humility in relationship to the complexity of alterity. That is, in many ways, the way I'd read the last part of his paper. I keep coming back to Sam's paper because I think it's the most concrete way in which something really different enters into the conversation.

What we've done ... basically is to create a protocol for trying to hold a particular way in which people might engage the past that is different from the basic narrative reflex. That first move is a non-narrative one. That first move is basically a practice of citation: taking images, quotes, anything that people can find in the archive that they are working with and constructing anywhere from one page to a twenty-page series of citations which act as a juxtaposition that embodies their response to the kinds of questions, contradictions, astonishments, and the insufficiencies to hold the past that they've been asked to engage in relationship to the archival material. We are asking people to, in a sense, represent their inability to create a narrative, where the narrative breaks down. This begins to open up onto what I would call the education of their sensibilities in terms of thinking about in what ways our lives are structured so that [they're] insufficient to hold the past, and what particular transformations might be necessary in our thinking. In a way, the past becomes a very difficult past because it opens up challenges to the sufficiency of our own frames of understanding to incorporate and hold a representation.

LEE: I'm trying to grasp what it is that is not narrative here exactly in your response ...

SIMON: The first response is ...

LEE: ... bafflement, amazement, you mentioned.

SIMON: ... astonishment and contradiction. I mean my understanding, and I may be misreading Jörn's position, but Jörn says clearly that narrative is not simply text and that there are narratives in visuality, absolutely. The basic organizing notion of narrative is some logic of synthesis within which a logical statement can represent the relationship between a series of events that have occurred through time. You are trying to tell a story and the notion of story has an underlying logic of synthesis associated with it. That is the notion of narrativity that I think is being discussed here. When you signal the breakdowns of that, through juxtaposition, juxtaposition as a form can hold onto issues of breakdown and contradiction in ways that stories cannot. It is not that stories or narrative aren't important. I'm just saying that there is ... [an] alternative for the process of remembering ..., which doesn't centre only on the production of narrative itself. There is another moment that is quite important. I am trying to argue for the importance of that moment and gesturing towards Mark [Phillips] and Sam and the kinds of things they have to say.

RÜSEN: First of all, I would say that there are constitutive non-narrative elements for any historical narrative. In that respect we do not have a dissent. Listening to you, and of course I have to digest your arguments, I would say two things. First of all, for me a narrative is an answer to a question. You described the question and the question is that there were experiences of difference which have a temporal indication which are astonishing, which are disturbing, and that is what you are focusing on. Disturbing means they do not fit into the pre-given historical framework of reference ... Now realizing this insufficiency, there is a type in my theory which is really based on that. I call that 'critical sense generation.' That means 'destroy the narratives!' This means that, even in a dialectical way, a procedure of historical sense generation is still related, and let's say constituted, by the narrative paradigm. It is a destruction of a narrative but even this belongs to, in my theory at least, that very complex *narratology* of history. So that is my offer to you to come to a peace treaty!

WERTSCH: I think probably for a lot of these discussions we are going to have to resort to something called 'functional dualism' or 'multiple functionality' because, your [Rüsen's] statement just now, for you a narrative is an answer to a question. There is a sense in which I agree. I think it also, at the same time, serves another, at least one other, function. What tends to happen in a lot of our discussions is that we privilege one or the other. At an earlier discussion we spoke about how neuroscientists are suddenly included in a lot of these discussions. When they talk about memory, for example, I think, to the extent they are talking about narrative at all, they are talking about a different function of narrative, dealing with what I would call its referential function. It never usually enters their discussion at all that you would think of one narrative answering another, whereas, if you talk to people in the collective memory business or historical consciousness, as with Barbara Hernstein-Smith, narrative is the dialogue among memories. So, this is not to say I agree with everybody and we are all happier, but I think that narrative and many other terms, memory, for example, have multiple functions and it makes sense then to try to look for this multiple functional picture and realize what is highlighted in one case or another. Psychology just doesn't raise this issue of the dialogic function of narrative. They look at narratives as the way of grasping together information for referential appearance ... I think Roger is getting to issues here about the inherent limitation of narrative as a kind of a textual resource. Narratives can be as dangerous as they are useful. You do not just want narratives to wrap up things and get us off the hook in a simple way, but they have a tendency to do that. But, it is very hard to imagine memory in non-narrative form beyond very beginning steps; I mean first struggling towards a narrative with the limitations built into it is part of the problem.

LORENZ: I have a question for clarification. Would you [Simon] clarify the way you use the term 'remembrance'? What I got from your paper is that you confront people with archives. In what sense do you apply the notion of remembering related to this type of experience?

SIMON: Obviously remembering is not remembering what happened to you. I have used different terms at different times. I started off using the word 'commemoration,' but that seemed to be a bit too celebratory for many people. The reason why I chose commemoration is that when I first got into working in this area I knew that commemoration primarily was about a set of particular social activities located in time and space where people came together to do something in relationship to recalling of the past. So when I'm using the term 'remembrance' – not so much remembering, but remembrance – I am actually talking about particular activities. The creation in time and space of particular activities where people are organized through a particular set of norms and a particular

set of agreed upon rules about how they are going ... to engage in a
practice of recalling the lives of people who lived in other times and
spaces. That recall is not such an individual recall; it's a recall that's
organized in the performance of people being, as competent members,
able to participate in remembrance activities in that space, the
performative aspect. This is sort of an educator's question in the sense
that I'm interested in creating public spaces, whether it is in schools or
not, within which new possibilities for learning from remembering can
actually take place ...

The notion of hope is extremely important and the function of utopia
I am not ready to give up personally. There is a dual track that I want to
pursue around these issues. One concern with politics is at the level of
the decisions around issues of power related to distributions of resources
and equity and so forth. Another [concern] ... has to do with ... how we
confront and understand differences and what does it mean to engage
each other in relationship to difference, I think the kind of thing that
Sam gestures towards. One of the interesting pieces that was very influential for me in rethinking the notion of the range of possibilities of
constituting hope was worked by Andrew Benjamin, a philosopher, in
the first chapter of his book *Present Hope: Philosophy, Architecture, Judaism.*
He takes up a Levinasian position which basically articulates the idea
that the possibility of futurity lies in the rupture of the 'always the same.'
There is a need to constitute the present as insufficient in order for
futurity to be possible. There is a moment of hope in the very coming to
grips with the notion of the insufficiency of the present in relationship to
history and remembering ... The reconstituting of the very possibility of
different terms in the present is actually a hopeful moment because it
provides the ground for the possibility of futurity that is impossible if the
present continues on as always the same. So that there's another kind of
thinking about hope which is obviously a post-modern conception which
I think I want, and I'm trying to hold that together with more traditional
modernist conceptions of hope rooted in messianic visions as important
ways of thinking about the function of history.

RÜSEN: Well, for me the last fifteen minutes of the discussion is of
extreme interest ... I think we can agree that the way of future-relatedness of socialism and nationalism is not worthwhile to regain or revital-
ize. That is not the point of your argument. I understand you in a way
that the collapse of both kinds of future-relatedness is a chance for a
completely new, categorically new, future perspective in dealing with the

past. The problem is that the way we do it, the post-modern way, is just missing the point. Post-modernism is not hope, but hopeless. For hope, there must be something 'pre.' If 'pre' something, then there is future relatedness. But 'post' is just the contrary. In nationalism and socialism and in the traditional modern way of future relatedness of historical consciousness there is a hidden teleology. Somebody here even used the notion of 'telos' in order to characterize hope. The point is teleology means that the future relatedness still is bound by constraint coming from the past. It is a narrow future. What we have to bring about is a non-telelogical future perspective. And here I would not speak of insufficiency. Insufficiency means we go some steps further and we have it. Can we go beyond the possibilities pre-given by experience to something radically different and new? It is a non-teleological future perspective. If we introduce this into the field historical consciousness then the whole logic of making sense of time is changed. Because then we construct or we tell narratives of the past from the future perspective that is beyond the historical experience. And that might be what you find is the way people do it. Whether that is narrative or not, that is not so important. It is a really new way of making the future a sense-bearing principle of dealing with the past and that might bring us in a secular way back to some traditions of religious transgressing of the horizon of experience; changing the origin in favour of some unknown, hoped-for future. But I think today, in the work of collective memory or historical consciousness, there is an issue of secular historical work, of doing history in a post-teleological and pre-hopeful way!

PART III

The Politics of Historical Consciousness

It is one thing to theorize about the relationship of academic historians and the shaping of collective memory through state institutions; it is quite a different thing to study how this relationship actually works. In this era of accelerated social, cultural, and political change, regimes around the world struggle to remake what is taught in schools, presented in museums, and represented in monuments. As conceived by office-holders responding to various political pressures, the question is 'What deserves to be remembered?' The problem is one of collective memory: less George Washington, more Sojourner Truth; less Voertrekkers, more Stephen Biko; or less Japanese internment, more D-Day. The task then becomes one of constructing the *lieux de mémoire* to assure remembrance.

Peter Novick noted the increasing engagement of historians in the public sphere some time ago.[1] At times historians find themselves at odds with pressure groups, as when American veterans lobbied for the cancellation of the Enola Gay exhibit at the Smithsonian. At other times, historians' own ranks are divided, as when the Canadian Broadcasting Corporation incensed Canadian veterans with revisionist docudramas on Canada's role in the Second World War. There were vocal members of the profession on both sides, as well, when the U.S. Senate condemned the National History Standards originally commissioned by the National Endowment for the Humanities.[2] Historians engaging in these battles, whichever side they take, deploy the tools and standards of the discipline as their chief weapon: if the claims they make wield the weight of 'the truth' it is because of the methods that lie behind them. But the public turf on which these wars are waged are subject to rules of engagement quite different from those of the academic symposium. And the claims of collective memory, of special debts to the legacies of the injured and the dead, often trump the historians. With even just a few examples, it quickly becomes clear that there are no general rules for the dynamics of these engagements.

Nonetheless, we can learn something from each case. Tony Taylor, director of the Australian National History Project (now the Commonwealth History Project), provides an insider's view of the attitudes and activities of federal politicians, academic historians, and schoolteachers during the past decade. He concludes (1) that the political interest shown in school history by a conservative federal government (1996–2001) stems from nineteenth-century liberal values, manifested in different forms by different politicians; (2) that many academic historians have recently lost touch with school history, leaving a few senior, influential academics to play key roles in reviving the subject in the schools; and (3) that schoolteachers remain cautiously (and perhaps justifiably) sceptical about both the academics and the politicians. In every jurisdiction, these players constitute the bare minimum. To them may be added any number of organized groups whose members seek an imagined redress for past debts and wrongs through a legacy in the historical consciousness of future generations.

In the closing chapter, John Torpey brings a critical lens to the whole phenomenon. The uneasy fit between the politics of collective memory and the discipline of history has become an issue because of the surge of interest in the past expressed in a variety of ways by many sectors of the population at large, coinciding with a broad questioning of the authority of experts – accountants and doctors as well as historians. The sense of breakage drives people off in quest of roots, foundations, and solid connections to the past in order to define identities that are no longer given. If this loss cannot be redressed fully by the work of historians, movie producers and marketing specialists leap at the opportunities it affords. Torpey argues that the inflated gaze backward is a substitute satisfaction that has arisen in response to the collapse of the future-oriented collective political projects of socialism and the progressive nation-state. He reminds us of the power of more future oriented narratives, which dominated historical consciousness less than a generation ago.

Notes

1 Peter Novick, *That Noble Dream: The 'Objectivity Question' and the American Historical Profession* (Cambridge: Cambridge University Press, 1988).
2 Edward T. Linenthal and Tom Engelhardt, eds, *History Wars: The Enola Gay and Other Battles for the American Past* (New York: Metropolitan Books, 1996); Gary B. Nash, Charlotte Crabtree, and Ross Dunn, *History on Trial: Culture Wars and the Teaching of the Past* (New York: 1997). Senate of Canada, 'The Valour and the Horror: Report of the Standing Senate Committee on Social Affairs, Science and Technology,' 1993.

Disputed Territory: The Politics of Historical Consciousness in Australia

TONY TAYLOR

Setting the Scene: Remembering Gallipoli

April 25th is a sacred day in the Australian calendar. It marks the occasion of the Gallipoli landings in 1915 when Australian and New Zealand Army Corps (ANZAC) soldiers and sailors, together with British and French troops, began their ill-fated Great War campaign against the Turks, an eight-month conflict that resulted in a total half a million casualties on both sides.

Anzac Day is commemorated as a national holiday, in remembrance of a tragic occasion (almost) universally considered to have drawn the parochially inclined post-Federation states together in the development of an Australian national identity, still referred to (subject to a variety of interpretations) as the 'Anzac spirit.' Each year, hundreds of thousands of men, women, and children march in cheerful but respectful fashion through the streets of Australian cities and towns. Each year, thousands of Australians travel to the remote Gallipoli Peninsula to witness a dawn ceremony of remembrance. There are few comparable events celebrating the histories of other nations. Unlike the 4th of July in the United States or the 14th of July in France, for example, Anzac Day is not a celebration of a remote, but pivotal, historical triumph. It is an emotion-charged commemoration of an event just within living memory, an episode that, moreover, remains Australia's greatest military defeat.

In April 2001, approximately 15,000 Australian visitors, many of them youngsters, trekked to Turkey to commemorate the Gallipoli landing. Interestingly, this is a similar number to the complement of Australian

ANZAC Corps soldiers who originally landed in Gallipoli on the original Anzac Day.[1] This phenomenon, where many thousands of young people travel 16,000 kilometres to a remote Turkish peninsula to commemorate the traumatic founding of a nation, is but one telling aspect of a novel and vigorous interest in the past among Australians. And it is not just on that one day that the visitors come:

> Australian tourists are thickly spread in Eceabat (a nearby port) and surrounds – and with special purpose ... It's not just on Anzac day that visitors converge, although naturally the dawn service is well patronised ... Year round, the visitors come ... There is an air of tranquility and deep sorrow here.[2]

It seems an odd thing to do, to celebrate the birth of one's own nation by travelling to the other side of the globe to visit a national *lieu de mémoire*. On the other hand, if military campaigns are to be thought of as providing defining moments in the development of national identity (the Battle of Britain, the Plains of Abraham, Gettysburg, Koniggratz; Tsushima), the travelling comes as no real surprise. Australia is fortunate enough never to have fought a conventional war on its own territory, but during the Great War, two-thirds of Australia's all-volunteer forces became casualties in overseas campaigns, and Gallipoli is regarded as a monument to that level of sacrifice as well as to the creation of a nation.

Gallipoli and the Politics of School History

One visitor to Gallipoli in April 2000 had been the Conservative-Liberal prime minister John Howard.[3] Shortly after leaving the Turkish peninsula, Howard arrived in Paris for a tour of Western Front battlefields. The prime minister, an admirer of Margaret Thatcher and Robert Menzies and a politician with an unapologetic reputation as a strongly conservative ideologue, then made some off-the-cuff remarks. He commented that, in his view, school history in Australia was deficient because 'there was perhaps a little too much of an emphasis on issues rather than on exactly what happened.' He stated that he had been inspired by the large numbers of young people at Gallipoli: 'They all had a simple, uncluttered pride in what had happened. I haven't seen that kind of, sort of unqualified love of a country and a country's history in my life before.'[4] He further remarked that it was possible for Australian children to go through school and not know anything about the development of Australia's 1901 Federation or the world wars. Such impromptu, doorstep comments represented a surprisingly interventionist response from Howard, until then not known for taking too much interest in educational issues.

These prime ministerial remarks were significant in three respects. First, Howard's observations represented, at the highest political level, a public endorsement of the significance of school history in defining national identity. Second, his remarks were, in essence, a typically conservative view of what history education is about, namely, a transmission-based learning model focused upon the acquisition of key facts and the commemoration of significant events of national importance. Finally, and more important, the doorstep comments seemed to be setting a clear political agenda for history education and for the development of historical consciousness in Australia.

This agenda, it could be argued, was based on Howard's world view, described at one stage by a leading historian as 'a largely benign story of heroic achievement,'[5] a revisiting of nineteenth-century Whiggish progressivism. That being the case, Howard's comments, although brief, created a furore back in Australia, where academic historians, history educators, and teachers challenged what seemed to be a conservative political attack on school history. Peter McPhee, of the University of Melbourne, represented the prevailing view of many in the history community when he disputed the prime minister's 'simplistic understanding' of history because, 'while there was a factual basis to history, history is not just facts.'[6]

Howard's remarks on school history, however, while they were unexpected and contentious, are less surprising if we consider the background to his Paris comments. The year 2001 was to mark the centenary of the Federation of the Australian colonies, a celebration dear to the prime minister's heart. Howard, self-described as 'the most conservative leader the Liberal Party has ever had,' is an ardent nationalist (although a committed monarchist still). Demonstrating a keen interest both in memorializing Federation and in remembering Australian participation in both world wars, his speech came at a time when the survivors of the Gallipoli landing had dwindled to but a handful, thus diminishing any direct connections with events in 1915. Importantly also, Howard's own father and grandfather had fought in the same battalion during the Great War battles on the Western Front, providing a very personal link with those events.

Thus, while it could be argued that Howard's attitude to history represented a new, politically motivated, and ostensibly nationalistic interest in school history, it was also representative of a personally inspired view of what constituted history education. At the same time, it could also be suggested that the prime minister was using the examples of Gallipoli and the Western Front as a way of establishing a clearly conservative trend in historical explanation, with this new, traditionalist direction then being allowed to influence school history through political pressure on the curriculum.

An explanation for this turn of events might be found if we examine the contrast between the prime minister's views on history in the year 2000 and his publicly expressed views before his 1996 electoral success.

Before his first general-election victory as party leader in 1996, Howard, a lawyer by training, had shown little overt interest in school history while showing great interest in historical interpretations of current controversies, an interest that reflected his firm middle-class values but had little direct effect because of his role as an opposition leader. However, once in office, he almost immediately waded into what was for him a new arena with a hard-hitting traditionalist analysis: in his 1996 Sir Thomas Playford Memorial Speech he accused 'cultural dieticians in our midst' of an 'insidious attempt to rewrite Australian history in the service of a partisan political cause.'[7]

At the same time, in his Sir Robert Menzies Lecture in Melbourne, Howard referred to an ongoing public debate that had become known as 'The Battle of History.' This debate, he asserted, was part of a Labour plot to establish a politically correct version of history, in his view a failed tactic that he described as being 'without substance, without honour and without success ... because it was seen by the vast majority of Australians for the divisive, irrelevant and prejudiced attack that it was.'[8]

Since 1996 the prime minister, together with his foreign minister, Alexander Downer (who has a degree in politics and economics), have maintained an interest in broad historical debate, which was taken right into the Olympic arena in 2000. For example, in October 2000 the prime minister commented that 'the negative view of Australian history which is portrayed by some of our detractors like Robert Hughes [author of *The Fatal Shore*] has been delivered a huge serve [attack] by the result of the [Olympic] Games'[9] and (almost contradicting himself) 'I think it is very wrong of people to try and hijack the atmosphere of the Olympics for their particular version of history. I think that it a hugely wrong thing to do.'[10]

Foreign Minister Downer too had already joined in the crusade against allegedly left-leaning historical interpretation. 'History is a very powerful weapon,' he remarked in 1996; and, in commenting on a 'Labour' view that links with Asia had only recently been developed during Labour administrations, Downer said, 'There is no Labour tradition in foreign policy. Labour hasn't been in power often enough in the 20th century to have one.'[11]

The conclusion has to be that Howard and his colleagues, exasperated by the activities of what the prime minister perceived to be an un-Australian, leftist cabal, chose, in his Paris remarks, to redress the balance at a time when political attitudes to history and to school history had reached the forefront of Australian public debate, a phenomenon that was itself a major turnaround after decades of apparent neglect of the discipline at the school level.

History: A National Inquiry

This high-profile revival of interest in school history among politicians, including Howard, stemmed in part from recent polls and surveys that had apparently shown a disconcerting lack of awareness among Australian citizens of the major characters and events in their own nation's history. For example, a 1997 survey by the Centenary of Federation Council had shown that only 18 per cent of those interviewed knew the name of Australia's first prime minister (Edmund Barton), while 43 per cent of interviewees did not know what Federation meant. These 'horror story' survey results (which had their parallels in Canada, the United States, and the United Kingdom) had, among other factors, provided the impetus for a major (and unexpected) National Inquiry into School History (1999–2000), funded by Howard's federal government.[12]

In November 1999, Dr David Kemp, the Commonwealth Minister of Education and Head of the Department of Education Training and Youth Affairs (DETYA), announced the setting up of the National Inquiry into School History. The announcement caught the education community unawares, since school history had not figured at all as part of the major reform strategy agreed upon earlier that year at an important Adelaide ministerial conference by Kemp and all state/territory ministers of education.

Members of the history community were gratified at the news. There had been a growing anxiety among academic historians, who claimed that the study of history in schools and in universities had been under siege for at least a decade, resulting in a loss of interest in schools and declining numbers of students taking the subject at university. These anxieties had been expressed repeatedly in public and professional forums, so much so that Kemp, himself a former lecturer in politics and history, finally agreed to hold an inquiry to examine what was actually happening in the schools.

Considering the provenance of the Inquiry and the sudden nature of its proclamation, notwithstanding a sense of relief that school history was being taken seriously, there was some suspicion among the history community that party politics may have been behind its announcement. As it happened, that was not to be the case, at least as far as the Inquiry was concerned. The same could not be said for the broader historical debate.

Party Politics and School History: 'Balancing' the Debate

At first glance, the idea that senior conservative politicians should take such an active interest in school history by setting up a national inquiry, at a time when there tended to be a sharper focus on more functional curriculum issues such as literacy, numeracy, and information-technology skills, seemed curious. This phenomenon is more explicable, however, when we examine the backgrounds of key Australian political figures a little more closely.

First, in recent years, for good or for ill, Australia experienced an unusual level of interest in history, and even a strong advocacy of historical studies, among its senior politicians. On the Labour side, the former treasurer (1983–91) and prime minister (1991–6), Paul Keating, a working-class autodidact with a passion for Mahler and French Empire clocks, offered a 1992 (50th anniversary) revisionist view of the 1942 Fall of Singapore which then excited some British military historians because of its vituperative, anti-imperialist nature. Moreover, Keating's main prime ministerial speechwriter was Don Watson, a historian of some standing in the academic community. Keating's career as a public commentator on historical issues is summed up neatly by academic historian Greg Pemberton:

> Famous for his pungent and controversial comments on Australian history, Keating used history frequently and effectively to pour scorn on previous conservative governments' records, accusing the Liberals of being the party of an outdated Menzies-era, Anglophile past while Labour was continuing to lead Australia on an independent path into engagement with economi-

cally booming Asia. Who can forget Keating's formidable parliamentary response to [a conservative manifesto] *Fightback* in February 1992 when he ridiculed 'the two Johnnies' – John Hewson [then conservative leader] and John Howard – for harking back to a 'golden age' of the 1950s and for the 'tugging of the forelock' by the 'Menzies and Caseys' to the British establishment after the imperial defence system, in which they believed, collapsed in Singapore in 1942?[13]

The list of historically minded politicians goes on. The then leader of the Federal Labour opposition, Kim Beazley (a former Rhodes Scholar), remains a military history buff. Labour Premier of New South Wales Bob Carr (who has a master's degree in history) had established a pioneering New South Wales History Council. Carr also received a Fulbright award for his services to history. Interestingly, Carr, a conservative Labourite, echoed the Howard view when he once commented, 'Patriotism springs from a knowledge of your country's history.'[14] Finally, Geoff Gallop, Labour Premier of Western Australia, another former Rhodes Scholar, is a political scientist with an interest in history.

In the Liberal/National Party camp there are fewer politicians with a formal background in history, but what they may lack in numbers they make up for in importance. Not only did Howard consider himself the 'History Prime Minister,' but the then education minister, David Kemp (who has a doctorate in political science), is firmly and publicly committed to the belief that historical understanding is an absolute prerequisite for an informed electorate in a democratic society. Tony Abbott, one of Kemp's close colleagues (and yet another former Rhodes Scholar), commented that Kemp 'is a man who is committed to the principles of a liberal conservative political philosophy and the values of choice, excellence, more competition and a better appreciation of our country's history. These are all the things which David has in the marrow of his bones.'[15]

Indeed, one of Kemp's major initiatives, before the National Inquiry, had been the historically based *Discovering Democracy* civics education program, which distributed curriculum kits to every school in Australia and also provided professional development for participating teachers. The seriousness with which Kemp and his conservative associates regarded civics education may be gauged by the budget for *Discovering Democracy*. Between 1997 and 2001, the Commonwealth government committed $29 million to the program.

Moreover, in announcing the 1999 National Inquiry into School History, Kemp referred back to *Discovering Democracy* when he suggested that '[t]he recent Republic Referendum, and Remembrance Day have once again highlighted the growing desire of young people for greater knowledge of the history of our country and our democratic process.'[16] To highlight the need for an inquiry, Kemp pointed out that, despite this high level of public interest, the number of students studying Australian history at the senior school level was in steep decline, a phenomenon, it was implied, that was especially to be lamented in the context of three recent, divisive controversies about Australia's past.

The first of these controversies was the unresolved issue of reconciliation with indigenous Australians, a discussion that divided politicians into two broad camps, not always on a party political basis. On the one hand, many (mainly Labour) politicians supported the view that some form of public recognition of past wrongs should be promulgated by the federal government, and indeed many state governments had already done so. Reconciliation, it was suggested, might comprise a minimalist recognition in the form of a national apology or, following Canadian parallels, reconciliation might even go as far as a treaty and compensation.

Many federal (mainly conservative) politicians, by contrast, opposed even the notion of a public governmental apology, arguing against what seemed to be irrelevant biblical notions about the sins of the fathers (errant settlers) being visited on their children (Australians today). Chief among the opponents of formal/legal reconciliation was Prime Minister John Howard. This reconciliation debate had, among other things, provoked a close examination of the Australian past and arguments about historical events such as the early-to-mid-twentieth-century policy of state-sanctioned removal of children from Aboriginal families for enforced adoption in non-Aboriginal homes. The raising of this particular historical phenomenon provoked a huge 1990s outcry and a national commission of inquiry, and then became categorized as the 'Stolen Generation' debate.[17] The Howard government's position was that there had been instances of forced adoption, but these had been limited in number and, in the context of their times, were understandable, if mistaken, actions.

The second controversy was the republican debate of the late 1990s, which eventually resulted in a 1999 national referendum. Prominent among the critics of the proposed Republic of Australia was Prime Minister Howard. However, his (controversially) monarchist views and the preparation for the referendum provoked another vigorous public debate about Australian history, particularly an examination of Australia's relationship with Great Britain, first as a colony, later as a dominion, and currently as an independent nation, albeit with a British Queen as head of state. Howard's anti-republican view, based on the notion of the organic growth of the state, was classically Burkean in its thinking and, that being the case, his main complaint was that there was not enough discussion of the historical background to the great successes of the Australian constitutional monarchy.

The third debate centred on the 2001 celebration of the Centenary of Federation itself. Here there was bipartisan support for a year of rolling festivals, but as the festivities unfolded in 2001, a division then became clear between the Howard view and the views of less conservatively minded public figures, including the governor general, Sir William Deane. It was Deane who, on several key public occasions, commented at length about the self-congratulatory nature of the Federation celebrations, which he contrasted with unresolved issues in Australian society, including past and present treatment of indigenous Australians. Deane was joined by other commentators. Some came from the left, as with Kim Carr's article 'Federation: Behind the Triumphalism'[18] and Mungo McCallum's 'A Time to Party. Really?'[19] Some commentaries came from the right; for example, Gerard Henderson's 'Convenient Targets in the History Wars.'[20] Federation's triumphs were not an unalloyed success, if public commentators were to be believed.

The Political Viewpoint: Contesting the Territory

In a recent article, Philip Adams, one of Australia's most prominent liberal/progressive commentators, publicly attacked the prime minister's view of the territory that is history. Adams's position is, more or less, a convenient summary of the Australian left's perspective on Howard's opinions:

> In Australia, history's contemporary importance has to contend with a Prime Minister who remembers what he wants to remember of the past. He rejoices in the history of Gallipoli and tells us that military mess was, somehow, the making of us, that something called the Anzac spirit flows through our veins ... Yet he feels no grief for the ongoing problems of Aboriginal history. Anzac history is, for him, living history, but that other history he dismisses, denies and even ridicules as 'black armband' [history].[21]

Adams provided an interesting commentary on the symptom, but did little to explain the underlying cause. Indeed, if we consider the bitterness of the school history wars in the United States in the early 1990s,[22] as well as the narrow Thatcherite view of school history in the 1980s,[23] Howard's approach is quite moderate.

Howard was seeking a conservative correction in the debate at the national level, bearing in mind that there is a consensus that Australian historiography is dominated by left-liberal historians.[24] There are a few exceptions, mainly Geoffrey Blainey and Keith Windschuttle,[25] with some less-than-reliable assistance from conservative broadsheet and tabloid newspaper columnists as well as radio shock jocks. The robust Australian political arena would not countenance a Thatcherite monopoly on historical interpretation, but might accommodate a Howardian dichotomy. Being a lawyer, Howard's framing of the historical debate is adversarial and is based on assertion, evidence, and contradiction. It is his intention to challenge publicly the ground he considers to be unfairly dominated by an opposing ideology.

Furthermore, Howard's historical vision resembles that nineteenth-century liberal advocacy of what is now referred to as trickle-down economics. It could be argued that, Howard, who was unable as a federal prime minister to influence state/territory school curricula, hoped to create a national conservative construction of Australian history, with the eventual aim that conservative representations might find their way into the classroom, where can be found the genesis of much of Australian historical consciousness. So, while the adults of Australia would be caught up in highly publicized and controversial national debates, students too would, of necessity, become involved in similar, conservatively constructed debates at the school level. This is trickle-down history.

There is one final point to make about the nature of Howard's intervention in historical debate in Australia. It could be argued that, unlike more established nations where historical discussion is about glorious or inglorious pasts, Australia is a nation whose national and international identity is still in formation, where debates about the past extend seamlessly into debates about the present and the future. For example, detailed discussion of Australia's past ties with Great Britain (good, bad, or indifferent) are seen as a necessary prelude to an informed debate about whether Australia should become a republic or remain a constitutional monarchy with a head of state who lives almost 20,000 kilometres away.

If that is the case, the unexpected involvement of the prime minister in historical debates makes more sense. His interventions in historical/political controversies may also be an attempt to change the very course of Australian history by shaping debates and events in a particularly conservative fashion.

Sharing Howard's political goals, but differing in his vision of education, Kemp believed not only that free and informed debate is a characteristic of a real democracy but that such a vigorous debate also has a place in the schools. Kemp was quite happy to allow a Monash team to conduct the National Inquiry (Monash University still has a mythical but outdated reputation as a politically radical university), and was at the same time happy to see Stuart Macintyre chair the National Inquiry Advisory Committee, notwithstanding Macintyre's close ties with the Australian Labour Party and his earlier role in the Labour government's *Discovering Democracy* program.

Despite, or even because of, these tensions, by the end of the 1990s there was a political consensus that detailed discussion of these kinds of historical issues could only be productive if, as Kemp had argued, the people of Australia had a strong grounding in historical understanding. Kemp and Howard were both suspicious of what they considered to be the prevailing historiographical orthodoxy, and both were of the view that this orthodoxy seemed to dominate the columns of major newspapers as well as the key current-affairs programs on television and radio. They were also both quite clear about the importance of school history. Yet while these key politicians did agree about the importance of school history, they each wanted different outcomes. Howard wanted 'balance' (that is, a conservative presence) in the broader national debate – with the teaching of the 'facts' to make up school history. In other words, he wanted the larger historical debate to be framed by conservative as well as by progressive polemics, and he wanted school students to have access to straightforward, 'issues-free' narrative to counterbalance 'progressive' views in the larger culture. His was a historical landscape to be viewed with uncluttered pride.

Kemp, although as 'dry' an ideologue as his prime minister, was more aware of the complex nature of the territory. Unlike Howard, Kemp has never engaged in high-profile national debates about major historical issues, preferring instead to foster historical understanding at the school level, which, he suggested, would lead to informed discussion among young people and adults. It could be argued that the first (Howard's) view was a purely political approach based on attack and counterattack, while the latter (Kemp's) view was the approach of a politician who understood the intricacies of historical explanation and held a more nuanced view of history education.

If school history was considered by leading members of the government to be too important to be left to the 'wrong' historians, there was despair among some politicians and others about how historical understanding might be fostered in a school system where the discipline appeared to be in decline. Indeed, when launching the Inquiry, Kemp remarked on the falling number of students taking history in the senior schools. But there was a second, less explicit, anxiety among politicians generally about an apparent dilution of primary and lower-secondary school history within a generic social-studies curriculum framework, a development that had its origins in educational change in the 1970s. Kemp's attack was on what he considered to be historical illiteracy, that is, a lack of understanding of key ideas in Australian history. Indeed, for politicians of all stripes, the national story is the alpha and the omega of historical consciousness.

The problem is that historical consciousness is a little more complex than that.

Historical Consciousness and School History

If, as Peter Seixas has suggested, historical consciousness can be broadly defined as individual and collective understandings of the past, the cognitive and cultural factors that shape those understandings, as well as the relations of historical understandings to those of the present and the future, it is the teachers of history who have a key role in the development of historical consciousness in Australia. Indeed, as far as the relationship between history education and historical consciousness is concerned, the arithmetic is inescapable. School history covers a big territory.

There are 9600 schools in the Commonwealth of Australia. In a population of 19 million, there are 3.22 million school students (K–12) of whom 1.88 million are in primary schools and 1.34 million in secondary schools. Australia has 215,000 teachers, half of whom are primary teachers. All primary teachers teach history. All secondary students will normally study history in one form or another until Year 9 at least.

There is more arithmetic. In 1999, for example, 38,918 Year 12 students, in their matriculation year, studied history seriously as a major part of their final year of schooling. They are assessed fairly rigorously at least over one, but usually over two years of historical inquiry.

The numbers speak for themselves. If we are looking for the origins of historical consciousness, and without wishing to discount other sources, the history classroom, for good or for ill, has to be considered the single most important formal element in the development of historical understanding, if only because almost every child in Australia will pass through the door of a history classroom.

However, as with their federal minister of education, many history teachers were discontented with the apparent decline of history in the school curriculum, the blame for which was laid at the feet of curriculum planners of the previous two decades.

The Politics of Progressivism and the 'Decline' of History Education

In the early 1970s, Australian history education had been in a dilemma. For over a hundred years, Australian school students had been brought up on the story of the British Empire. This meant, for example, that, while many Australian school students might study eighteenth-century sheep-breeding techniques in Derbyshire, they might not study the Great Shearers' Strike of the late nineteenth century, an event that had given rise to the formation of the Australian Labour Party.

Because of this remoteness from the Australian experience, school history in the early 1970s was considered by many students to be boring and, consequently, senior student numbers were falling. At the same time, because of its allegedly colonialist roots, progressive educators regarded history as an elitist and obsolete form of study.

Some progressives abandoned school history altogether in the 1960s and 1970s and it was these teachers, academics, and curriculum developers who pushed for a generic social-studies approach late in the 1970s. It might even be suggested that the social-studies movement established itself in opposition to the study of history. One prominent and influential critic of school history was Malcolm Skilbeck. In November 1976, Skilbeck, then director of the Canberra-based Curriculum Development Centre and the leading light of a school-based core curriculum movement, suggested, in dismissive and condescending fashion, that

> [h]istorical understanding, by contrast with knowledge of the classics, does not depend on the mastery of esoteric skills. Given some interest, a minimum level of literacy (which presupposes a very minimal capacity for rational thought) and application, anyone can understand history. That is one of the subject's charms ... [M]ore conclusive arguments ... are needed if teachers of history are to maintain and strengthen the place of historical study in the school curriculum.[26]

Accordingly, what then followed in many jurisdictions during the 1980s was the patchy replacement of discipline-based studies with integrated social studies. The perceived need to relate national educational efficiency to economic recovery and to introduce a national coordination of economically and socially relevant curriculum development led to a federally initiated Declaration of National Educational Goals in 1989. One of these initiatives was the consolidation of social studies and environmental studies as the social studies–based Studies of Society and Environment (SOSE).

SOSE was now one of eight outcomes-based Key Learning Areas in a proposed national curriculum, an approach that was rapidly taken up by most curriculum development agencies in the states and territories in a first round of locally based curriculum change during the early to mid-1990s. By and large (there were several local variations) SOSE comprised an amalgam of outcomes within 'strands,' which included Time, Continuity, and Change (history); Place and Space (geography); Culture (sociology and social anthropology); Resources (economics and environmental studies); and Systems (politics/law/sociology).

Thus, by the mid-1990s, SOSE, the post–social studies curriculum model, was the prevailing curriculum framework for the delivery of school history in all states and territories except New South Wales, a turn of events that gradually gave rise to serious criticism from a variety of interested parties including politicians and not least from academic historians, who were simultaneously anxious about the encroachments of vocationalism and managerialism in the university system and the effect of these encroachments on the study of the humanities.

Academic Politics and the Ownership of History: Priests of the Muse

Many academic staff in Australian universities had, during the 1990s, expressed disquiet at the direction of higher education under successive Labour and Conservative governments. Following the reorganization of Australian higher education in the late 1980s and early 1990s, there was a general feeling, among humanities staff particularly, that the alleged corporatization, bureaucratization, managerialism, and casualization of the new university system had corrupted its integrity and produced an emphasis on vocationalism and credentialism at the expense of the humanities disciplines. This was not an unfamiliar refrain in the universities of many developed nations.[27]

Under pressure to perform and obliged to be accountable within the closed circle of the university environment, many academic staff members drifted away from what had been an altruistic professional involvement in school curriculum. In particular, apart from local, individual personal involvement, there was, by the late 1990s, little formal or structural linkage between the community of academic historians and the communities of history teachers and history educators. There were three additional problems.

First, the academic history community in Australia is relatively small in numbers and scattered across a wide continent. There are currently about three hundred historians employed in thirty or so university departments or schools, and so this community is very thinly spread.

Second, because of an increased need to focus on history research as a prerequisite for promotion within the modern arts faculty, as opposed to academic engagement in history education, university teachers no longer have any professional incentive to involve themselves in curriculum planning, in textbook writing (which is generally not well paid in Australia), or in teacher professional development.

Third, complaints about academic workload have been increasing. History departments in many universities suffered a decline in staff numbers in the 1980s and 1990s, at a time when undergraduate populations were rising across the board, with a concomitant increase in workload pressures. For example, the University of Sydney had forty-one history staff members in 1988, reduced to twenty-six in 1996,[28] this at a time when there was an increase in the numbers of students opting for history, though not as a major field of study. Thus, within the university system, while work levels went up, the strategic importance of history as a humanities discipline went down.

As a consequence, even if professional links had once existed between academics and schoolteachers, because of these increased workplace pressures, instances of this kind of connection seemed to be in decline. There were some individual exceptions of course, but at first glance younger academic historians now appeared to be far less interested and much less involved in school history than were their predecessors.

Accordingly, it is not surprising that many academic historians felt that their discipline was besieged, that history in the schools was dying, and that they alone represented the last bastion of historical consciousness in Australia. As a result, during the mid to late 1990s, academic historians in Australia began to express public anxiety about this apparent state of affairs, that is, the declining significance of history as a major field of study both at the university level and in the schools. They looked back to the boom times of the 1970s, when university history was seen by some as a 'fundamental of liberal education' that would be 'integrated with the professional training of teachers.'[29] They lamented the decline in the status of the discipline,[30] and regretted the diminution in academic staff numbers.[31]

This descent was attributed to two causes. First, historians agreed with conservative politicians in expressing strong doubts about the value of a nationally based generic Key Learning Area such as SOSE, accusing it of being responsible for the 'dilution' of historical studies in school.

Second, there was strong evidence that the 1990s had witnessed a collapse in the numbers of students opting for history in senior secondary schools. Chief among those academics expressing disquiet were two prominent historians, Stuart Macintyre (Dean of Arts at the University of Melbourne) and John Hirst (Reader in History at La Trobe University).

An extreme solution, according to one academic historian, Alan Ryan, was to force students into an 'energetic national curriculum,'[32] a suggestion that was anathema to many teachers and system (state/territory) officials. Ryan, to his regret apparently, also blundered when, in the same article, he attacked schoolteachers for their poor performance. Without any evidence for his views, Ryan laid the blame for the decline in school history at the feet of the 'majority of history teachers in schools [who] were unlikely to have been our best students and ... [M]any of them are still teaching from notes that we had given them ten years before.' Historical study, it was suggested by some, was pre-eminently the territory of the academic historians, and school history needed scholarly management to make it both respectable and attractive.

If there was to be any formal resumption of an erstwhile collaboration between the two tribes of academic historians and schoolteachers, Ryan's article did little to help. This approach from an academic historian represented an exclusivist view of the creation of historical consciousness in which academic historians were, to use Horace's phrase, the real priests of the muse, and the teachers their handmaidens.

Not all academic historians had this sacerdotal view of their role in history education, but while Ryan's views might not be considered truly representative, they were published in a professional bulletin, which is the community sounding board for academic historians and many secondary school teachers.

The result was that many teachers, who actually constitute a substantial proportion of the Australian Historical Association membership, were livid that an allegedly sheltered workshop/ivory tower/out-of-touch university historian should advocate a national curriculum, moreso since they regarded such a centralist move as highly suspect in any case. More important, they were furious with Ryan for publicly suggesting that, when it came to reviving school history, university lecturers should take the lead from their allegedly inept school colleagues. Finally, the more sceptical teachers had a strongly held view that academic historians were arguing out of blatant self-interest rather than educational altruism. The accusation was that university historians simply wanted schoolteachers to provide them with more students so that the academics could keep their jobs.

Ryan's allegations, which, it was suggested, attempted to derogate the role of curriculum planners and teachers in providing good history, only served to inflame incipient mutual suspicions that existed between two groups who, although part of the same history community, were all too easily driven back into peevish factions. The consequence was that a growing gap now appeared between university historians and school-teachers of history, a dispute that threatened to create two tribes of history educators who had once belonged to the same community.

Indeed, if we examine the profession closely, it might be fair to suggest that the academic history community's approach to the contentious territory of history education falls into four main categories. First we have a small group of historians who are regularly engaged in the shared territory of curriculum design and development issues and who work closely with teachers, generally to their mutual satisfaction. Then we have another small group of historians who are persistent and consistent public advocates of historical studies and who respect the professional expertise of leading history teachers without necessarily comprehending it. Third, we have a much larger group of historians who are largely unaware of, or indifferent to, history education issues. Their hands are full just pursuing their own research and teaching. Finally, there remains a much smaller group of self-appointed public representatives of the history community who persist in following a well-meaning, but misguidedly Olympian approach to the management of their domain. For example, in 2000, a prominent academic historian remarked to the National Inquiry that curriculum officials needed 'to trust scholars to be professional and produce a school curriculum which is intellectually respectable in collaboration with teachers and students.'[33] In other words, the suggestion was that any initiatives in history syllabus design should lie first with academic historians, a remark about as tactful as a teacher commenting that teachers should be involved in outlining research strategies for their university colleagues.

Schoolteachers and History Education: The Politics of Survival

Ryan's article, in the Olympian vein, provoked a commotion[34] in the course of which nine leading teachers from various state and territory history subject associations responded. In summary, their arguments were based on the view that schoolteachers, jealous of their professional status and their territorial rights, were more interested in managing their own curriculum than in being tutored by academics. To put it simply and forcefully, teachers were not interested in being directed by university lecturers who had little or no understanding of, for example, what it was like to teach a Year 9, last double lesson on Thursday, in a portable classroom, when the outside temperature was 38C, the ceiling fans didn't work, and the Venetian blinds were jammed in the up position. These cultural and attitudinal differences came out quite clearly among teachers, particularly secondary teachers, interviewed during the National Inquiry, 1999–2000.

A key difficulty, and a matter of some exasperation to teachers, was the failure of some university historians to grasp that schoolteachers have to teach students across the whole ability range in almost all year levels, not just a small fraction of the more able young adult population. Moreover, it was pointed out that history teachers worked with students who have to be convinced of the value of history, most of whom are below school-leaving age, unlike university students, who are volunteers. Finally, teachers asserted, it was not their job to provide undergraduate students for university teachers.

The following comment represented the views of many teachers:

> School history teaching is not the same as academic history teaching. University lecturers only teach adults who have chosen to do history and who more or less have the skills. And they tell history teachers what they should be doing! The issues (school and university teaching) aren't the same.[35]

The conflict arose not only from a lack of opportunity for many overworked lecturers to have regular contact with schools, but also from the parallel impediments of overworked teachers to regular contact with universities.

The immediate concern of history teachers was not the state of history in universities and in society at large, but the more urgent and immediate survival of history in a school curriculum dominated by other more politically desirable initiatives, such literacy and numeracy, and by more socially desirable programs such as drug education and student health. One other concern that teachers expressed was the allegedly low (historical) skill and knowledge levels of new entrants to their profession:

> Look at the pre-service teachers who are coming into our schools ... They are people who want to teach, who love their students but they are naïve [*sic*] in their backgrounds. They'll be fine in lower high schools but beyond that? ... [They are not] able to take a single argument and go into it in depth with primary source material.[36]

The accusation was that new history and humanities graduates were poorly trained, and that recent generations of history teachers were, to paraphrase Eldridge Cleaver, part of the problem and not part of the solution, a belief that vigorously threw the ball back into the court of the academic historians.

Finally

Notwithstanding these occasional misunderstandings, there have been serious attempts to draw members of the history community together. For example, at a state level, the History Council of Victoria, chaired by the energetic and ubiquitous Stuart Macintyre, contains several representatives of the academic and the school communities. At a national level, the 2000 National Inquiry Report, *The Future of the Past,* made several major recommendations, all accepted by DETYA (now renamed the Department of Education Science and Training or DEST), including the suggestion that all members of the history community should work together harmoniously in advocating historical studies, in providing a focus for research into history education, and in collaborating in professional development activities. A National History Project (NHP), under the auspices of a federally funded (at $2.3 million) National Centre for History Education, has been set up (2001–3). The NHP attempts to draw these groups together in common activities, which include trial local professional-development consortia, an online history education journal, a nationally offered postgraduate program in history education, an association of history educators, and an online professional digest of best practice. Finally, two national seminars have been funded by DETYA/DEST to discuss history education issues. These seminars, in June 2001 (in Canberra, on teaching and learning Australian history) and April

2002 (Brisbane, on teaching and learning regional and global histories), were each attended by fifty individuals who represented the
academic history, schoolteaching, history education, and curriculum
design communities.

The lasting value of these highly successful national seminars has yet
to be determined, but there were two anecdotal responses to the 2001
seminar. The first of these concerns a prominent academic historian
who, for the first time in her career, joined an intense discussion group
that contained primary school teachers of history. She described the
experience as a 'real eye-opener.' The second anecdote concerns the
state/territory curriculum designers, who announced, with some plea-
sure, that the initial national seminar was the very first time in their
careers that the history education curriculum officials from the eight
jurisdictions had actually met each other to share common issues in a
positive fashion.

As far as the author knows, at this stage, the National History Project is
meeting political as well as professional expectations. David Kemp has
been replaced as minister by ex-medic Dr Brendan Nelson, but there are
no apparent changes in policy direction. Prime Minister Howard remains 'hot' on history: in April 2002, he and Alexander Downer joined
in a public debate about the proposed removal of ANZAC graves in
France to make way for a new airport. Howard stated, 'There are more
Australians buried in France than [in] any other country other than our
own and therefore, any campaign to keep sacred the memory of those
people who died in France is a campaign that has my total support.'[37] Re-
funding (from 2003 onwards) for the National History Project is, of
course, at the whim of electoral fortunes and shifts in government
policy, but at the time of writing, the NHP seems to be on track.

The teachers remain cautious about it all. There still exists a tension
between the enthusiasm that many teachers of history have for their
subject, the ambivalent feelings they have towards academic historians
(deference/exasperation), and the case-hardened suspicions they have
about government initiatives. It was even suggested that Kemp had
wanted to bring in a national version of the 1999 New South Wales
history syllabus, which featured mandatory Australian history at Years 9
and 10. One consistently strong rumour was that the Inquiry was a conservative attack on the (progressive) SOSE approach to social studies.

These defensive and sceptical responses were only to be expected.
Many Australian teachers are still shell-shocked after a decade of constant curriculum change, downsizing, and school closures. There have

been bitter industrial struggles in New South Wales. In Victoria, during a conservative state government administration (1992–9), over 8000 teachers were laid off without replacement and over 200 schools were closed. At the same time, across Australia, curriculum support services have been shut down, assistance for professional development has largely been redirected to state/territory system priorities only, and now, because of poor planning, there are huge teacher shortages in several jurisdictions.

Under these conditions, some history teachers were wary of any federal initiatives in history education, partly because they are sceptical about any government proposals, but also because they are guarded about the funding relationship that exists between the National History Project and civics education (the NHP is funded mainly out of a Discovering Democracy budgetary allocation). In addition, top-down projects do not excite teachers, particularly in the face of managing the daily grind in each individual school. Glossy curriculum projects parachuted into the school system with little on-the-ground support invariably fail to inspire, and tend to end their days on the dustier sections of school library shelves. Thus, despite its potential, school-based enthusiasm for the National History Project is still tempered with caution.

Notes

1   The cove where the ANZACs landed was eventually renamed Anzac Cove by Kemal Ataturk, who·had been in charge of the Turkish troops who stopped the first ANZAC landing before it reached its objectives. The renaming was in honour of the ANZACs who had fought there. In return, Australia built a monument to Ataturk adjacent to the War Memorial in Canberra. One of the key agencies in propagating the Anzac myth on the world stage was Peter Weir's 1981 film *Gallipoli,* which starred, among others, a young Mel Gibson. Weir's film takes an anti-imperialist line, as did its predecessor *Breaker Morant* (Bruce Beresford's 1979 film about the Boer War). *Gallipoli* is shown every April night at a cinema close to the memorial site at Anzac Cove. Mel Gibson has since moved on to greater things but, as an actor, his anti-imperialism still comes through in such films as *Braveheart* and *The Patriot.*

2   *The Weekend Australian,* 3/4 February 2001.

3   There are two major parties in Australian politics. The Liberal Party is roughly equivalent to the British Conservative Party but operates in coali-

tion, with the assistance of the small, rural National Party. The other major party, the Australian Labour Party, also has its obvious British equivalent. There is a small, progressive centrist group of Democrats and an even smaller, but currently more influential, Green Party who operate independently of the major parties.

4 *The Australian*, 28 April 2000.
5 *The Australian*, 28 November 2000.
6 *The Australian*, 1 May 2000.
7 *The Age*, 10 October 2000.
8 Sean Brawley, '"A Comfortable and Relaxed Past": John Howard and the "Battle of History,"' *The Electronic Journal of Australian and New Zealand History*, www2.h-net.msu.edu/anzau/journal/articles/brawley/htm. Brawley has written a very clear and valuable commentary on events up to and including 1996.
9 Gerard Henderson, *The Age*, 10 October 2000.
10 *The Australian*, 21/22 October 2000 – the issue was Olympic-ceremony performers wearing T-shirts supporting indigenous Australian causes.
11 Greg Pemberton, *The Australian*, 12 June 1996.
12 Tony Taylor, *The Future of the Past: The Final Report of the National Inquiry into School History* (Canberra: DETYA, 2000).
13 *The Australian*, 12 June 1996. Geoffrey Bolton, a prominent historian also remarked that Keating had a 'readiness uncommon in recent prime ministers to take note of recent trends in historiography and to use them in the service of promoting a particular myth of nationalism' (Brawley, '"A Comfortable and Relaxed Past,"' 2). Keating, according to his biographer Don Watson, had a personal involvement in the Singapore issue. His father's brother had been captured and was, in Watson's words, 'murdered on the Sandakan death march.' Don Watson, *Recollections of a Bleeding Heart: A Portrait of Paul Keating PM* (Sydney: Knopf, 2002), 120.
14 *The Daily Telegraph*, 1 May 2000.
15 *The Australian*, 14/15 October 2000.
16 DETYA Press Release, 18 November 1999, Canberra.
17 See, e.g., Robert Manne, 'White Lies,' *The Age*, 31 March 2001. Manne is an important political commentator who, while ostensibly a 'small c' conservative, can often propose, in a serious and logical fashion, radically progressive views, much to the fury of his conservative colleagues.
18 *The Age*, 5 January 2001.
19 *The Age*, 8 January 2001.
20 *The Age*, 10 October 2000.
21 *The Australian*, 21/22 July 2001.

22 Gary Nash, Charlotte Crabtree, and Ross Dunn, *History on Trial* (New York: Knopf, 1999).

23 Rob Phillips, *History Teaching, Nationhood and the State: A Study in Educational Politics* (London: Continuum International Publishing Group, 1998).

24 See, e.g., Henderson, *The Age*, 10 October 2000, and Brawley, 'A Comfortable and Relaxed Past.'

25 Geoffrey Blainey, author of several key works in Australian history, is a controversial figure because of his publicly espoused conservative views on immigration and indigenous issues. Keith Windschuttle is a productive historian and commentator of the Jack Granatstein variety.

26 Martin Skilbeck, 'The Nature of History and Its Place in the Curriculum,' *The Australian History Teacher* 6 (1979): 3–4.

27 See, e.g., Tony Taylor, J. Gough, V. Bundrock, and R. Winter, 'A Bleak Outlook: Academic Staff Perceptions of Changes in Core Activities in Australian Higher Education,' *Studies in Higher Education* 23, no. 3 (1998): 255–68 and R. Winter, Tony Taylor, and J. Sarros, 'Trouble at Mill: Some Perceptions of Quality of Academic Work Life within the Australian Unified National System,' *Studies in Higher Education* 25, no. 3 (2000): 270–94.

28 Stuart Macintyre, 'History,' in *Knowing Ourselves and Others: The Humanities in Australia into the 21st Century* (Canberra: National Board of Employment, Education and Training, 1998).

29 J. Roe, 'Presidential Address,' *Australian Historical Association Bulletin*, 1999: 14.

30 Alan Ryan, 'Developing a Strategy to "Save" History,' *Australian Historical Association Bulletin*, 87 (1998): 39–50.

31 Macintyre, 'History.'

32 Ryan, 'Developing a Strategy.'

33 Taylor, *The Future of the Past*, 144.

34 *Australian Historical Association Bulletin*, 1999.

35 Taylor, *Future of the Past*, 79.

36 Ibid., 69.

37 *The Age*, 13 April 2002.

The Pursuit of the Past:
A Polemical Perspective

JOHN TORPEY

'Time is not a single train, moving in one direction at a constant speed,' notes the Trieste writer Claudio Magris. 'Every so often it meets another train coming in the opposite direction, from the past, and for a short while that past is with us, by our side, in our present.'[1] Magris's metaphor captures nicely the ordinary state of things with regard to our posture vis-à-vis the past. Time may be experienced as 'full' or 'empty,' depending on one's historical and social location, but it usually appears, at least, to move forward at a more or less constant rate, with occasional digressions into previous experiences that may be recalled fondly, wistfully, dismissively, indulgently. Yet the past thus remembered, while perhaps movingly present, does not thereby lose its quality of remoteness. Under normal circumstances, the past remains simply part of the stock of ideas upon which people draw to organize and make sense of their lives, but hardly the predominant part. Most people maintain a balance between past, present, and future that allows them to move forward in their everyday lives, despite the unhappy memories that past experience may hold, along with possible trepidation about the future.

That balance seems to have been upset in recent years. There is no reason to aspire to the ahistorical rumination of Nietzsche's cow – which is untroubled by remembrance of things past and can thus live blissfully, vigorously in the present – yet Nietzsche's fears of a surfeit of history are entirely apposite to our current situation.[2] The more usual attitude toward the past suggested by Magris's remark throws into sharp relief the peculiarity of our contemporary relationship to former times. In recent years, the distance that normally separates us from the past has been strongly challenged in favour of an insistence that the past – a very particular past, as we shall see – is constantly, urgently present as part of our everyday experience. Indeed, a rising chorus of memory entrepreneurs asserts that the ordinary relationship between past and present described by Magris does not and indeed should not exist. This outsized pursuit of the past is part of a larger sense that, as George Steiner has put it, 'the dishes are being cleared' on that epoch of Western culture that can be understood in terms of a narrative of hope and progress.[3]

We are being buried under an avalanche of history – but a history conceived as far different from the heroic, forward-looking tales that underpinned the idea of progress for two centuries. Instead of the illuminated manuscripts decorated by latter-day monks for the edification of the faithful that had characterized history under the sign of Hegel, we are presented with tawdry chapbooks containing narratives of injustice and crime. These censorious histories, often closer than their mythopoeic predecessors to the real story of how we got where we are now, have helped promote extensive efforts to make whole what has been smashed en route to the present.

As a result, many countries – especially the more developed, and especially the more privileged groups within those countries – are confronted today with the task of digging themselves out from under the burden of that history. That redoubtable historian Karl Marx once famously said that the past 'weighs like a nightmare on the brain of the living,' and that this is especially so 'just when they seem engaged in revolutionizing themselves and things.'[4] The sort of 'revolutionizing' that is currently taking place may not be what Marx had in mind when he penned those lines. Yet the contemporary intellectual and political preoccupation with the past is, indeed, a response to massive social transformation, as his prescient comment would lead us to expect. I want to argue that this intensive and often vengeful concern with the past is a response to the collapse of the future, along the lines suggested by Steiner.

In what follows, I discuss the contours of this remarkable situation and the factors that account for the current concern with exorcizing the spirits of the past. I argue that the chief and defining aspect of our contemporary historical context is its 'post'-ness, its quality of being 'after' other, more future-oriented projects – most particularly, socialism and the nation-state – that animated the energies of large constituencies during the preceding two centuries. Deprived of these narratives of progress, our era is marked by a pervasive mood of 'enlightened bewilderment,'[5] lacking any firm direction adumbrated in a vision of a society better than the 'really existing' variant. At the moment, the only utopian vision around is that of a more thoroughly market-based society, extending the 'great transformation' to those areas of the world that have been shielded from the naked power of markets heretofore.

We live, in short, in an age distinguished by the (temporary) abeyance of what *New York Times* columnist Thomas Friedman has called 'big idea politics.' That is, we lack a collective dream capable of energizing large numbers of people on behalf of that dream. A galloping individualism replaces the collective visions that animated the 'Fordist' class politics of the twentieth century, while a diffuse and inchoate solidarity with one's putative 'diaspora' or with anonymous global 'others' supplants identification with political projects associated with nation-states. This all has its positive sides, to be sure; the burgeoning idea of 'human rights' bears witness to a proper concern with the fate of humanity as a whole. But there are also serious costs entailed in the fact that wide segments of the intelligentsia, as well as a good deal of the broader public, now deride these more 'middle range' collective projects as overweening, illegitimate 'grand narratives.' When the future collapses, the past rushes in.

The Collapse of the Future I: Socialism

Those of us in the Euro-Atlantic world live in an era whose mental parameters are shaped by the end of Communism and the attendant international rivalries of the Cold War. To be sure, despite its moments of high drama, the Cold War was in many ways a profoundly apolitical era during which ideological conflict came down to endorsing one of two mutually exclusive alternatives – capitalism or Communism, anti-Fascism or anti-Communism.[6] This Manichaean thinking led to extensive blindness toward the faults of each side's respective partners in international affairs. Such thinking helped to smother attention to past misdeeds on both sides – those of Germany and Japan as they were transformed after the war from fascist enemies into allies of the 'Free World,' on the one side, and those of the Soviet Union, which quickly transmogrified from ally to enemy, on the other. *Realpolitik* argued against airing out these old wounds, and the heroic visions of a prosperous capitalist or an egalitarian communist tomorrow kept eyes turned firmly toward the future. The dynamics of the Cold War thus banished much discussion of what meanwhile have come to be known as 'the crimes of the past' to the murky twilight of the struggle between Communism and the 'Free World.'

That struggle paired two countries that embodied divergent but quasi-messianic projects for the future of the world. One was a former colony, born of revolution, that had been a role model for many people struggling for freedom from one or another imperial yoke (including at one time even Ho Chi Minh). The other was a newly influential Eurasian power that increasingly assumed the mantle of progressive humanity after the Second World War. Between them, they had been seen as the vanguard of the global future at least since Tocqueville's time. Yet in the world circa 1945, the position of the United States as the self-appointed leader of the world's colonized and dispossessed masses was called sharply into question. After the Second World War, the Soviet Union inherited the anti-colonialist banner from the United States, which in turn had stepped in to replace a declining Old World as global hegemon.

From the point of view of the broad masses outside Europe, the Soviets' (enormous) contribution to the defeat of Nazism and their espousal of the anti-colonial cause after the war were thus of a piece. After all, as Marx had noted in his discussion of 'primitive accumulation,' the extermination and enslavement of the indigenous populations of the Americas, the 'looting' of the East Indies, and the massive stimulation and expansion of the slave trade in Africa had heralded 'the rosy dawn of the era of capitalist production.'[7] Race and racial domination have been at the heart of the capitalist enterprise since its very inception,[8] and the Soviets' stance on these issues appeared to be considerably more compelling than those of the racially retrograde United States or a Europe hanging on, often brutally, to 'a dying colonialism.'[9] Accordingly, W.E.B. Dubois, the leading voice of pan-Africanism at mid-century, admonished his readers that if an 'ultimate democracy, reaching across the colour line and abolishing race discrimination,' could be achieved 'by means other than Communism, [then] Communism need not be feared'; otherwise, there was no alternative to 'the method laid down by Karl Marx.'[10]

Much of 'the West' was of course tainted among the world's non-white masses for its rapaciousness and savagery in the course of the creation of the white-dominated modern world. (Recall Gandhi's quip in response to the question of what he thought of Western civilization: 'I think it would be a good idea.') The Allies' shortcomings in the arena of race relations generated considerable hand-wringing among Western opinion-makers about the political advantages this situation might give to the Soviets after the war. Whether ideologically close to the Soviet Union or not, communists were frequently among the most engaged participants in the freedom struggles of blacks in the United States and South Africa.[11]

Ultimately, the challenge posed by the very presence of the Soviet Union and of socialist movements to the *soi-disant* 'Free World' was critical to the transformation of racist practices in the United States, helping to create a favourable context for the success of the Civil Rights Movement in the 1960s.[12] With the decline of a vibrant socialist movement and of the USSR since the early 1990s (and for that matter since the end of the 'Bretton Woods boom' in the early 1970s), progress in global race relations has stagnated. Africa, in particular, has been largely reduced to being a backwater of foreign-policy concern. Recent successes in convincing some of the wealthier countries to forgive the debts of some of the world's poorest nations, and to make available medicines for the treatment of AIDS therein, may help. But these measures hardly amount to a major redistribution of wealth and power to the predominantly non-white Third World.[13]

More broadly, of course, the challenge of socialism was arguably decisive in pushing the capitalist democracies to institute welfare and other policies that blunted the sharpest edges of the market economy. Welfare states came to be the norm in the more industrialized countries in the aftermath of the Great Depression. In part this was an indigenous reaction to the devastation wrought by the slump on the populations of these countries. But it was also a response to the perception that the Soviets, who had notably abolished capitalism, seemed not to endure the same shocks from the global economy during the 1930s. In addition, of course, socialist and communist parties throughout the West pushed for policies that softened the blows of capitalism's 'creative destruction.'[14]

The collapse and discrediting of socialism and Communism has resulted in widespread befuddlement among the forces that had once been allied with the future, so to speak, about how to understand themselves in the post-Communist age. Some of those who have seen their faith disintegrate along with the Soviet bloc may have retreated into quietude, whereas others have undoubtedly found new ways to express the convictions embodied in what may now have been proven to be misguided hopes. Some of the latter have surely been among the legions of those protesting against 'globalization' in Seattle, Prague, Washington, Goteborg, and Genoa, many of whom are of course too young to have had any mature memory of Soviet communism. As an organized political force, however, socialist or communist movements have become largely irrelevant in the most developed countries, and anti-globalization movements have not yet developed the institutional stability to replace them as a major force for social change. The old is dying, and the new has not yet been born.

Others from the once-socialist fold – particularly those most strongly charmed by Communist promises of a redeemed humanity that were betrayed by the Soviets and their minions – have nonetheless gone to great lengths to denounce *post mortem* the seductions of communist utopianism and the disastrous realities of its Soviet incarnation.[15] Their aim in the battle for control of the past is to nail irretrievably shut both the coffin of Communism and, more broadly, the revolutionary tradition stemming from the French Revolution. This counter-revolutionary thrust, advanced with rapier intellect by François Furet, has gone hand in hand with a strong revival of totalitarianism theory, the approach that sees Communism and Nazism as two species of a larger and unprecedented twentieth-century political genus. As a form of political analysis, totalitarianism theory was inaugurated by Hannah Arendt, who saw the two major movements as both unprecedented and tied together by their use of 'ideology and terror' as tools of government.

Yet it is worth noting that, for all their shared commitment to the notion of totalitarianism, Arendt and Furet differed sharply in their attitude toward the revolutionary heritage in modern political culture. The excesses of Communism did not vitiate the idea of revolution for Arendt, who lionized the American version in which she found refuge from Nazism, whereas they did so for Furet, who found lamentable the consequences of its French variant for his own *patrie*. In contrast to Furet, Arendt thus remained committed, in a Jeffersonian vein, to the revolutionary tradition as an affirmation of (Arendt's term) 'man's' ability to escape the stagnation of unfreedom, of the human capacity to 'start something new.'[16]

In a manner more reminiscent of Tocqueville, Furet and his followers hope to put an end to the chronic instability produced by the shimmer of revolution and the other abstractions promulgated by intellectuals – in the French tradition, *maître-penseurs* with a privileged insight into political truth. Herein, according to Furet and his epigones, lies the error of those led astray by the Communist illusion – an error they are loath to see repeated. The weakness of left-wing politics today suggests that they have done their work successfully, or perhaps that they are simply the owl of Minerva alighting in the dusk of *etatist* socialism.[17]

The political interregnum created by the shrivelling of the socialist challenge has been filled to a considerable extent with identity politics and the 'politics of recognition,' a shift that has led to seismic disputes over the extent to which culture is relevant to progressive politics.[18] These debates have yielded many important insights, but the point here is that a good deal of the discussion of identity and recognition has taken place in and through the idiom of coming to terms with past injustices. The upwelling of attention to the past has had important elective affinities with the preoccupation with 'identity.'[19] This is perhaps unavoidable. Any reasonable understanding of the inequalities facing non-whites in the world today must involve some attention to the racist practices and policies that underpinned five centuries of white supremacy, not to mention the fact that women have had to face an even longer period of 'masculine domination.'[20]

Still, the outpouring of concern with culture, identity, and memory bespeak a retreat from an unjust, but also refractory, social reality. These preoccupations thus resonate with the impulse underlying the current obsession with the 'socially constructed' nature of just about everything.[21] The repeated incantation that the social world is 'socially constructed,' and hence apparently infinitely malleable, reflects a weakening of the idea of social structure that was essential to a broad, cross-class vision of politics. To the extent that it transcends the merely rhetorical, the insistence on the socially constructed nature of various social categories constitutes a kind of sociological libertarianism, a refusal at the level of ideas to come to grips with the hard realities of wealth and power.

Similarly, we have witnessed the emergence of a 'memory industry' that, largely emancipated from the evidentiary requirements of a pedestrian positivism, opens the door to all manner of unanchored conjecture regarding the supposed contents of people's recollections. Memory emerges with such force on the academic and public agenda today, according to one critic, 'precisely because it figures as a therapeutic alternative to historical discourse.'[22] Such discourse is constrained by the unpleasant facts that bestrew the canvas of the past, whereas memory talk allows for a subjective reworking of those events combined with the bland prospect of 'healing.' The excavation of memory and its mysteries salves buried yearnings for a presently unreachable future. Taken together, the interconnected concerns with memory, identity, and 'social construction' amount to defensive responses to the bewilderment induced by the collapse of an edifying, invigorating conception of a common destiny. Such responses are a reflection of the contemporary forward march of the invisible hand, not a critique of it, as many of the practitioners of these pursuits seem to think.

The problem is that, for fairly obvious reasons, the pursuit of the past has generally been the terrain of conservatives; Edmund Burke is perhaps the leading example of the sensibility in question. The past has always been full of disasters for those on the bottom of the social ladder; until recently, moreover, their role in that past was met chiefly with the 'enormous condescension of posterity.'[23] Conversely, the past always seemed more glorious to those whose power and privilege are now being challenged. Because the present always and inevitably remains one of unnecessary suffering and inequality, to be superseded in a coming better day, the future is of necessity the temporal horizon of earthly (or any other) redemption. 'The meek shall inherit the earth'; 'the workers have nothing to lose but their chains, and a world to win.' But they need the future in order to realize those hopes, which is the best they have in the still-unjust present. It is no coincidence that Steiner's concern about the 'problematic' status of hope in our day stems from a view that the twin progeny of prophetic Judaism – Christianity and its secular sibling, Marxism – have atrophied.[24]

The Collapse of the Future II: The Nation-State

Yet it is not only communism that has proven to be an illusion. The idea of the nation-state, too, has been widely discredited, reduced to its historical role – not to be gainsaid, of course – as the platform for delusions of grandeur leading to tragedy. As the paradigmatic case of nationalism gone disastrously wrong, the Holocaust and its reception in opinion-making circles have done much to undermine confidence in the nation-state as a political form. In the Euro-Atlantic world, at least, the Holocaust has become the touchstone of contemporary historical consciousness, undermining the very idea of nationalism among the ranks of respectable opinion.[25] The human-rights agenda that received so important a boost from the international responses to the Second World War has further promoted a scepticism about the nation-state as a force for good in the world. This is an enormous change of sensibility since the heyday of the nation-state in the early twentieth century.

Max Weber noted, in his discussion of 'The Nation,' that it was usually related to the notion of the superiority or irreplaceability of the cultural achievements of a peculiar group.[26] This view of the nation is now routinely condemned in enlightened circles as a grotesque form of hubris likely to have been at the root of, or to issue in, one or another form of self-aggrandizing violence. The principal exception to this proposition involves those cases of national strivings tied to efforts to escape from some sort of imperialist or quasi-imperialist overlord. In other words, nationalists seeking to achieve the norm of self-determination that underlay the French Revolution, and that was reaffirmed by Woodrow Wilson after the First World War, still have a legitimate cause. National feeling among the already powerful, however, is to be looked at askance.

As a result, it is difficult at this point to imagine Hannah Arendt's view that 'the decline of the nation-state' – that is, 'the conquest of the state by the nation' – had led to 'the end of the rights of man.'[27]Arendt disputed the natural-law notion that we were 'born equal,' insisting to the contrary that we only became so as a result of laws that treat everyone the same. Hence, the preferential treatment of nationals over other humans that developed during the late nineteenth century and after represented for her a betrayal of the Declaration of the Rights of Man and Citizen. Likewise largely forgotten is the fact that a sense of common membership was crucial to the extension of the social rights that fostered equality in the face of capitalism's systemic inequities.[28] The nations associated with powerful countries are widely regarded today as illegitimate entities, mere brute victors in a process of 'internal colonialism.' Such nation-states are seen (not entirely inappropriately) as having been brought into being on the strength of injustices against others, including expropriation, murder, rape, and the destruction of once-vibrant cultures. The rights of minorities to 'their' cultures have thus been one of the most widely discussed extensions of the norm of self-determination in recent years.[29] Under these circumstances, the authority of the nation-state to mould its populace in the image of elite defenders of the national mythology has largely evaporated.

Among the more educated strata in the Euro-Atlantic world, at least, national(ist) histories – once the essential pedagogical bedrock of imagined national communities – have fallen under the suspicion of celebrating the narcissism of small differences and the banality of evil. Such histories are seen as responsible for the *ex post facto* glorification of those crimes today regarded as the most heinous, and as such unacceptable. This sensibility has also made the leap to other parts of the world, although there it may more readily get caught up in the vicissitudes of international power politics. An excellent example of this transformation in thinking about the history of the nation is the ongoing controversy over the content of school history textbooks in Japan, where the textbooks have been condemned by neighbouring countries such as China and South Korea as giving insufficient accounts of Japanese atrocities during the Pacific War.[30] In short, historical consciousness in the

Euro-Atlantic world and its fragments around the globe,[31] and in would-be democracies elsewhere, is now more likely to be bound up with a search for perpetrators and with the posthumous recognition of victims than it is to be rooted in the foundation myth of a *Volk*.

The identity-promoting authority of the nation-state has thus been replaced among substantial numbers of people in the developed world by a growing identification with the notion that they are members of a diaspora of one sort or another. Two leading analysts of world migration processes have recently defined a diaspora as 'a persistent sense of community between people who have left their homeland (usually involuntarily) and who may be scattered all over the world.'[32] Forced migration may be an important aspect of membership in a diaspora for some groups, but this element need not be significant in a group's experience for the notion of a diaspora to be relevant to their self-understanding today. Identification with a putative diaspora is likely to depend as much on the porousness of national identity in the 'host' states and on the political and economic situation in the homeland as it is on the causes underlying the groups' departure from their ancestral domains. In the Euro-Atlantic world today, the growth of diasporic consciousness reflects the fading of a cohesive, overarching sense of national belonging. This fragmentation is mirrored in the explosion of academic attention to transnational communities and to 'postnational' phenomena generally.[33]

Ethnic activists in putative diasporas have played a crucial role in foregrounding experiences of historical injustices in the Euro-Atlantic world in recent years. The activism of Jews in the United States with respect to reparations for Nazi crimes is too well known to require elaboration here. Iris Chang, author of *The Rape of Nanking*, is the daughter of Chinese immigrants to the United States, and she became involved in publicizing the atrocities committed by the Japanese during the Second World War as a result of her involvement with Chinese-American activists devoted to cultivating the memory of those events.[34] The Armenian communities in France and the United States, similarly, have played a decisive role in promoting the legislative recognition of the 1915 massacres as a genocide. Also important has been the African diaspora, which is of course of long standing in the Americas. Those who call attention to the connections between colonialism, the slave trade, slavery itself, and the continuing discrimination against those of African descent in the United States and elsewhere have done so in part by insisting on the community of identity and interests among the inhabitants of Africa and African-descended peoples elsewhere.[35]

Pervasive talk of a 'globalizing' world entailing the heightened geographic mobility of far-flung populations suggest that the developed world has become a melting pot absorbing hitherto unfamiliar peoples from around the globe. A mere glance at the faces of those walking the streets of Paris, London, Berlin, Sydney, New York, and Toronto indicates that there is much to this view. Yet the images of multicoloured, multi-ethnic populations have also helped stimulate a concern about identity and 'roots' among both those in motion and those receiving them. This sense of transformation and drift could scarcely fail to promote a concern about who one 'really' is, especially as politics in the world's powerful countries since the era of Reagan and Thatcher seems increasingly oriented to scaling back the scope and range of government activities. If 'the nation-state' offers its citizens less, and demands less of them (e.g., the shift away from conscript armies), it is hardly surprising that they would look elsewhere for the sources of their self-understanding.

This tendency has been especially prominent in a context in which the culturally savvy view the nation-state principally as a force for deracination and cultural decimation. This intensified search for the moorings of the self is precisely the response to contemporary developments that one might expect on the basis of Marx's previously quoted remark; the presence of the past *is* enhanced when people are in the process of 'revolutionizing themselves and things,' as they appear to be doing today. An essential element of that 'revolutionizing' is the declining authority of nation-states vis-à-vis other claimants on people's loyalties and, in the Euro-Atlantic world, the increasing individualization of people's ideas about who and what they are.

The Past after the Future

The discrediting of the twin forces that dominated twentieth-century history – namely, nationalism and socialism/communism – has promoted a pervasive 'consciousness of catastrophe' among the educated segments of Euro-Atlantic society. Against this background, Europe – once thought of as the homeland of the (capital-E) Enlightenment – replaces Africa as the 'dark continent,' while Henry Louis Gates celebrates 'the wonders of the African world' in a multi-instalment PBS series and accompanying coffee-table book.[36] The reversal of images, however appropriate in righting traditionally triumphalist and 'orientalist' histories, is strikingly symptomatic of the transformed sensibilities of our age. Fortified by postmodernist critiques of 'grand narratives' and the celebration of 'difference' over a universalism alleged to harbour intrinsically totalitarian impulses, the end-of-the-century meets *The End of Utopia*.[37]

We thus find ourselves in a post-socialist and post-national condition[38] that, sceptical of new blueprints for a heaven on earth, instead fixes its gaze firmly on the horrors and injustices of the past. In the conclusion of his magisterial *Passing of an Illusion*, Furet writes: 'The idea of *another* society has become almost impossible to conceive of, and no one in the world today is offering any advice on the subject or even trying to formulate a new concept. Here we are, condemned to live in the world as it is.'[39] This assessment underestimates the unfamiliarity of market capitalism to many of the societies that have been exposed to it since the Communist collapse – not to mention the amount of advice promoting that new kind of society that has been dispensed by the Harvard Economics Department. Unsurprisingly, however, given the real object of his ire, Furet sees only socialism as 'another' society. But even the creation of capitalism in societies that have not previously encountered it is a novel experience, if not a new idea.[40]

In the absence of any plausible overarching vision of a more humane future society, the significance of the past and of people's recollections of it become magnified; righting past wrongs tends to supplant the search for a vision of a better tomorrow. The reckoning with abominable pasts becomes, in fact, the idiom in which the future is sought. We might call this the *involution* of the progressive impulse that has animated much of modern history – the deflection of what was once regarded as the forward march of progress and its turning inward upon itself. Where can one now find analogues of those venerable early-twentieth-century expressions of optimism in the socialist future conveyed in the Italian socialists' *Avanti!* or the German Social Democrats' *Vorwärts*? Not since the Romantics has so much energy been spent on digging up the past, sifting through the broken shards, and pondering what people think about them.

Across wide segments of the intelligentsia and the public the pursuit of the future has thus been replaced by a veritable tidal wave of 'memory,' 'historical consciousness,' 'coming to terms with the past.' Perhaps never has so much intellectual and political firepower been trained on history as a battleground of political struggle and a field of scholarly exploration. Who today, ensnared in the riddles of the past or crushed under its bulk, could imagine the exhortation of those seekers after new worlds, the Futurists, to 'burn down all libraries so as to emancipate the senile spirit from the dead weight of the past'?[41] Nietzsche's acerbic remark that 'man would rather have the void for his purpose than be void of purpose' captures the remarkable intensity with which we have in recent years made a purpose of the past. As we pursue the past in this manner, however, we should be aware that this preoccupation is in substantial part a replacement for paradises lost.

Notes

1   Claudio Magris, *Danube: A Sentimental Journey from the Source to the Black Sea,* trans. by Patrick Creagh (London: Harvill Press, 1999), 39.

2   Friedrich Nietzsche, 'Vom Nutzen und Nachteil der Historie für das Leben,' in Nietzsche, *Unzeitgemässe Betrachtungen* (Frankfurt: Insel, 1981 [1874]); translated as 'On the Uses and Disadvantages of History for Life,' in Daniel Breazeale, ed., *Untimely Meditations* (Cambridge: Cambridge University Press, 1997).

3   George Steiner, *Grammars of Creation* (New Haven: Yale University Press, 2001), 3.

4   Karl Marx, 'The Eighteenth Brumaire of Louis Bonaparte,' in Robert Tucker, ed., *The Marx-Engels Reader,* 2nd ed. (New York: Norton, 1978 [1852]), 595.

5   Jürgen Habermas, 'Foreword,' *The Postnational Constellation: Political Essays,* trans. Max Pensky (Cambridge, MA: MIT Press, 1998), xviii; my translation.

6   Ken Jowitt, 'A World without Leninism,' in Jowitt, *New World Disorder: The Leninist Extinction* (Berkeley: University of California Press, 1992), 306.

7   Karl Marx, *Das Kapital,* vol. 1 in Karl Marx and Friedrich Engels, *Werke* (Berlin: Dietz Verlag, 1979), 779.

8   For a valuable discussion of the vicissitudes of race in the capitalist 'world system,' see Howard Winant, *The World Is a Ghetto: Race and Democracy since World War II* (New York: Basic Books, 2001). Following Michael Adas's arguments in *Machines as the Measure of Men: Science, Technology, and Ideologies of Western Dominance* (Ithaca, NY: Cornell University Press, 1989), George Fredrickson doubts that race was a central motivation behind European global conquest and colonization. See his *Racism: A Short History* (Princeton, NJ: Princeton University Press, 2002), 108–9.

9   Cf. Frantz Fanon, *A Dying Colonialism,* trans. Haakon Chevalier (New York: Grove Press, 1967 [1959]).

10 W.E. Burghardt Dubois, *The World and Africa: An Inquiry into the Part Which Africa Has Played in World History* (New York: Viking, 1946), 258.

11 See George Fredrickson, *Black Liberation: A Comparative History of Black*

Ideologies in the United States and South Africa (New York: Oxford University Press, 1995), esp. chap. 5.

12 See Mary L. Dudziak, *Cold War Civil Rights: Race and the Image of American Democracy* (Princeton, NJ: Princeton University Press, 2000) and Fredrickson, *Racism: A Short History*, 129–32.

13 On the relative stagnation of progress in race relations since the early 1990s, see Winant, *The World Is a Ghetto*. On the situation in the United States, along with a plea for a non-racial interpretation of the fundamental problems, see William Julius Wilson, *The Bridge over the Racial Divide: Rising Inequality and Coalition Politics* (Berkeley: University of California Press, 1999).

14 See Eric Hobsbawm, *The Age of Extremes: A History of the World, 1914–1991* (New York: Vintage, 1996 [1994]), 96 and passim. The term 'creative destruction' is Joseph Schumpeter's; see his *Capitalism, Socialism, and Democracy* (New York: Harper & Brothers, 1942).

15 See esp. François Furet, *The Passing of an Illusion: The Idea of Communism in the Twentieth Century*, trans. Deborah Furet (Chicago: University of Chicago Press, 1999 [1995]) and Stéphane Courtois et al., *The Black Book of Communism: Crimes, Terror, Repression*, trans. Jonathan Murphy and Mark Kramer (Cambridge, MA: Harvard University Press, 1999).

16 See Hannah Arendt, *On Revolution* (New York: Viking, 1963).

17 For a more extensive discussion of the *Black Book of Communism*, see my 'What Future for the Future? Reflections on the *Black Book of Communism*,' *Human Rights Review* 2, no. 2 (Jan.–March 2001): 135–43.

18 For a sharply critical view of identity politics, see Todd Gitlin, *The Twilight of Common Dreams: Why America Is Wracked by Culture Wars* (New York: Metropolitan Books, 1995). For a recent iteration of the debate, see the exchange between Richard Rorty and Nancy Fraser in *Critical Horizons* 1, no.1 (February 2000): 7–28.

19 For a devastating critique of the use of the notion of 'identity' in recent social-science writing, see Rogers Brubaker and Fred Cooper, 'Beyond "Identity,"' *Theory and Society* 29, no. 1 (February 2000): 1–47.

20 See Pierre Bourdieu, *Masculine Domination*, trans. Richard Nice (Stanford: Stanford University Press, 2001).

21 See Ian Hacking, *The Social Construction of What?* (Cambridge, MA: Harvard University Press, 1999).

22 Kerwin Lee Klein, 'On the Emergence of Memory in Historical Discourse,' *Representations* 69 (Winter 2000): 145. Klein's article does for 'memory' what Brubaker and Cooper do for 'identity.'

23 The phrase is E.P. Thompson's; see his *The Making of the English Working Class* (New York: Penguin, 1968 [1963]), 12.

24 Steiner, *Grammars of Creation*, 7.

25 Charles Maier has noted that, outside the Euro-Atlantic world, where the problems have been of a different nature, the Holocaust narrative is seen as a 'parochial' preoccupation. See his essay 'Consigning the Twentieth Century to History: Alternative Narratives for the Modern Era,' *American Historical Review* 105, no. 3 (June 2000): 826. Accurate though it undoubtedly is at the level of popular historical consciousness, I suggest certain limitations to this view in my essay '"Making Whole What Has Been Smashed": Reflections on Reparations,' *Journal of Modern History* 73:2 (June 2001): 333–58. For an outstanding study of how the Holocaust came to assume its paradigmatic status and the implications of this fact for our ways of thinking, focusing on the United States, Germany, and Israel, see Daniel Levy and Natan Sznaider, *Erinnerung im globalen Zeitalter: Der Holocaust* (Frankfurt am Main: Suhrkamp, 2001).

26 Max Weber, 'The Nation,' in Hans Gerth and C. Wright Mills, eds, *From Max Weber: Essays in Sociology* (New York: Oxford University Press, 1946), 176.

27 See Arendt, *The Origins of Totalitarianism* (New York: Harcourt, Brace, 1973 [1951]), chap. 9.

28 See T.H. Marshall, 'Citizenship and Social Class,' in his *Class, Citizenship, and Social Development*, ed. Seymour Martin Lipset (Garden City, NY: Doubleday, 1964 [1949]), 71–134. On this point, see also David Abraham, 'Citizenship Solidarity and Rights Individualism: On the Decline of National Citizenship in the U.S., Germany, and Israel,' manuscript, Shelby Cullom Davis Center for Historical Studies, Princeton University, 2002.

29 See esp. Will Kymlicka, *Multicultural Citizenship: A Liberal Theory of Minority Rights* (Oxford: Oxford University Press, 1995).

30 For updates on the controversy, see the home page of the Center for Research and Documentation on Japan's War Responsibility, at http://www.jca.apc.org./JWRC/center/english/index-english.htm. See also the relevant essays in Laura Hein and Mark Selden, eds, *Censoring History: Citizenship and Memory in Japan, Germany, and the United States* (Armonk: M.E. Sharpe, 2000).

31 By this I mean to refer to settler societies such as Australia and South Africa. The idea of European 'fragment' societies was first developed in Louis Hartz, *The Founding of New Societies: Studies in the History of the United States, Latin America, South Africa, Canada, and Australia* (New York: Harcourt, Brace, Jovanovich, 1964), part 1.

32 Stephen Castles and Mark J. Miller, *The Age of Migration: International Population Movements in the Modern World*, 2nd ed. (New York: Guilford, 1998), 201.

For an in-depth discussion, see Robin Cohen, *Global Diasporas: An Introduction* (Seattle: University of Washington Press, 1997).

33 For representative examples see Peggy Levitt, *The Transnational Villagers* (Berkeley: University of California Press, 2001); Yasemin Soysal, *Limits of Citizenship: Migrants and Postnational Membership in Europe* (Chicago: University of Chicago Press, 1994); and Habermas, *The Postnational Constellation.*

34 Chang notes that her involvement in the cause of commemorating and seeking reparations for the Rape of Nanking was galvanized by her attendance at a 1994 conference of the Global Alliance for Preserving the History of World War II in Asia in Cupertino, CA; see Iris Chang, *The Rape of Nanking: The Forgotten Holocaust of World War II* (New York: Basic Books, 1997). The website of the Alliance for Preserving the Truth of Sino-Japanese War, a member of the Global Alliance, can be found at http://www.sjwar.org.

35 Randall Robinson, *The Debt: What America Owes to Blacks* (New York: Dutton, 2000).

36 Mark Mazower, *Dark Continent: Europe's Twentieth Century* (New York: Knopf, 1998).

37 See Jean-François Lyotard, *The Postmodern Condition: A Report on Knowledge* (Minneapolis: University of Minnesota Press, 1984); Russell Jacoby, *The End of Utopia: Politics and Culture in an Age of Apathy* (New York: Basic, 1999); and Susan Buck-Morss, *Dreamworld and Catastrophe: The Passing of Mass Utopia in East and West* (Cambridge, MA: MIT Press, 2000).

38 Nancy Fraser, *Justice Interruptus: Critical Reflections on the 'Postsocialist' Condition* (New York: Routledge, 1997) and Soysal, *Limits of Citizenship.*

39 Furet, *The Passing of an Illusion,* 502.

40 For one analysis of the nature of the 'transition from socialism to capitalism,' see Gil Eyal, Ivan Szelenyi, and Eleanor Townsley, *Making Capitalism without Capitalists: The New Ruling Elites in Eastern Europe* (New York: Verso, 1998).

41 Steiner, *Grammars of Creation,* 329.